Our bayonet was twelve inches long, its handle four more, and it weighed a pound. It was of dulled blue steel, an unlovely thing, and unloved. But the Japanese bayonet is a beauty of gleaming steel, longer than ours is by several inches, with a point upturned in a cruel curve. Their officers glory in their Samurai swords, but the troops worshiped their bayonets with a fanatical devotion. These bayonets were now brought most forcibly to our attention; for the next three years and more we were never allowed to forget them. "Don't stop for water, they just stuck a fellow" was the word passed. We looked at the moving column up ahead, and there as that column divided itself like a swift, rushing stream around a rock in its bed, we saw a pitiful, crumpled figure lying in the road, his bright blood reflected against the shining sun.

"Let the chow alone, they just got another!" was barked at me as I was stuffing my shirt with C rations from a roadside dump. I looked up, and there was a man in the ranks passing by, supported by a comrade and trailing a few drops of red in the gray dust....

I Am Alive!

A United States Marine's Story of Survival in a World War II Japanese POW Camp

**U.S. Marine
Sergeant Major Charles R. Jackson**
Edited by Major Bruce H. Norton, USMC (Ret.)

PRESIDIO
PRESS

BALLANTINE BOOKS • NEW YORK

A Presidio Press Book
Published by The Random House Ballantine Publishing Group
Copyright © 2003 by Maj. Bruce H. Norton, USMC (Ret.)

Grateful acknowledgment is made to ASSEMBLY Magazine for permission to reprint an excerpt from an obituary article written by Alexander G. Kirby. Copyright ASSEMBLY Magazine, Spring, 1972.

www.ballantinebooks.com

ISBN 0-345-44911-8

Manufactured in the United States of America

First Edition: June 2003

OPM 10 9 8 7 6 5 4 3 2 1

DEDICATION

It is customary to dedicate your work to someone—this shall be no exception. After due thought, these stories and articles are offered to the following:

First Lieutenant Asaka, Infantry, Imperial Japanese Army: His stern and rigid treatment was tempered by a real regard for our welfare while I was imprisoned in Japan; an enigmatic figure, we think he saved many lives entrusted to his care.

Soochow, the little Marine mongrel mascot: His keen ears often detected bombing and strafing planes ahead of the air raid warning. Unlike most other dogs, who gave warning by scurrying for shelter with their tails tucked between their legs, this little fellow stood his ground, barking furiously at the sky raiders before he would take cover. By doing so, he saved the lives of many of his Marines.

Last, to "Big Ray" Foss, a civilian employee at the Cavite Navy Yard, who, when the going was really rough, shared his starvation rations with Soochow and kept the little dog alive.

—Charles R. Jackson

To Darice, Bruce, and Elizabeth—my wife, son, and daughter—to whom I owe so much.

—Maj. Bruce H. Norton, USMC (Ret.)

"I AM ALIVE!"

At the lowest point of our despair, in the bleak and bitter cold of a copper mine in northern Japan, a chief petty officer of the U.S. Navy was given an opportunity to write a prisoner-of-war card to his wife. He was allowed ten words— he used three: "I AM ALIVE!" This laconic message, classic in its poignant pregnancy of suffering and despair, pictures only too dreadfully well what it meant to be a PRISONER OF THE JAPANESE ARMY!

CONTENTS

SHORT STORIES

Contents

ACKNOWLEDGMENTS

I want to express my gratitude and sincere thanks, first to Dr. David M. Goddard for allowing me permission to edit and publish his uncle's stories; Maj. Gen. John S. Grinalds, USMC (Ret.) and President of The Citadel, the Military College of South Carolina, Capt. John S. Coussons, USN (Ret.), Col. Thomas Palmer, USMC (Ret.), Col. Philip W. Leon, USA (Ret.), Col. John G. "Tony" Lackey, III, USA (Ret.), Maj. Edward Y. Hall, USAR, Col. James A. W. Rembert, Col. Richard D. "Mick" Mickelson, USMC (Ret.), Special Agent Craig M. Arnold, FBI, Mrs. Janis W. Breazeale, Ms. Crystal M. Lottig; Mrs. Jacqueline Chocas, Mr. James S. Simons, Mr. Richard M. Cutler, Jr., and Mrs. Rosalba H. Norton for providing me with their critical reviews; to Maj. Jim Capers, USMC (Ret.), and G.Sgt. (Gunnery Sergeant) Joe Singh Rodriguez, USMC (Ret.), for their investigative expertise; to Mr. Carlton Shokes, Ms. Mary Chapman, and Mrs. Erika Larsh, from The Citadel's Information Technology Services Department, for their great patience and professionalism; Mr. Fred J. Graboske and Mr. Charles R. Smith, at the Marine Corps Historical Center, for their advice and support with this project; and Ms. Kerry Strong and Dr. Jim Jinther at Quantico, Virginia, for their assistance in providing those photographs that have enhanced Sergeant Major Jackson's work.

To all of these good people, I am indebted—*Semper Fidelis*.

—B.H.N.

FOREWORD

This book, in the opinion of many, is one of the most remarkable records of Marine Corps history written after World War II. Charles Ream Jackson's ability to present his collection of fascinating observations as a prisoner of war in an honest, clear, and chronological order has made my task as editor a most enjoyable experience. To that degree, I have tried to maintain the integrity of his original manuscript as much as possible.

The transformation of this Marine's extraordinary story, moving from his recorded remembrances originally typed on onionskin paper, now turned brown and brittle with age, into book form, began in 1994.

While I was serving as director of the Marine Corps Command Museum, in San Diego, California, Mrs. Margaret McRae Jackson brought her husband's collection of notes and short stories to me. She hoped they could become a recorded part of Marine Corps history, and to ensure that happened, the original pages of Jackson's stories were forwarded to the Marine Corps History and Museums Division, located at the Washington Navy Yard.

Ironically, Charles R. Jackson and his wife, Margaret, had for many years lived in the coastal town of Pacific Beach, a few miles north of San Diego. Margaret, in 1992, realizing that her own health was rapidly deteriorating, wanted to be certain that her husband's written account of his time as a Marine POW survived.

With assistance from Dr. David M. Goddard, Charles R. Jackson's nephew; Mr. Fred J. Graboske, the Marine Corps

History and Museums Division's chief archivist; Ms. Sheila
Biles, library technician for the Special Collections and
Archives Division at the United States Military Academy
Library, and Dr. J. A. Jinther, photographic archivist at the
Marine Corps Research Center, Quantico, Virginia, a more
complete picture of Charles R. Jackson's twenty-eight-year
military service has now been documented.

As Jackson states, there have been a number of books
written about the American prisoner of war experience, his-
tories of men brutally killed, tortured, and starved while in
the hands of their Japanese captors. Most of these books
have been written by historians who were most fortunate in
never having personally experienced the horrific effects of
"being a guest of the emperor." Here is a significant exception!

I AM ALIVE! is a fascinating series of stories—personal, graphic observances coming from one Marine sergeant major who, as a prisoner of war during World War II,
credits his own struggle and survival not only to his fellow
prisoners of war, but to several of his Japanese captors!

As editor of this work, my inclusion of Jackson's personal history, as background, is offered to assist the reader
in getting to know and understand this remarkable man. It is
readily apparent throughout his recollections that Jackson
was a devoted Christian, and true to his Marine Corps motto
of *Semper Fidelis*—Always Faithful—he, too, managed to
"keep the faith" during his extraordinary and heroic ordeal.
It is the documented history of compassionate, courageous,
and spirited individuals such as Charles R. Jackson that help
define the term—UNITED STATES MARINE.

—Maj. Bruce H. Norton, USMC (Ret.)

INTRODUCTION

My name is Charles R. Jackson. I am a professional Marine, with nearly twenty years' service in our Corps. Prior to that, I served for eight years [as a commissioned officer] in the United States Army. While in the Marine Corps, I have served in China several times, in the Philippines, Japan, Guam, Hawaii, [on] most of the West Coast and at a few of the East Coast naval stations in our own country, as well as in Nicaragua, Panama, Haiti, Cuba, Puerto Rico, and the Virgin Islands. I have also been seagoing, and have had at least a year's service on transports in my wanderings.

I left Pearl Harbor in October of 1940 for duty in Shanghai with the 4th Marine Regiment. We evacuated that troubled city and landed in the Philippines a week before the war began. We saw a bit of Bataan and a lot of Corregidor, and then came more than three years of dreary imprisonment. Surrender found me working for the Mitsubishi Company in one of their copper mines located some four hundred miles northwest of Tokyo.

This [book] is written in the quiet and peace of an old Virginia town, without benefit of notes or references, except in a few cases where specifically stated. My experiences are still vivid enough to be remembered clearly. A critical reader may find minor errors in numbers of troops, dates, and certain happenings, but these recollections are as accurate as I am capable of making them.

While a prisoner, I suffered from partial blindness, the direct result of prolonged starvation. An Army Medical Corps doctor, Lt. Col. Warren A. Wilson, procured for me, after some ten months of helplessness, a pair of eyeglasses from one of our dead. With these glasses I was able to sew my clothes, do my work, and read such books as our meager stock provided. Had it not been for these blessed volumes, I doubt my capacity to have pulled through, mentally. Physically, I will always bear an eternal gratitude to the doctors who were my fellow prisoners. They saved thousands of lives, these unselfish gentlemen and physicians. Never, during those dark days when the worst in us came to the surface, when it was a case of "dog eat dog" for survival, did I see or hear of a mean, cruel, or selfish act on the part of these splendid men. The Red Cross food and medicine, scant as they were (for the Japanese seldom allowed them to be issued), were the means whereby most of us who survived are alive today.

Among the diseases I recall having, generally at one and the same time, and all the time, were pellagra, ulcers, "dry" and "wet" beriberi, malaria, dysentery (both bacillic and amoebic), amblyopia of the eyes and bursitis in the shoulders, scurvy, and arthritis. (Chronic diarrhea, internal bleeding, and malnutrition I hardly count as diseases, I was so used to them.) On two occasions my weight was 95 pounds or less. My average weight might have been 125 pounds. During the only break I ever got, a kitchen police job in the galley, my weight went up in those five lucky months to 165, only fifteen pounds below normal.

And yet, I was only an average prisoner as far as diseases went. The weak and dispirited died early. We who survived must have been incredibly tough, with the most intense desire to live.

Strange as it must seem to some of you, I bear no hatred toward the Japanese, except for a few individuals with whom I came into close contact and earned their disfavor. Judged by our own standards, there were even some "good men" among our enemies. *Remember that these people were but ninety years removed from a medieval society;* considering that, we were lucky not to have been killed when we surrendered. The Chinese and Korean forced labor prisoners were treated far worse than we were.

In the Bataan campaign our forces did cruel and evil things that would have justified severe reprisals. In the Corregidor surrender, whose terms I understood included turning over all installations intact, we grossly violated those terms by destroying all we could in the few hours left to us. There was no punishment for that.

As I said, there are a few Japanese against whom I bear a personal grudge, and it would not be true to deny it. Yet, on the whole, I think I can safely speak for most of the fellow prisoners whom I knew, and say that we bear them no ill will. Apart from systematically starving us, there was a strange mixture of kindness and cruelty, with the former predominating. One sometimes thinks that they themselves did not have too much with which to feed and clothe us, for the blockade cut off essential food, medicines, and other supplies for the whole nation.

I have come out of this nightmare of over three years in jail in pretty good shape except for my eyes. I now know I have cataracts in both eyes, and they are increasing in size. One of our doctors, Lt. Col. Albert A. Weinstein (who died 25 February 1964), once remarked to me that the most amazing thing he had observed among us prisoners was the incredible toughness of the human body and how hard it was to kill.

In telling these tales of other people, I have tried as much as possible to keep out the personal element. This was difficult to do. I was too much a spectator, and sometimes a participant, in all of them except one. (I shall tell you of this one when I write it.) These are primarily character sketches of different men of different races, along with a little dog and five gallons of rum, which I thought to be outstanding. I have tried to add enough narrative and background to keep the reader's interest. In closing, I repeat I cannot hate the Japanese.

—Charles R. Jackson, 1948

BACKGROUND . . .

Charles R. Jackson was born on 14 July 1898 in Dinwiddie County, Petersburg, Virginia, the firstborn son of Capt. Montgomery Chamberlayne Jackson and his wife, the former Isabel Biscoe. Their home was located at 30 Corling Street, Petersburg, Virginia, where Captain Jackson was, in 1917, president of the Jackson Coal & Coke Company.

Charles had a brother, Montgomery Chamberlayne Jackson, Jr. After graduating from high school, both brothers attended Virginia Military Institute, where Montgomery graduated in 1920 with a baccalaureate degree in science. He served in the U.S. Army and by 1956 had risen to the rank of colonel. He was employed by the U.S. Life Insurance Company in Carmel, California, and died on 6 June 1972.

Charles R. Jackson attended Petersburg High School, where the records show that he studied "Arithmetic, English, History and Civil Engineering, in Primary School, and concentrated on Algebra, Plane geometry, English, French and Drawing during his last year of high school." He also studied drawing at Smith Art School in Petersburg under the guidance of Mrs. Judy Smith.

At VMI, which he attended for two years, Charles pursued a degree in civil engineering.

Charles R. Jackson applied to the U.S. Military Academy at West Point, New York, and was admitted on 14 June 1917. He was a "second alternate appointee" of Congressman Walter S. Watson from the Fourth District of Virginia, and his father, Capt. M. C. Jackson, was listed on his application as his guardian.

5

An accelerated curriculum was in effect at the time of Jackson's cadetship due to personnel shortages caused by World War I. Charles R. Jackson graduated on 1 November 1918, ranked number 178 in a class of 284 members.

Charles R. Jackson's class returned to the academy on 3 December 1918 to pursue a postgraduate student officer's course, from which they graduated on 11 June 1919. During the period of 13–20 July 1919 he toured the battlefields of France, observing the Belgian, French, and Italian fronts and the Army of Occupation. He traveled through Germany from 17–27 September before returning to Camp Benning, Georgia, as a student officer at Infantry School in October. He resigned his commission on 19 January 1920, but was reappointed a second lieutenant of infantry on 1 July 1920 and promoted to first lieutenant that same day.

The Howitzer, the yearbook of the Corps of Cadets, published by the Class of 1921, which graduated on 1 November 1918, shows two photographs of Cadet Charles Ream Jackson, nicknamed Charlie, or Jack.

Beneath his *Howitzer* photograph it reads:

> *"Will call any place in the city in my unlettered wagon, and buy or sell Old clothes, rags, bottles, and sacks." Did you ever see that legend over a junk shop door? Diogenes says that Jackson is the man who first patented the idea. Could he develop a Neapolitan brogue, he surely would be in his element, for he is the most accomplished scavenger in the Corps, and has amassed a fortune in clothes, shoes, leggings, b-plates, gloves, bell-buttons, and gray rags.*
>
> *Charlie has considerable talent for drawing and printing. The vast amount of ice cream he has eaten in payment for artistic hop-cards may partially explain the precocious "embonpoint" that has given the Kaydet store so much trouble. Glance through this book and see for yourself that Goldberg—or Broberg—has nothing on him.*
>
> *He has other remarkable talents, notably that of kiss-*

*ing the boot. His efforts in this line have been of avail,
but as Stevenson tells us, "the true success is to labor."
"Ditch the boodle boys, here comes Jackson."*

He served with the 22d Infantry at Fort Porter, Buffalo,
N.Y., 30 November 1920 to 3 March 1921; at Fort Jay, N.Y.,
from 4 March to 20 May; at Fort Porter, N.Y., 21 May to 16
September; at Fort Benning, Georgia, on detached service,
from 17 September 1921 to 1 June 1922; at Fort Sam Houston,
Texas, with the 23d Infantry, 1 June 1922 until he was returned
to the grade of second lieutenant on 15 December 1922.

He transferred to the Coast Artillery Corps on 8 June
1923. He served at Fort Ruger, Hawaii, with the 16th Coast
Artillery from 1 October 1923 to 16 September 1924; at
Fort Shafter, Hawaii, from 16 September 1924 to 27 July
1925. He resigned, for reasons unknown, on 27 July 1925.

Civil History: Engineer, E. I. DuPont de Nemours Co.,
Hopewell, Virginia, 1920; student, Cornell University, Ithaca,
N.Y., 1920; Member, Eleusis Fraternity and Cornell Society
of Engineers; Engineering Sales Department, Standard Oil
Company of California, San Francisco, 1925; Engineer, E. I.
DuPont de Nemours Co., Parlin, N.J. and Flint, Michigan, 1927.

For reasons known only to Charles R. Jackson, but to his
everlasting credit, he enlisted in the United States Marine
Corps as a private on 3 September 1927.

Jackson's Marine Corps career began when he enlisted at Detroit, Michigan, as a private. He served in
China for a total of almost three years, Nicaragua one
year, and the Philippines for one year. He now was a first
sergeant, but became a temporary sergeant major on
14 August 1940. Meanwhile, he was sent to Pearl Harbor on 2 July 1940 and to China on 14 November 1940,
then returned to the Philippines on 1 December 1941.

When the Japanese invaded Luzon after the
Pearl Harbor attack, he was active in the fighting in
Bataan. His unit, the 4th Marines, was stationed on
Corregidor. Jackson was verbally given the rank of

lieutenant colonel, but no papers were issued, and after the war no records of this were available. I think that Charlie was correct. When I was in 6th Army headquarters, 1948–51, I remember someone asking me if I had a classmate who was a Marine officer on Corregidor, but unfortunately I had to reply that I did not know.

"During the fighting on Corregidor, Charlie was awarded the Silver Star on 13 April 1942 for his bravery in saving the lives of his comrades while under direct enemy fire. He was also awarded the Purple Heart on 2 May 1942 and a Gold Star in lieu of a second Purple Heart on 6 May 1942.

"After the surrender of Corregidor, Charlie was taken [by the Japanese] north to Cabanatuan [POW camp]. There he managed to escape from the Japanese and helped organize a Filipino guerrilla unit to harass the Japanese. When the Japanese organized a major retaliation against the guerrillas, Charlie started south to Luzon, hoping to work his way to Borneo or to Australia. While traveling south he contracted malaria and became unconscious. He had given away most of his supply of quinine. When the Japanese found him, they gave him quinine and recaptured him. He was held in Manila for a while, and then was sent to Japan. There he worked in a copper mine and in the scrap metal department of a Japanese steel mill until the end of the war."[*]

In a letter written in 1992, asking to describe Sergeant Major Jackson, Mr. Joseph E. "Frenchy" Dupont, Jr., of Plaquemine, Louisiana, recalled:

The thing that I remember most about [Sergeant Major] Jackson was that we enlisted Marines had a nickname for him—we called him "Chowbanger" Jackson. In China, the chowbanger was a food prepared on the

---

[*]*Assembly* magazine, spring 1972, obituary article by Mr. Alexander G. Kirby, pp. 103–4.

street corners by the lower-class Chinese. They would have a bamboo yo-yo pole about seven feet long, and on one end would be a little charcoal-burner stove and on the other end would be their supplies. They would walk down the street with this pole and it would bounce, so that on the upswing they would take their steps, and could carry its weight when both feet were on the ground.

Whenever Sergeant Major Jackson would go on liberty, and we would pass by him on rickshaws going downtown, he could be seen on the street corner eating these chowbangers with the Chinese coolies and the lower class of Chinese people that were around. A chowbanger, as best as I can remember, was a fried, doughy substance made from rice flour and some other ingredients.

We thought he should have eaten in a better situation, down at our club, as we did, rather than out on the street corner with the Chinese coolies. Of course, no one ever called him "Chowbanger" to his face.

Sergeant Major Jackson was the sergeant major of the 2d Battalion, 4th Marines, and in my capacity as a private first class, I had very little association with him. I did have an occasion at one time to go to his quarters. I can't remember the reason why, but it was after I was transferred into the Battalion Intelligence Section and became part of Headquarters Company, 2d Battalion.

I remember going into his quarters and I saw him without his shirt on, and to my surprise he was covered with tattoos all over his body. He had a spread eagle on his chest, and the wing tips went off to his shoulders. On his back was a large Chinese dragon extended from just below the nape of his neck, down his back, in a curling design to where his pants came to well below his waist.

With this thought in mind, I can remember that he never appeared in the barracks with just a skivvy shirt on. He always wore long-sleeved shirts, possibly to hide the fact that he had these tattoos. In regards to his physical appearance, he kept his hair cut very short. He was always dressed immaculately. He was a rather large man, as I recall, and always made a good presentation as a Marine. He was not a sloppy person. He was always neat and properly dressed.

I have one other story about Charles R. Jackson that I believe is worth sharing:

We evacuated Shanghai on November 28, 1941 and went to the Philippines and landed at the Olongapo Naval Base. On Christmas Eve, after the war had started, we were bombed by the Japanese. The naval base was hit pretty hard, as was the little barrio outside the base.

The word came down that the Japanese were driving down our way, and we had to leave Olongapo for fear of being cut off from the rest of the Regiment. The bombing began on Christmas Eve, and by morning everyone had begun the evacuation. Being assigned to the Battalion's Intelligence Section, along with a Lieutenant Sidney F. Jenkins and five other Marines, we were the last ones to leave Olongapo with Lieutenant Colonel Anderson.

We were all riding in a truck with Sergeant Major Jackson, Lieutenant Colonel Anderson and Lieutenant Jenkins, driving down the Bataan Peninsula toward Mariveles where we would bivouac before going over to the Island of Corregidor.

As we drove along, we passed by the remains of a bombed out cabaret, a small nightclub. It had been badly damaged by a bomb, but part of it was still standing. Colonel Anderson suggested that we stop, as it was Christmas Eve, and that we all go inside and have a Christmas drink. All of the Filipinos had taken off to the hills and there was no one around. Half the walls had been knocked down, but the bar was still standing, although it too was in pretty bad shape.

We went inside and one of the Marines began to fix drinks for all of us. It was Colonel Anderson who suggested that we gather around a piano and sing Christmas carols. Lieutenant Carol knew how to play the piano, and Sergeant Major Jackson had a pretty good voice. I remember one of the carols we sang was, "O Come All

Ye Faithful." The real title was "Adeste Fidelis," and he sang it in Latin. He said, "Dupont, do you know that the Christmas carol, Adeste Fidelis, is the oldest of all the carols? It was written back in the Middle Ages and the author is anonymous. No one knows who wrote it." I remember that well, and it stayed with me. I was surprised to hear him say that, and I often wondered whether or not he knew what he was talking about. I thought it very strange that a sergeant major in the Marine Corps would be so knowledgeable about church music.

Years later, I had occasion to talk with Fred Koenig, who was a member of our Battalion Intelligence Section, and I asked him if he could remember anything about Sergeant Major Jackson. He said, "Yes, I remember my impression of Sergeant Major Jackson was that he was a very well educated, refined man, but he never acted that way around the troops. He maintained his usual demeanor of a Marine Corps sergeant major who was rough and tough, and didn't want to appear to give the impression that he was interested in things other than Marine Corps activities."

Fred Koenig, known as "Bones," later told me that he had gone on liberty with Sergeant Major Jackson. This was the first time I had heard this. According to Bones, "Jackson talked about the arts, music, and literature. But when he was back in garrison with the troops, he used the rough and tough language that the rest of us did."

Two articles, appearing in the United States Military Academy's *Thirty-Five Year Book* and *Fifty Year Book*, respectively, published by the Class of 1919, offer additional and supporting information about Charles R. Jackson:

Commissioned Warrant Officer Charles R. Jackson, USMC:

Charlie, the Missing Marine, has finally been located; retired after thirty years service, and living in San Diego. After resigning from the Army, for the

second time, in 1925, Charlie enlisted in the United
States Marine Corps, and served in all enlisted grades
from 1927 to 1945, when he was promoted to the
rank of commissioned warrant officer (infantry). He
retired in 1951. Charlie was captured on Corregidor
and was a prisoner of the Japanese for over three
years. He had the unusual distinction, as a Marine, of
receiving a Silver Star from the Army, for volunteering and rescuing wounded under heavy enemy artillery fire. To his citation the Commandant of the
Marine Corps added a highly commendatory letter.
(Charlie expressly requested that the fact of this
award and commendation is withheld from the Class
in this yearbook, but we have disregarded his request
because of the pride that Class will feel in his
achievements.) Charlie continues his interests in ancient history and lectures on his hobby in a California
university. He and Margaret have no children; but
they have equivalent grief—they raise Siamese cats.*

And from the *Fifty Year Book*, published in August 1969:

Charlie's unique military service is outlined in the
Thirty-Five Year Book. He was recommended for the
Medal of Honor for his service at Corregidor, but received instead the Silver Star, apparently because too
many became eligible by being involved in the action.
There were only two survivors out of twelve. Since his
retirement in December 1951, Charlie has done a considerable amount of studying especially of ancient history, and has been a guest lecturer in that field at a local
university. Charlie's eyesight has been failing for several
years until he can no longer see as he would like to, and
he is faced with the possibility of total blindness within a
few years. He says he has had a full life and an enjoyable
one. Margaret and Charlie Jackson have no children.

Thirty-Five Year Book, Class of 1919, Washington, D.C., October 1954, p. 60.

1

THE STORY OF FATHER McMANUS

Father McManus is dead. When a prison ship, the *Enote Maru*, carrying American prisoners of war, was sunk by our own bombs and torpedoes, Lt. Frank McManus of the Chaplain's Corps, United States Navy, went down to his grave in the deep, blue Pacific.

Thus perished an obscure Catholic priest. I do not know the details. I feel sure, if there was a spark of physical strength left in the frail, starved body of the man, he died helping others to live. He came from somewhere around Boston, and I hope his people get to read this tale, for Father McManus was a saint out of the early days of the Christian Church. I can never forget him.

I once read Thucydides, the most sublime of historians, an Athenian of classical Greece. To borrow a phrase he applied to another sage of antiquity, "He consulted the light of reason before that of the faith had arisen." Parts of a speech he puts in the mouth of Pericles come to our mind. They seem to fit Father McManus so well that we are copying down the oft-quoted words of the old Greek:

We are not suspicious of one another, nor angry with our neighbor if he does what he likes; we do not put on sour looks at him, which, though harmless, are not pleasant; . . . For we are lovers of the beautiful, yet simple in our tastes, and we cultivate the mind

13

without loss of manliness. . . . For we have a particular power of thinking before we act, and of acting, too, whereas other men are courageous from ignorance but hesitate upon reflection. . . . Reflect that this empire has been acquired by men who knew their duty and had the courage to do it, who in the hour of conflict had the fear of dishonor always present to them, and who, if they ever failed in an enterprise, would not allow their virtues to be lost to their country, but freely gave their lives to her as the fairest offering they could present at her feet. . . . For the whole Earth is the sepulcher of famous men; not only are they commemorated by columns and inscriptions in their own country, but in foreign lands there dwells an unwritten memorial of them, graven not on stone, but in the hearts of men. Make them your people.[1]

This priest thought before he acted, and acted, too. Many a man who wears a medal for bravery will freely admit that he acted upon ignorance; had he reflected, there would have been no gallant deed. Raw, physical courage is the commonplace on the battlefield; the records are studded with deeds of nineteen-year-olds, the best of battlefield age. Quiet, unsung moral courage is more valued and rare. No doubt the name of Lt. Frank McManus, Chaplain's Corps, United States Navy, is suitably inscribed in the bronze and stone of the written records, but among the prisoners of war who knew the man for his deeds there is an unwritten memorial, graven in their hearts. To make him an example is asking too much of weak flesh, but those who knew him are better men for that privilege.

And now to the tale. I must of necessity put a bit of myself into it, for I was there at the time.

Much has been written of Cabanatuan Military Prison Camp Number One, Nueva Ecija Province, Philippine Is-

---

1. Thucydides, *Peloponnesian War*, chapter VI. Extracts from Pericles' funeral oration (Crawley's translation).

lands, and much of it is true. In April of that dreary year of 1943, the mental state of the prisoners was at low ebb; the physical but little better. Nearly all the weak and broken-hearted were now dead; the tough and wiry were alive. The death rate had been, among some 5,000 men, about 28 per day. Red Cross food and medicines had been allowed to come in, so that now only one man or so died per month! (Executions now and then are of course not counted in the death rate.)

The Japanese are a strange mixture of kindness and cruelty. I know I shall never understand them. Nearly half of the 5,000-man group was permitted to be in the hospital, under our own doctors. (These unselfish physicians worked day and night with meager equipment and few drugs to save lives.) No hospital patient worked on outside details.

The 2,500 so-called "well" men were divided into three groups of about 800 men each. Each unit had about 250 officers, of whom few worked, and 150 enlisted men, clever and adroit, who had gotten the inside jobs. They hung on to them like grim death.

Of the 400 left in a group, the Japanese allowed about 100 sick to be marked "quarters"; they either worked at easy inside jobs in that status, or, in the more severe cases, were allowed to *ya si me*. (We thought more of that Japanese army word for "rest" than we did for food, starved though we were.)

That left 300 to a group, 900 for the camp, men not sick enough to make the highly prized "quarters" list or clever enough to secure inside jobs, to work [on] The Farm. This place was simply hell. (From now on, any reference to The Farm will be capitalized; my leg alone will never let me forget it.)

Happy was he who worked in the commissary, the galley, or the food supply room. While he lacked ordinary American food, he could gorge himself on inferior third-grade rice, decayed and evil-smelling salt fish, stringy carabao (water buffalo) meat now and then, and native vegetables, often rotten or spoiled. We were sure that some of these men were also filching more than their share of the Red Cross food issue, for they had charge of it.

How we hated (and wistfully envied) them all!

The Japanese stayed on the outside of the barbed wire, turning over the running of the inside of the camp to the prisoner officers. It was either the most fiendish of clever, diabolical moves to sharply cleave officer and man or else it was done in ignorance. We suspect the former.

Second lieutenants received twenty pesos per month; the higher grades more. Privates and noncommissioned officers who worked The Farm got ten or fifteen centavos.

(I repeat the words; "The Farm" is capitalized on purpose. That evil place is indelibly inscribed in our memories. Even today, after release, when there is no armed guard ordering us around in this land of plenty, most of us shudder to think of The Farm.)

The Farm fed outlying garrisons of the Imperial Army and the camp guard of six hundred or so men; the prisoners got what little was left. There were signs all over the place saying, ANY PRISONER PICKING UNAUTHORIZED FOOD WILL BE SHOT. In spite of this, we stole whenever we could. No prisoner was ever shot, but some few were caught, brutally beaten, and tortured.

The prisoner officers ran a camp commissary, selling such divine delicacies as atrocious native tobacco, crude "*caromata* pony" sugar, dirty native syrup swarming with dead insects, rancid coconut oil, raw peanuts, strong-smelling duck eggs, and once in a while a puny chicken or a stringy duck. He who had twenty pesos or more each month lived in what we "have-nots" thought was luxury; but he who earned from The Farm, at the most, three pesos [per month] could buy but little. The "haves" seldom shared with the "have-nots." It was, to use our expression, "dog eat dog!" (The commissary food was in addition to the scanty rations the Japanese allowed us in the mess lines.)

Americans under such conditions tend to become mean and selfish. Every form of black market and petty racketeering came to the fore. Quite justly, the Japanese derided us for it. Hatreds grew that will never die out among us; we try to forget them but we cannot. The gulf between the officer prisoners, our natural leaders in any escape plan, and their men became so enormous that, incredible to relate, as far as we know, no such design was ever seriously thought of except in rare, individual cases.

Who has not heard of "R.H.I.P.," meaning, "Rank has its privileges"? Too large a number never forgot it, but failed to remember its corollary, "But it also has its obligations." Under the dismal life we led, who could blame the officers? Human nature was there in the bleeding raw. I probably would have acted the same, and maybe worse, had I been in a position to do so.

An ugly picture has been delineated; it has been necessary to do this to explain Father McManus when I come to tell you [of] what he did.

Now in this April of 1943 there is a change in the guards, for the worse. The garrison commandant, one Lieutenant Colonel Mori, was relieved; some four hundred of his veteran Japanese soldiers were replaced with a like number of half-savage aborigine conscripts from the island of Taiwan. Mori was not too bad, unless one was being executed. He always tortured the victim from twenty-four hours to a full week before the firing squad and death brought a welcome release. To give the devil his due, he did seem to hold in the sadistic impulses of his men to some extent.

His successor was a weak, white-haired old major, a reservist, I heard. In appearance he seemed benign and kind, but he could not control the fiendish cruelty of his men, even had he desired to do so. The second-in-command, a captain, ran The Farm. It was told of him that he had said, "To work Americans, beat like carabao." The regular soldiers were bad enough, but the native young Taiwanese were ferocious in their uncontrolled cruelty.

The daily detail for The Farm had been about 900 men. Now it was stepped up to 1,500. This increase resulted in a great scurrying around to fake illness and get in the hospital, or at least to make the "quarters" list. The officers eased some of the special-duty men out of their sinecures. Now even some of the latter had to go to work, and junior captains and lieutenants took over some of the outside details, but not The Farm. Some of these details had always included fine officers who volunteered for such jobs as woodcutting,[2] fence building, and ditch repair, but such work was decidedly not The Farm.

Work gangs were of thirty men each with a junior officer who, as supervisor, did not work. Senior officers looked after several groups. Overall, as overseers, were Japanese farming specialists. At the head of them was the "Beat like carabao" captain, who had an assistant in the person of a three-star private, a perfect cartoon-type figure with buckteeth and glasses and a look of restrained ferocity. We called him "Air Raid." He was a most unpleasant person. Who among us that knew him shall ever forget him?

In addition to the perimeter guards around The Farm, there were four or more Taiwanese to each four-bull gang of thirty. We called them the "torture squads." Let a man slow up and they pounced on him. For forty-five minutes, prisoners were required to slap each other until blood came, hold heavy farm tools at arms' length until muscles screamed with pain, hold these same tools over their heads until they nearly collapsed, and then finish up by kneeling on the ground with a tool handle between the back of the thigh and the calf of the leg. Try this sometime, if you can, for five minutes, and see if you can walk afterward! Often to all of this was added a clubbing with what we prisoners called, with sardonic humor, "Jap vitamin sticks." The grim threat of being shot or bayoneted if one faltered was always there. A man who went through this felt the results for over a week. (We know one man very, very well whose clubbing on the thigh lamed him for some three years. Even today he can feel the effects. The man—myself!)

Naturally, there was very little "soldiering" on the job.

2. Maj. Reginald H. Ridgeley, USMC, later a major general, was one of the woodcutters.

You had to "keep your head down and your tail up" unless you wanted a good working-over. We may add that all Japanese tools are built to make you work in this position; it is natural to them, but how foreign to us, and it made our backs ache cruelly.

To the hazards mentioned above was added what seemed to be a quota system of men to be tortured. If no one was caught loafing, about four men were picked out of each group of thirty, *"pour l'encouragement des autres!"*

Every trick and device of the malingerer was brought into play in order to make the "quarters" list. But what could the doctors do when only a certain number of men were permitted to be so marked? This small number was decreased daily by the stern orders of the conquerors. Men who had malaria and a fever of over 102 degrees were dosed with a little quinine (there was never enough) and sadly told they must go and work in the blazing sun. The heat of the dry season was pitiless. Mild symptoms of beriberi, scurvy, pellagra, and amoebic dysentery were not enough to make the "quarters" list. If one could produce positive, non-encysted stool, with blood, one could make the hospital, but not otherwise. A fair guess would be that the average weight of the men, all suffering from malnutrition, was about fifty pounds below normal.

One hardy soul was reported to have been detected eating large green flies from the latrines around the dysentery barracks, hoping to get a positive specimen and the comparative paradise of the dysentery hospital. I knew of a young officer,[3] a second lieutenant, assistant leader of a dysentery barracks, who feared his job would be given to a senior and that he might then have to work at The Farm. He actually used to pay a Marine "quarters" case for his stools and then take them to the dispensary for a microscopic examination. It was funny in that the Marine's own stool, every time the doctors looked it over to shake him loose from the hospital, was

3. 2d Lt. Richard Roth, USA Reserve, 92 C.A.

always positive, but the samples submitted by the lieutenant were all negative!

Among the black market operators and "Big Dealer Kings," along with the professional gamblers who were listed to work The Farm, the price for a sick man on "quarters" to take their place for half a day's work had been only a few pesos. Now it rose to ten; for a starving man, this might mean enough commissary food to save his life.

And now, at long last, we come back to Father McManus.

One day in my agony of "head down and tail up" with a Japanese pick whose handle was about half the length of an American-made one, I saw to my utter surprise Father McManus working alongside me. He wore the rags of a private. Barefooted, he worked in the sharp gravel and had on no lieutenant's insignia. I had known him personally but slightly, though fairly well by reputation, for he had been a member of the USS *Canopus*'s gallant crew, whose tale will long live in the annals of the navy. He was much underweight, and I felt sure that, like some very, very few other officers, he had been giving away his pay to starving men.

"Chaplain, what on earth are you doing out here? Are they making the officers work The Farm now?" I asked out of the side of my mouth, for it was dangerous to let the "torture squad" catch us talking while working. It meant the usual forty-five minutes of their careful attention.

"Oh, I want to keep my sanity," he replied with a cautious glance toward the nearby sentry. "You know, there are few ailments that a pick and shovel will not cure."

I studied his gaunt, emaciated frame and watched him pant and sweat. I thought, "You glorious, splendid saintly liar! You must be taking a sick man's place."

There was no further talk with the good priest, for the danger was too great. (It may be superfluous to point out that I addressed him as "Chaplain." Had I been of his faith, I would have called him "Father.")

That night I roused myself from my apathy and sought information. I found, as I well knew I would, that Chaplain McManus had for some time been making rounds of differ-

ent barracks, asking the officer in charge of each one to put
him in the place of his sickest man who had to work. He removed his officer's bars before he fell in with the detail, for
the Japanese might not have permitted him to toil in the
place of an enlisted man.

It is possible that there were a few, a very few, other officers who emulated Father McManus and volunteered to
take a sick man's place in the labor party being taken off for
the day to The Farm. When The Farm was first started, 1st
Lt. John Paul Flynn, late of Company L of the 3d Battalion
of the 31st Infantry, with an unhealed head wound caused
by shell splinters in the Cabcaben area of Bataan, imprudently took the place of a sick man for The Farm's working
party. Poor Flynn got the attentions of the torture squad; a
broken thigh on a man of about forty-five does not heal as
quickly as it does on a younger man. For the next two and a
half years that I knew "Old Dobe," I seldom, if ever, saw
him walk; the few times that he did, it was with a cane and
a pronounced limp.

Perhaps, and I hope so, there were other officers who followed the example of Lieutenant Flynn and Father Mc-
Manus. Among the dull, dreary clods that were once men,
whose sole topic of conversation was food and *ya si me*,
such sublime self-sacrifice went unnoticed and unsung by
the majority. But I did hear some praise of Father Mc-
Manus. The language was bitter, with short and ugly little
four-letter words, unprintable, when they compared him
with other and younger officers.

After a few months of The Farm, a kindly doctor, Lt.
Col. Jack Schwartz, MC (Medical Corps) Chosen Race,
USA, got me into the heaven of the dysentery hospital. In
the dull, unending days, my mental faculties began to slip,
like those of so many others. I thought no more of Father
McManus, for all my waking thoughts and dreams were
about food.

Later, when I could no longer hold on in the hospital, I
was shipped out to Japan. The Japanese feed their sick, soldiers and civilians alike, only half what they gave me as a

well man. I thought that Japan would be a civilized country, with more food, so I asked for a detail to the Flowery Kingdom. I got it. There was a little more food, with some suffering from hunger and a lot from bitter cold, but it was better than The Farm.

When a Red Cross Christmas package was given to us in the copper mines of northern Japan, for a brief interval we did not discuss the eternal subject of food. We ceased our prattle about chocolate malted milks; and the name of Father McManus came up. We spoke of him in admiration and some wonderment. One prisoner, Pvt. Walter M. Lee, said he had once seen him beaten and tortured for the usual forty-five minutes. The man remarked that so many men were getting worked over in those days that the incident was not thought worthy of comment, if spoken of at all.

Once, long ago, in the days of my pious youth, I was forced to make some studies of the early Christian Church. The Lives of the Saints seemed rather dreary reading. Perhaps I wondered what force, what principles, or what impulse could cause a martyr to embrace joyfully the cruel claws of ravenous wild beasts before the jeers and catcalls of the Roman populace in the Flavian Amphitheater.

In the marvelous days following release, my joy was tempered by the news of Father McManus's death. With a full stomach and a bulging waistline, I reflected upon the man. Curiously, I opened a copy of The Lives of the Saints. There was no longer any wonder at the faith that could exalt the primitive Christians to die so horribly for an ideal.

It was a great privilege to have known and worked alongside Father McManus. I no longer wonder; I know the answer; I have seen it in a living man. I have walked with a saint.

2

THE STORY OF CAPTAIN FLEMING

Major Elmer Pearce Fleming, Field Artillery, U.S. Army, is a released prisoner of war. He, too, was a "guest of the emperor" for a bit longer than he cares to remember.

I received a letter from him the other day. He is on leave in Columbia, South Carolina, amidst the rolling hills and green woods of that fair state, where life is good. He is with his wife and the little son he never saw until he got out of jail. We Marines wish him well, for he is a fine soldier. He told me that the Regular Army is giving him a permanent commission, which shows much wisdom on the part of the War Department.

I also learned that he has been decorated with the Bronze Star for what he did while he was a prisoner. From what I personally know of his activities, he richly merits it.

He used to tell us, in the dreary days of that terrible winter in northern Japan, that he would like to remain in the army. He was a boy captain then; now, since he is out, he has been made a major. I should refer to him by his new rank, but to some five hundred of us, he will always be our "Captain" Fleming.

He is a tall fellow, nearly six feet, with an elastic spring in his walk. (He always kept that walk, while we who had the "beriberi shuffle" used to wonder how he did.) He has a frank, boyish, open face; he cannot tell a lie and get away with it. With those lean legs, he would look good in the

impeccable peacetime uniform of a major of Regulars, with
a pair of seventy-dollar boots by Peal of London, 487 Ox-
ford Street, N.W., patronized by General ["Black Jack"]
Pershing, et al.; but alas, gone are the days of Sam Browne
belts and boned boots, resplendent with spurs, leather
guards, and chains. But he would still look good in any uniform, for he is a born soldier.

One used to hear certain "professional" Virginia gentlemen say it took three generations to breed one of the tribe.
A hard, old soldier-emperor of Rome[4] once remarked, "A
man is his own best ancestor." We think the remarks of the
Virginia gentlemen and the emperor Tiberius both apply in
this case.

Some of us Marines are suspicious around officers of the
U.S. Army. Probably we have too much esprit de corps, a
phrase defined by one of our famous fighting officers who
used to write articles for the papers as "esteeming your own
corps and looking down on others." Until we get to know
them, we are naturally wary of the army. They do not speak
the same language we do. Later, when our dead have lain together on the battlefield, we grudgingly admit them to our
fellowship. They are rather liberal in the matter of buying
drinks, like the soldiers of Scotland; and we Corregidor
Marines will commit assault, battery, and mayhem on the
brash person who disparages the 59th and 60th Coast Artillery Regiments, or the 91st and 92d Filipino Scouts,
whom we know well.

I never got a chance to know Captain Fleming's regiment. It was some obscure outfit of the Philippine National
Army with a sprinkling of American army officers, largely
reserves, to stiffen them. In those days of March 1942, when
I was not ducking bombs and scorning the scattered fire of
the 105mm cannon on the Cavite shore some seventeen
thousand yards away, I used to stroll down the cliffs above
James Ravine on the island and watch the flashes of the big
Filipino one-five-five guns as they helped repel the assault

---

4. Suetonius's *Lives of Twelve Caesars: Tiberius* (Thomson's translation).

of the Japanese on the little Bataan Peninsula, right in our backyard.

Day by day those flashes grew closer to us, for the Bataan lines were cracking. Wracked by malaria and starvation, by shell and bomb (the latter was worst of all, for the US soldiers had no aviation of their own with which to strike back), they were finally overwhelmed. In April the flashes drew closer and closer to us; on the ninth day of that month, Bataan was no more. We knew it on Corregidor; we saw them blowing up the ammunition dumps in a last effort to keep the Little Yellow Men from using our own shells against us. Then came a deep calm and quiet, but not for long. By two o'clock in the afternoon the amazing Japanese had run their artillery up to Cabcaben; we soon knew what it was to have some 290 cannons firing on us. Of the "Death March," we got a few gleams of broken light in spite of the curtain that was dropped over the fate of our comrades. We had plenty of our own troubles, which were mostly concerned with trying to keep alive.

Captain Fleming survived the Death March, for he was a tough youngster. I feel sure that he was never very hungry or sick with malaria. "R.H.I.P." is all very well when its obligations are lived up to. Let the right type of rank do its duty by the file, and the latter will see that the former has its privileges, with a fierce pride and joy. Enlisted men have decided feelings toward their combat officers who share their dangers; either they hate and fear them or they worship the very ground they walk on. I think Captain Fleming's men worshiped him.

I heard that they helped him on the march, for he had been wounded. This was only meet and fitting, for he stuck with them on the march to Camp O'Donnell, not leaving them to try for a truck ride as many other officers did. He and his men were shrewd enough for each one to pick up an extra canteen of water from the dead. They stuffed their gas masks with C rations and rice, and they perhaps got hold of a few medicines. Fleming has a long head, and he must have realized much sooner than other officers just what he was up

against. Many of the men in that march without his foresight are dead; it took more than a strong body to keep alive
when you were a prisoner of the Japanese.

Captain Fleming never told me this; he was always very
vague and modest about what had happened in his battalion,
and about his wanderings from Camp O'Donnell, Cabanatuan, and Clark Field before I met him.

I learned a bit about him now and then from men who
had known him; I can guess the rest, and perhaps I am not
far from the truth. He was a mapmaker of sorts, and every-
place he went, he mapped the area. In due course of time,
via the underground, these maps reached American headquarters. They came in handy in the later Philippine campaign of 1944 and 1945, for they showed new airports,
revetments, and storage dumps. No doubt this mapmaking,
fraught with the certainty of torture and death if detected,
helped Captain Fleming earn that Bronze Star.

I dragged a bit of this from him, but not too much. Huddled together over a tiny stove in the barracks in Japan, our
fronts warm and our backsides freezing, and both sick in
that dreary prisoner of war camp at Hanowa, Akita Prefecture, the barriers between officer and man were somewhat
lowered. Man is a gregarious animal who likes company;
our captain liked us; and we talked of everything from
"shoes and ships and sealing wax," except of the one all-
absorbing topic, food. Captain Fleming always kept his sanity, and he helped me to keep mine, for if one began to talk
about food he was beginning to go crazy. I tried to draw him
out about his war experiences; I thought, like a fellow traveler in a smoking car, he should unveil his own inner
thoughts. He never would and I resented it; he always was
the reserved gentleman, as a real army officer should be.

I first met him in the Old Bilibid Prison in the city of
Manila. I, who had been so often to Manila in better days,
who had so often listened to the old "Sunshiners'" tales of
the "days of the empire" and Bilibid, had once in a while
passed its grim walls in a *caromata* behind a pint-sized

pony and courteous driver. Now I found myself locked up in the Bilibid.

The Bilibid Prison was used as a clearinghouse and hospital for the prisoners. Here broken men were sent from the outlying hells of Nichols, Clark, and Las Pinas [Air] Fields, and from other places of nightmare memory. Here men but little better off were "processed" (this was a new war term I first learned here) to be sent out as replacements. Here bewildered or hopeful men, a little tougher and wirier than these replacements, were gathered for the unknown mysteries of the trip to Japan or Manchuria.

Today they call those ships they traveled in "prison ships," and folks shudder when they read about them. Our trip was not so bad, for I heard of only one man who died as a result of it. (I think he was the tall skeleton I saw being carried by Captain Fleming through the Tokyo Station. But this is getting a little ahead of the story.)

In Bilibid Prison they took us off in companies of 200 men, 1,035 finally for the trip. I marched with my pitiful baggage through Manila and the port area and down to the docks. I saw the Japanese cutting a gate through the east side of the lovely old Walled City. I guessed it was for defense, but they always had needed a traffic gate there. I passed cavalry; fine horses and beautifully kept, for this fold are kind to their animals and cruel to men. There were lots of 105mm guns, a little shopworn, but I reflected that these guns helped take Singapore, the East Indies, and our Philippines—they looked dreadfully capable. I saw a Filipino yanked off his bicycle, tied, and beaten. Idle inquiry revealed that he had made a "V" sign at our column.

On our march we halted and rested briefly on the lovely green sward of the Luneta [Hotel] while trucks picked up the men who had fallen out. "Malaria patients" was the word passed along the ranks. It felt good to be in the hands of humane people, regardless of how rough they had been in the islands. After all, Japan was a civilized country, a land of plenty. They make the war pay for the war, of course, just like old Napoleon used to do; what they do in the Philippines is different from what they do in Japan. Now I am in the anteroom of the empire. Things will be changed, of course, and all for the better, I thought. In the midst of these idle musings I came to the docks and the *Noto Maru*.

A big, new fifteen-thousand-ton motor ship she seemed, fine lines she had; the sailors and Marines looked at her with an appreciative eye. They marched us on board and we clambered down the ladder into the upper forward hold, arranging ourselves around the bulkheads. "Sit on your baggage, move backward, pack together a little more," the interpreter yelled at us. Finally, all 1,035 of us were jammed into that one hold. It measured about 70 by 140 feet, and we were held tighter than sardines in a can. We thought we would be distributed into other holds later, so we settled down resignedly to "sweat it out." In that heat, this is exactly the right expression.

After a while the hatches were partially closed and latrine buckets were lowered. It began to dawn on us, with horrible reality, that we were to make that long voyage in just that one hold. And a few hours before, we had been thinking that the Japanese were a civilized folk!

Food was served twice a day in buckets lowered to us. It was more and better than we had had for a long, long time. A level mess kit of steamed rice and barley, a quarter of a canteen cup of fish soup, and a canteen of water. Just twice a day we had this little amount. It is not much to eat, you will not gain weight on it, but you can live on it for a long time. As Doctor Weinstein, one of our doctors, remarked more than once, the human body with a will to live is a tough thing to kill. If you eat food like this for several months, some of you may die of scurvy, beriberi, and pellagra, all aggravated by just plain malnutrition.

We made out our mess details from men we hoped would be honest in dividing the food; there was great political work to get these jobs. We gave ourselves "chow numbers" so that there would be a fair, rotating division on the precious seconds.

When night came we tried to sleep. Think of sleeping

like a lot of snakes as you uncover them in a den, just before the spring has awakened them. A few fortunate men were assigned by the senior officer prisoner to jobs topside at the head of the ladder. Our desperately sick pneumonia men were laid on deck under heavy guard, with the senior medical officer prisoner, Dr. (Capt.) Dan Golenternek, MC, to help care for them; the rest of us went through that hideous night waiting for the ship to sail, whenever that might be.

In order to get to the latrine buckets, one had to crawl over hundreds of men, wait in line, and then crawl back again. Men began to go out of their minds, the crawlers were bitterly cursed, and fights started. And dysentery broke out almost at once!

A big, tough army lieutenant, named Sense, or something like that, from Spokane, Washington, near our corner, stuck a bar of soap in a sock and said that he would hit all fighters on the head, regardless of who started the fight. He certainly did it, too. A Marine private and a sergeant fought over some trivial thing, forgotten now. The big officer crowned them both. The sergeant said, "You might as well stand by, sir. I am going to hit him again." He did, stood meekly for his slugging, and sat down quietly. How we roared with insane laughter at the goings-on of creatures that once were men. But we thanked our gods for officers like him; he kept men sane and prevented killings. (The private did not make it back, for he died in a mine accident at Hanowa.)

Lieutenant Sense, Doctors "Dan" and "John,"[5] and, I later learned, Captain Fleming, stayed in that hold handling those snarling beasts all of that trip.

Thirteen days it was; Fleming was only about fifty feet away from me, and I never saw him. Think of that—a thirteen-day trip with a fellow traveler, and I never saw him. The Japanese let the other officers on deck during the daylight hours to get life-giving sun and air. When the horrid din belowdecks annoyed the Japanese, the senior officer prisoner, an army captain named Samson, used to step partway down the ladder and, in a quavering, plaintive voice, beg them to desist. He was ignored and profanely abused. He always began his orations with a "Bear with me, men"; we knew that he and the other junior officers on deck were begging the Japanese for cigarette butts and extra food or water; we hated them for this.

"Bear with me" and his type I would like to forget, and I think I should. My hatred was caused mostly by envy. I probably would have acted as he did, had I the rank to do it.

The trip was without much incident; a day and a night in Olongapo Harbor; a few depth bombs dropped by the destroyer escort; and two ten-minute periods on deck, in glorious sunlight, in some nameless Taiwan harbor. (Our guards refused to tell us the name of the place.) The stench that arose from that awful hold must have annoyed our captors, for we were sloshed off with saltwater from a hose on deck. Just a little thing, but how much we appreciated it; just two saltwater baths from a fire hose!

During all of those thirteen hideous days and nights, Captain Fleming, Lieutenant Sense, and Doctors "Dan" and "John" stayed in that hold. We repeat this for emphasis. It was the physicians' duty to do so, to save lives and sanity, and it was to be expected of them. Sense and Fleming did not have to stay there during daylight hours. Smoking was forbidden down there, while it was permitted on deck. They could have groveled to the guards, gotten friendly, and obtained a bit of waste food or a cigarette butt contemptuously thrown down on the deck. But to their eternal credit *as men*, they stayed in the hold.

I want to forget that voyage.

On a clear day in early September 1944 we came to Moji, at the China end of the Inland Sea. A pretty land Japan is, until you look at it close up. It photographs beautifully. But houses and shrines are of unpainted, flimsy wood. After mature consideration, from our year there, we give it as our fixed opinion that it is the world's largest poorhouse.

On a vacant lot in the railroad yards our new guards made us lay out our belongings. We thought it was the usual search for security reasons, to make sure that carefully hoarded cakes of Red Cross soap were not hidden. Soon the word was passed that in the 1st Company, guards were taking up soap and other things. "Bear with me" lacked the nerve to protest. His type could not be expected to do anything about it. Captain Fleming and Lieutenant Sense protested with vigor, risking a beating. The thefts stopped and some articles were actually returned.

We saw a few Dutch prisoners, furtive-looking and cowed. We tried to talk to them, but they avoided us. None too well fed looks, shabby in their dress; they filtered through us here and there like slinking animals. We began to think this was not the civilized land we had imagined, even those of us whom the voyage had not disillusioned.

Now came a five-day trip on the trains—narrow-gauged, dirty, and crowded. The [Japanese] army fed us better than the ship had, but gnawing hunger was always present. There was never enough to eat. We still crawled over one another to reach the toilet, where we still stood in line, but we had blessed sunshine and fresh air. We recall the stations, Hiroshima and an overnight stop, Kobe, Osaka, Nagoya, and Tokyo. In the capital we changed trains while Captain Fleming and Doctors "Dan" and "John" argued with the Japanese over our precious Red Cross medicines. In the end the Japanese confiscated only half of them, but it took guts even to dare to protest to them. The Japanese had issued these medicines in the Bilibid Prison, and they were on the scant side.

And, as I said before, here I saw Captain Fleming, near the head of the column, supporting the still taller figure of a gaunt prisoner, his hollow eyes bright with fever. It was no trouble to carry him, for hunger and starvation had brought his weight down to less than a hundred pounds.

Now and then along the route we dropped off work details, fifty men here, a hundred there. Lieutenant Sense of Spokane, the big soap-and-sock man, was left at some

nameless town. I regretted losing him and wished he had remained with us; I felt so secure in his strength as a buffer
between our captors and me. Men follow a leader; he was
one. "Bear with me" left obscurely, forgotten and unwept.

A trip on an electric train across Tokyo to another station; another steam train, and we bowled along northward in
driving rain. And so, in a mountain village hidden by saw-
toothed peaks, we came to Hanowa, Akita Prefecture, and
our journey's end. There were some five hundred of us left,
and for eight of them, there would be no returning. Only
eight would never again know sugar, pork chops, potatoes,
and white bread in plenty, and all the other foods they so
wistfully dreamed of. In plain little white pine boxes, their
names lettered in both English and Japanese, we would rev-
erently take their ashes home. For so small a number of
deaths we can thank Doctors "Dan" and "John," Captain
Fleming, and a certain First Lieutenant Asaka of the Japanese Imperial Army, who was our camp commandant for
most of our stay.

For some ten days we rested and received more rice than
we had gotten in a long time. But there was no rest for Captain Fleming, in charge of making out many rosters, details,
and the thousand-and-one other things the Japanese wanted
from him. He was "Skipper," first sergeant, police and property sergeant, mess sergeant, company clerk, and runner, all
in one. When the guards told him what they wanted, Captain
Fleming would first send word by some noncommissioned
officer. Obedience from sullen and beaten men was slow. If
orders were not promptly carried out, mass punishment
would quickly follow. We all knew it, but our mental state
was such that we did not care. So, if men were to be kept
from being beaten and slugged, Captain Fleming must do
everything himself.

A few men were chosen for the galley and the inside
jobs. How we hated and envied the men who got those jobs!
"It's the old Clark Field gang that were with Captain Fleming on detail before," we muttered. We all felt the sting of
not being chosen. Yet these men had worked with him be-

fore, and he knew what they could do. How otherwise could
he have chosen them? We knew these reasons, yet we hated
him for choosing them. To such a state of mind had over two
years in prison reduced us.

Had we reflected, we would have remembered that, when
officers were picked by senior fellow prisoners to go out to
the work camps from Cabanatuan, some of them volunteered from a genuine desire to help those bewildered,
beaten men; that others were sent out because, as agitators,
they openly denounced privileges and extra food for the favored few when there was so little food for all; that some
were disliked for the usual reasons that people dislike one
another; and that some asked to go out for reasons that they
were sick of the sullen, dispirited monotony of the same
faces; the same talk and the same routine. I never asked
Captain Fleming why he had gone out so early, but I ought
to have known. That man went out to help others.

We began to work the mine. It was a forty-five-minute
climb up that mountain; we were fagged out when we got
there. Both the Japanese and we seldom called it the mine;
it was always the *yama*—the mountain.

Certain of us hated Captain Fleming for his springy
walk, his alert, boyish looks, and his unfailing faith in ultimate Allied victory. Our sick drooped around with heads
lowered between their shoulders, like the dismal vultures of
Nicaragua. Our well dragged their feet with the unforget-
table beriberi shuffle and tried by devious ways to make the
sick list. We felt that no prisoner had the right to look so
keen and fit, or to keep so neat and clean. We knew Captain
Fleming for a better man than we were, and we hated him
because of it.

The dreadful winter was soon upon us. The first snow
was on 10 November 1944. The snow covered all, with
drifts over fifteen feet deep. To the despair of imprisonment,
the eternal gnawing hunger, and the harassment of tired
men by brutal guards after a long day at the *yama* was added
the torture of bitterly cold weather. Fires were tiny and few,
fuel was scarce, and sometimes there were no fires at all.

The fortunate sick stood their morning *bango* (formation), slid into bed with all of their clothes on, covered up their heads, and got out of bed only to eat or go the latrine during the daytime.

Captain Fleming ran all of the camp details. There was no rest for him. He protested about things as they were, and he continually asked for more food, medicines, clothing, and fuel. Often his requests were punished with a slapping, for he had "offended the honor of the Japanese army." How easy it would have been to sit back when a detail had been ordered out and let the guards come in the barracks to speed up the slow ones with clubs and bayonets! How the sick men, and men not sick, whom the kindly doctors had placed on the "quarters" list, hated and cursed him!

He did not eat any better than we did. He was never seen sampling food in the galley. He always got enough hot water to keep clean and shaven, and to wash his patched and threadbare clothes, but we never begrudged him that little extra. The Japanese allowed him a soldier-prisoner for orderly duty to take care of his laundry and do some of the runner duty; we suspect that Captain Fleming gave him some extra food from his own plate now and then. We know that he shared with the orderly a few drags from precious butts, and so we hated and envied PFC L. B. "Willie" Williamson.

When "Willie" had a little food left over, not often of course, he furtively gave it to the more emaciated of the prisoners, for the others would not have understood. We used to see the orderly's eyes follow Captain Fleming's figure with a sort of doglike devotion; master and man, each loyal to the other.

Soon after we arrived our camp commandant was changed, for the worse, we thought, until we began to learn better. Captain Fleming was not as diplomatic as we would have liked him to be; he was young, with a boyish impulsiveness that the years to come will, we fear, replace with suavity. The impressive, exclusive dignity of First Lieutenant Asaka refused all interviews with his prisoner captain; orders—and there are many with the Japanese—came through the camp interpreter. (I will tell the tale of this worthy individual, a good man, elsewhere.) Often they were supplemented by instructions from First Sergeant Takahashi, the second-in-command. The interpreter and the *gunso* were both kind to us, on the whole; we wish them well in the dark days to come in the Flowery Kingdom.

Doctor Dan, who had joined us just before Christmas, with his marvelous diplomacy, together with Doctor John, tempered and taught our young captain. The other officer, 1st Lt. Richard T. Pullen, one of the better types of army lieutenants, worked the *yama* and did extra work as camp interpreter. Gentlemen all, we liked to think that they never talked each other out, and for Captain Fleming there was never too much time for talking. The Japanese always wanted him for some new orders to be carried out.

We men did not give any of these officers our own food, for we knew they would have rejected it with kindly thanks; but there were always little gifts of tobacco for them, tiny and precious. Perhaps some were offered for political reasons, for there were always fellows hoping for a job in the galley, or to make the "quarters" list, but often a man would press a whole cigarette or a short one on Willie. There would be a furtive hand placed in Willie's pocket, a half-ashamed "For the captain" or "For the doctors," and usually a "Take a drag for yourself," for by now we were beginning to like and trust him.

Lieutenant Asaka we now regarded with mixed feelings. Although he was tough, frozen-faced, and more of a stickler for the proprieties than most Japanese officers, we began to realize that he was trying to take good care of us. We knew the doctors worked well with him. Captain Fleming he outwardly ignored, yet Fleming must have influenced him, and our lot began to be a bit easier.

Our weaker men could talk of nothing but food, food, and more food. The topic was all-absorbing. Our stronger men fought against it. If you talked too much about food, your mind would stray into a world of half-darkness peopled with bakery shops, grocery stores, and soda fountains. While handling heavy machinery in the *yama* you might slip and cripple a comrade in your trance. Whenever we got a chance to talk to Captain Fleming, we would try to bring the conversation around to the one burning, important thing that preyed so continually on our waking and sleeping thoughts; always he gently steered us away from it.

We got a few other officers, among them a fine young Australian flier, Flight Lieutenant R. H. Thompson, and a couple of British captains, Capt. I. C. Spotte and Capt. C. Willoughby. Fifty of their clean-cut men came with them. We learned to like the sterling qualities of our English cousins, fellow prisoners with us. Captain Fleming's duties were lightened in some ways by their arrival, but the increasing loss of weight among us, with attendant malnutrition and its effect on weakened and sick minds, gave him much concern, and his burdens actually became heavier.

He tried his best to stop the black market and to curb the big dealers among us; it was hopeless, but he never stopped trying. We were always ashamed of ourselves for this weakness, but so many of us took the attitude, "If I don't trim this sucker, someone else will." It was the old "dog eat dog," so familiar to all of us. It is a side of our character I would like to forget.

Toward the end we got a new senior prisoner officer, Lt. Col. A. J. Walker, Air Corps, U.S. Army, a grave, austere type of army officer. A good man he was, one of the best. How well I remember the night he quietly talked the guards out of torturing some of us, for some petty trash discovered by the sergeant of the guard in our barracks. As we stood with our heavy trash boxes over our heads, arms aching, he came out and slowly said, "Lower your burdens; the sentries will not beat you while I am here." This fellow was good, but we still think Captain Fleming was better, for by now we had begun to really understand all that he had been doing for us. There was no letup in his industry, for he now had more time to work with tortured minds, fighting to resist the almost irresistible drag-down into the half-world of dreams of food.

Now, like a great clap of thunder, came the news of surrender. Lieutenant Asaka told Captain Fleming, who passed it on to us. There was to be no yelling or cheering. There was none.

Two days later came a ceremony of quiet dignity. Asaka told us the official news and we gave him a perfunctory hand clapping. Our lieutenant colonel took full command, with Captain Fleming as his adjutant. Our guards left; we took their rifles. For a few days we saluted our officers. It was a long-withdrawn privilege; now we could show our own form of military respect. I am ashamed to relate that in a few days the novelty wore off, and we saluted our own American officers no more. But Asaka, the Japanese, silent and inscrutable, who remained with us without his samurai sword, we saluted to the last.

Our final glimpse of Captain Fleming was in the railroad station in Shinagawa, telling Asaka good-bye. His step was still springy, his boyish face ablaze with the happiness that was his, for he was soon to meet his wife and the little son whom he had never seen. (Alas, the boy, when he saw him, was mentally handicapped!)

I heard that in Manila he was able to give the War Crimes Commission an elaborate set of records that he had kept, day by day, of all the food we had received, worked out to the last fraction of a kilogram per man, all medicines, and all the clothing. He risked death to keep such records. We all knew of them, but I thought that in the delirium of release they would be thrown away. These records, along with the maps I spoke of earlier, got him the Bronze Star.

Here, safe in the United States, a lot of us wrote to him. I got a personal reply, and I felt sure he answered all the others. And, as I said, he told me the army was going to keep him. Someday he will be a general.

We Marines hold a slight resentment against him. He would make a fine Marine officer. But it does not matter so much, for after all, we cannot hope to have *all* of the good officers.

3

THE STORY OF LIEUTENANT ASAKA

I sometimes think I ought to hate the Japanese. As one of their prisoners for three years and four months, I saw some hideous things. As a direct result of what they did to me, I must wear glasses for the rest of my life. Prolonged malnutrition induced the formation of cataracts in my eyes, which had to be removed surgically. I now wear contact lenses to replace my natural lenses and have to wear strong glasses for reading.

I do not pretend to understand the Japanese. Perhaps I was in the Orient too many years. I know, for instance, that the longer I remained among the Chinese and the more I learned of them and their language, the less I understood them. I feel the same way about the Filipinos. And I am sure that I know but little of the Japanese, for, as their prisoner, I studied them with dreadful intensity. May you never be required to study them as I did!

I think the casual visitor writes the most informative books about the Orient. We may laugh at the writer who, after two months or so, a mere flying visit, turns out a readable book on some special part of the Far East. We "old China hands," however, like to read them. Maybe the fresh impressions of these writers are the best. Perhaps our long years among the most perfect servants in the world blunt our sense to what is going on around us each day, making us incapable of putting down what the Chinese are actually thinking about and doing.

And I really think the Japanese are the same way about us. Did you ever notice, in the days before this war, that no member of the diplomatic corps of the Empire of the Rising Sun was ever a doyen, the senior member of the representatives of the different nations in a capital? Hardly any diplomat ever remained more than a few years in a post before he was moved. Most people thought that the reason for this policy was that when you get to know people you begin to think like them and act like them, and become less hard in pressing for every advantage for your own country. It is wise, therefore, to shift the diplomat before he is in one place too long.

I suspect a different reason—that the Japanese know they will likewise never understand us, so after two years or so, they bring their representatives back to Japan for a breathing spell and then send them out to a different land. There were Japanese, plenty of them, long resident in the Philippines, for instance, who were agents or spies. These gentry rendered able service to their empire during the war.

This brings me back to my subject, First Lieutenant Asaka of the infantry of the Imperial Japanese Army. The camp interpreter, a kindly soul (he was a teacher of English and a Christian), always pronounced his name "As' sa-ka," with a sibilant hiss and accent on the first syllable. Asaka was our camp commandant in Japan for eleven months. I have tried to hate this man—I think at times I ought to hate him, yet I cannot bring myself to do it.

At the beginning there were some five hundred of us enlisted men and four officers: a splendid young army captain named Elmer Pearce Fleming, whom we hated before we really got to know him; a pretty fair army first lieutenant named Richard T. Pullen, whom I had known very well on Corregidor; a too kindly senior army medical officer, Maj. John Jackson, who was no diplomat in dealing with the Japanese; and a mighty fine junior army doctor, 1st Lt. John

E. Lamy, who had to follow his senior's lead. We had all come by prison ship from the Philippines to Japan in that fall of 1944; we had come by train a thousand or more miles from Moji and Shimonoseki through Tokyo to our camp in the mountains, and here we were in the northwest corner of Honshu Island at a place called Hanowa in the Akita Prefecture, working in a copper mine for the Mitsubishi Company.

We rather liked our first commandant; he let us *ya si me* for the first ten days after we arrived and he fed us well. We received some new work clothes, sparingly issued, and he addressed us in good English. He was a fresh-faced, rosy-cheeked youngster, a second lieutenant, and while he was tough and strict like all Japanese officers, life was not too bad. The terrible damp cold (lasting seven months of the year) had not yet set in. After three years of the warm islands in the southern seas we had forgotten all about cold weather.

A month of this and the commandant was relieved. He took with him his own interpreter, whom we did not like at all. We heard this fellow was mission-educated and of a low social class, which was perhaps why he so loved to slap the prisoners around. He was replaced by First Lieutenant Asaka, from some infantry regiment. The number we have forgotten (it's of no real matter), and we got a new interpreter, one Shoshichi Yamanouchi, whom I have recorded to be a kindly man, even according to our standards.

I well remember Lieutenant Asaka's first formation. The Japanese call it *bango*, and to them it is a most important military ceremony. (They always made it so, even for us, and how we came to hate it!) The silly-looking interpreter, for he was never a soldier in any sense of the word, read to us the new commandant's proclamation. Behind him, ramrod stiff, stood Asaka. His uniform was of good serge and well fitted. Some five and a half feet tall he stood, and his face was strong in character. We never at any time saw him smile, nor was there ever a gleam of sympathy or understanding in his eyes. His coat was empty of any ribbons. His age could not be determined.

Later we came to learn that Lieutenant Asaka spoke very good English, but he never spoke it to us while we were his charges, unless he wanted something done in a great hurry. All commands were given in Japanese; all lengthy warnings, after Asaka had spoken them, were translated into the weird English of the interpreter, with the grim figure of the lieutenant standing rigidly by.

We knew he was a real soldier; the few professionals among us instantly recognized him as a member of a fellow craft; but we knew we were in for it. In certain ways, we were not mistaken.

It seemed as though every time a group of Japanese, military or civilian, got together, they held a *bango*. They loved them. You form in line, two ranks. The senior yells *"Kiotski!"* then *"Kashara naga!"* and you all look directly at the inspecting officer. He salutes, holding the salute while he very slowly turns on his heels from one flank to the other. It seemed to me that it showed the respect the Japanese officer had for the men in his command. After the salute is over comes a *nori*, where you look to the front again. Then follows *ya si me*, the military "rest," and you slap your left foot some six inches to the left front. Your hands are held, fingers rigidly extended and together, with the middle finger along the trouser seam. Then follows *bango*, where you count off in Japanese. (You had better make it loud, snappy, and correct, or you get slapped.) The commander then slowly walks around you on his inspection and resumes his post. The same ritual is then repeated, with the exception of the counting off, and is followed by the welcomed dismissal of *wakaru*. A final salute is made to the noncommissioned officer calling his last command, and you are through. (How terribly those Japanese commands and numbers are seared in my brain!)

Asaka always held a longer *bango* and saluted us better than any Japanese officer I ever saw. What a proper soldier he was, and how we hated him for it!

Since he never wore a decoration, the rumor spread around that he had been reduced from the rank of captain for some failure in battle on the southern front and condemned to spend the rest of the war guarding prisoners and eating his heart out. This was why he was so mean, we thought. I think a bit differently about the man now. Release has cleared the perspective of my vision.

Lieutenant Asaka's first order was to turn in all bladed knives. Most of us did so; we feared him. Loss of these knives was a real hardship. They cut fingernails and toenails and were useful in a thousand other ways. Mess kit knives, honed down and stropped to razor-edge sharpness, were used for shaving. Some men, with infinite pains, had made a good semblance of razors from American bayonets. After this order, shaving with what little we had left was torture, so most of us shaved only once per week. Even on shakedowns after this, knives were sometimes found in barracks. They were taken up, but no one was ever punished in any way. Asaka must have been aware that we had some knives, for how otherwise could we have kept clean-shaven?

No doubt the order about the knives came from higher authority. The good soldier ordered it carried out, the better soldier never condescended to blame it on headquarters, the wise soldier did not look too closely for its observance, and the kind soldier did not punish its violators as long as they were not flagrant.

Lieutenant Asaka, as far as I know, never hit but one man. At an inside *bango* one night, for it was too cold to be outside, he found trash hidden in the barracks. He was terribly strict about cleanliness, but we just never would keep the place the way he wanted it kept. He crowned the section leader, navy chief boatswain's mate Robert "Frenchy" Marechal, over the head and arm with the scabbard of his samurai sword, and the blow really hurt. After that, we helped "Frenchy" out a bit more in his work area, but only for a short while. Some men said Asaka was drunk when he did it. His second-in-command, "Gunso" Takahashi, on the whole a bit of a good egg, used to tip us off that the "Old Man" was in his cups now and then, and to stand by for "rock and shoals."[6] If he ever was intoxicated, none of us could ever tell it, for if he did imbibe too deeply, he had the old soldier's faculty of carrying his load with a military jag, which means to those who have never soldiered, to carry your liquor without detection.

I recall a poem of my school days with a refrain that appealed to me after I took up the martial life:

> Bacchus' blessings are a treasure,
> drinking is the soldier's pleasure,
> Sweet the treasure, sweet is pleasure after pain.[7]

If Lieutenant Asaka was tipping his saki, one could not blame him, for the man was doubtless longing to be with the fighting forces at the front, where there was honor and glory. Surely there was none to be had in a prison camp.

[Perhaps] First Sergeant Takahashi simply told us about his drinking to buck us up a bit when Asaka threatened him with punishment for our lack of discipline. Soldiers, regardless of their color, have certain similar characteristics in all armies. The saying that the "Old Man" is real mean when he is drunk is an old trick to secure a good inspection.

And, in connection with the inside *bango* for prisoners in cold weather, it may be noted that Lieutenant Asaka always, regardless of the weather, personally held the *bango* for his own guards outside.

During the day we toiled in the mine. Some labored topside, but most men toiled underground. It was a terrible

---

6. "Rock and shoals" is a navy term referring to the Articles for the Government of the US Navy. The term derives from Article XIX, Rules and Regulations for the Government of the Navy, 1862: "If any officer . . . shall, through inattention . . . suffer any vessel of the navy to be stranded, or run upon rocks or shoals . . . he shall suffer such punishment as a court martial shall adjudge." The term came to be applied to those Articles for the Government of the Navy, enumerated in *Naval Courts and Boards*, that were required to be read periodically to ship's crew.

7. John Dryden. *Alexander's Feast*, lines 55–60.

climb up that *yama*, and a man had done almost a day's work in getting up the mountain before he touched his tools. Each section of forty men had a Japanese guide who took them up, stayed with them all day, and brought them home. At all times soldiers guarded us. Some guides were good, some fair, and one or two were downright fiends. Asaka looked us over at the *yama* frequently, descending into the shafts and laterals. The workmen were always scared to death of the military, so we were always tipped off when the lieutenant came by and we pretended to be working at top speed. I wonder if we really fooled him. I thought so then, but now I'm not so sure.

Most of the prisoners—*holio*[8]—were sick by anyone's standards. Unless you were one of the favored few who worked in the galley (how we hated—and envied—their sleek bodies and well-fed looks), your weight was around forty pounds below normal.

There was a Japanese medical second lieutenant who called in now and then—we called him the "Black Prince," for he was swarthy—and he looked us over. He spoke to us in Japanese and to our doctors in a weird jargon he thought was German. Some forty of us were marked "quarters" by this man, which meant we were given inside jobs in the barracks.

All of us were tough and wiry despite our ailments. Had we not been, we would have died long ago in the Philippines. Our dysentery bugs had arrived at a sort of agreement with their hosts; if they reproduced too much they would kill the host, and then where would they be? Perhaps germs are smarter than we realize! But we were fighting a losing battle with starvation and sickness; we do not think many of us could have survived a second winter under such terrible conditions. Blessed release saved us. Our senior prisoner doctor, Major Jackson, was too kindhearted. All of us were the most adroit of fakers at sickness; we think we fooled even the

8. "Flower sniffer," a contemptuous term for a man who would save his life in battle by suffering.

major. The "quarters" list grew amazingly, and soon over 300 men were on it. The mine management had gone to some expense in building barracks for 500 men; 300 were now on the sick list. They must have put pressure on Lieutenant Asaka, for he really clamped down. The "Black Prince" came in and only his original 40-odd patients were left on "quarters." Both our doctors, Jackson and Lamy, were relieved of their medical duties and put to work as inside laborers.

Care of the sick was turned over to a sergeant of the Imperial Medical Corps, a man ignorant of his duties who spoke no English. We knew some of the military and work jargon, but none of the medical terms in Japanese. A few hardy, persistent souls sweated out the sick call *bango* and fewer yet made the coveted list. The sick men were required to work in the mine. Just at this time an inspection party of the big brass came up from Tokyo; a man with pneumonia, a First Sergeant McCarthy, Air Corps, U.S. Army, was sent up to the *yama*, and he died right after he got back.

Captain Fleming made a vigorous protest to the Japanese colonel. We heard he got slapped for it, and there was a big row. Our senior medical officer was immediately sent off to some Tokyo prison hospital; we got a new one, a Capt. Dan Golenternek, MC, USA, a physician of the same high standard, but a born diplomat in dealing with both the prisoners and the Japanese. He was of the Chosen Race (may his Jehovah bless him and cause him to prosper wherever he may be today) and a better man for that particular time and place could not have been found. The ignorant sergeant, "Cyclops" by nickname, was relieved and resumed his job of trying to see that the "quarters" list did not grow too long. This worthy man, urged on by Doctor Dan, got a hospital built for us, and medicines, and certain delicacies for the very, very sick, so we came to think a bit differently about the "Cyclops."

Doctor John, who fitted in perfectly with Doctor Dan's programs, was relieved of his camp laborer's job and went back to his quiet way of saving our lives and our sanity.

As the dreadful winter got worse, the "quarters" list

grew, and the hospital was filled to its forty-bed capacity. The snow piled up in fifteen-foot-high drifts. To bitter cold would be added raw dampness, and soon more men were staying in camp than were going to the *yama*. Lieutenant Asaka had plenty of pressure put on him by the mine owners about this; he gave Doctor Dan a lot of growls, but the list stayed the same.

When the spring thaw finally came in late May, our doctors gently shook us loose, one by one, from the list, and we went back to work. But by then Lieutenant Asaka had a good hundred of us working on a special detail down at the railroad yards in the town, where the work was fairly easy and there was no terrible *yama* to climb.

At the beginning of winter, Lieutenant Asaka had issued us heavy British overcoats, loot from captured Hong Kong and Singapore. We even received an occasional heavy khaki shirt. We guessed the Japanese army gave him those. The mine workers gave us gloves, socks, heavy warm caps, straw work mittens and overshoes, and certain other odds and ends. In each case of issue, we had suffered for lack of them before the mine workers gave them out.

The mine began to issue tobacco. "Hair" tobacco we thought to be a sort of synthetic nicotine-flavored rice straw; "hard rolls" were atrocious Japanese cigarettes. The average issue, once it was started, might have been three "hard rolls" a day, or their equivalent in "hair." This issue started in December, and we could credit Asaka, but we never knew. He never told us anything. We wondered.

For a smoker, tobacco is a drug. I have seen many men die of starvation, trading small bowls of precious rice for cigarettes or enough tobacco to roll them. It was also degrading to see Americans walk with a bent-over stumble, eyes fixed to the ground, looking for a cast-off cigarette butt. It was more degrading to see a man hang wistfully around a Japanese smoker, his eyes bright with anticipation, making you think of a spaniel dog. But it was far more degrading to hear the eternal cries at mealtime of "Four hard rolls for rice now," "Three hard rolls for rice tomorrow,"

"One hard roll for soup now," and "Half a hard roll for soup tomorrow."

Lieutenant Asaka was responsible for a commissary where we could spend the pitiful small wages we received from the mine and army. The Japanese themselves had nothing, for they were starving, too. At first we were sold a vile sort of red pepper and a worse brand of anise powder to flavor our rice. The men liked the pepper but hated the anise seed. With the coming of tobacco, morale shot way up. Men even began to speak kindly to one another at times and, most remarkable of all, there was heard an occasional polite phrase. Just how many items the mine furnished and how many came from the army we never quite knew, but Lieutenant Asaka supervised the distribution through Captain Fleming. Very fair it was, too.

The black market that we had learned so well in the Philippines came with us. Like the poor, it was always with us. Big dealers arose, and everything was based on the value of "hard rolls." When soap, socks, and gloves were issued, many of them were traded with the civilians at the mine for tobacco. They used to envy our plenty wistfully, we who had so little! Men traded even precious blankets and leather shoes at the mine, in the dead of winter, for tobacco. Lieutenant Asaka was always putting out orders against this practice, but it flourished just the same. Perhaps he realized the futility of trying to change American nature and overlooked a great deal.

The trouble with us, as far as army discipline in the barracks was concerned, was that we did not have the eager obedience of cadets. In America cadets generally come from the best of families; they are very young; they are animated by traditions and ideals and commanded by handpicked officers; their reward is a commission to lead other men. The whole Japanese nation seems imbued with the cadet idea, which is one of the secrets of their disciplinary success. We simply would not act as cadets at any time, hence the Japanese marked us down as surly and refractory.

Lieutenant Asaka demanded this cadet type of discipline,

but could not get it. The guards were changed about once per month; they were young recruits for the most part. The lieutenant had to train and discipline them before they could handle us properly, which is why they were ignorant in their brutalities, and low and cunning in their thievery. There was always speculation about how good or bad the new guards would be. We were required to salute and bow in their peculiar Japanese fashion every time we passed their guardhouse; it became quite a dangerous hazard. After a hard day's work, the sentries continually harassed us in our barracks in addition to harassing those near the guardhouse. We feel certain Lieutenant Asaka spurred them on, yet from a professional soldier's outlook, his attitude was only natural. He was a good soldier. I once idly watched him conduct a guard mount for his men in the bitter cold. Without benefit of overcoat or gloves, he talked to them for a long half hour, officer and men vying with each other in ramrod stiffness at attention. I would rather like to forget all about those guards.

One of our men, a hospital patient, had some ability as an artist. Not being the best type of American, he foolishly drew a series of pencil sketches of sexy female subjects and sold them to the young guards for tobacco. Lieutenant Asaka, during one of his periodic shakedowns of the guards to ensure they were not dealing with or stealing from us, discovered these pornographic works of art. The owners were smartly slapped in public, where all could see it done. The hospital patient, being sick, was merely reprimanded by the medical sergeant. A Japanese soldier guilty of such an offense would be beaten up, even if he were sick. This incident showed a creditable side of Lieutenant Asaka.

His brig, however, was a thing of horror. It consisted of three tiny cells, dark and unheated. With the Japanese, confinement is not simply the loss of liberty; there is punishment with it. The fear of the brig was always with us. In the dead of winter, every man who entered it got severely frostbitten hands and feet. In every case, our fearless doctors bearded the ogre in his den, and the sufferer completed his sentence in the comparative ease of the hospital. We know that by Japanese standards our brig was not as hard as those in which the Japanese were locked up, but we were not Japanese. We shall always hold the existence of that brig against Lieutenant Asaka. Yet, except for an escape attempt near the end of our imprisonment, we recall no one who was ever put in the brig unless he stole from a comrade, stole from the food stores allotted to our common mess, or snatched food from a passing woman or child on the way back and forth from the *yama*. With few exceptions, I think most of the men who made it to the brig richly deserved it.

The fuel supply was always short, often pitifully inadequate. From what we saw of the Japanese civilians, they fared but little, if at all, better than we did. Orders were continually being issued against stealing from the mine; we ignored them to smuggle in precious fuel. Huddled and crowded around a tiny stove, trying to heat water and cook in homemade tin cans what refuse we had been able to get from the mine, we fought and snarled at one another like wild beasts. If caught with fuel by guards at the gate, you might be punished, but not too badly. Yet, here is a very strange thing: once we had the fuel inside, and used moderate care in concealing it, we were not bothered. Lieutenant Asaka must have had continual complaints from the mine workers about the serious theft of coal and timber, yet he did very little to try to stop it; a perfunctory search was all. By now most of us were expert thieves, and it took more than a routine search to catch us. The astute old sailor, "Frenchy," had his forty thieves bring in coal hidden in their mess gear; they were never caught.

After a while I began to notice that the prisoners had started to call Lieutenant Asaka the "Old Man." I first heard "Frenchy" use this term—he who had been slugged by this Japanese officer. When his men call an officer the "Old Man," the term is one of affectionate respect.

Now, here is something difficult to believe, and we are still bewildered by it. Orders came down from Japanese high command to execute all prisoners of war in the event of an amphibious landing on the four major Japanese home islands—and Lieutenant Asaka actually told Captain Fleming about it! Naturally some us decided we were going to do something to forestall the executions, or at least try to take as many Japanese soldiers with us to their deaths as we could before we were all killed. An army first sergeant, one Jack Boyd, was the leader of a group that brought in dynamite, fuses, and blasting caps stolen from the copper mine. In some mysterious way, Lieutenant Asaka found it out and all of the explosives were taken up. We stood by in fear and trembling, for it would have been fairly easy to locate the guilty ones. Yet, all we got out of it was a sharp reprimand at a *bango*, with a threat of the death penalty if such a thing ever happened again. In the Philippines there would have been torture and shootings; here there was nothing. Perhaps Lieutenant Asaka did not care to have such slackness on the part of his prison guards publicly disclosed, and for that reason he smothered the offense. We gave him a good mark for this incident.

Lieutenant Asaka was careful in his issue of the Red Cross food. He made it last for months instead of giving us one big feast at Christmas, as had always been done before. Even the little we received increased our chronic diarrhea to awful proportions, but we all recovered. How we loved the rare and unaccustomed food! We hated Asaka intensely for withholding the Red Cross issues, but upon reflection we realized that his method was for our own good. It was a constant source of worry for him to safeguard the food from his own men and from the other prisoners. Only his strong hand restrained the hungry men, both Japanese and American, from stealing. (Oh, Doctor Dan, was not your fine Italian hand concerned in this?)

As the [naval] blockade around the dying empire tightened, the food supply got smaller. Capable, far-seeing Lieutenant Asaka built up a reserve. His proud nature would not let us know that his beloved army was losing the war, but his actions and advice to take care of the food betrayed him.

As the dreaded *ni ju ku san*—"Mister" B-29—came closer, fire precautions and plans for the evacuation of wounded were given to us. We never knew of any bomb shelters being built for us around the barracks, yet I am sure that, behind that inscrutable mask of a face, Lieutenant Asaka had found some way to take care of us when the bombers came.

The entire nation went on a general 10 percent rice reduction; so did we. Lieutenant Asaka's face grew tense and gaunt. We know that he and his guards lost weight. Yet how simple and easy it would have been for them to take their fill of our supplies, for they were in charge of us. They had command of life and death over us; what could we have done?

Then came the end, a glorious surprise. On the fourteenth day of August there was an air raid alarm; then it was over and we were not sent to the *yama*. The next day was the same—no work. On the sixteenth, Lieutenant Asaka informed the officers of the surrender, and Captain Fleming told us not to make any demonstrations. Two days later, in his last *bango*, in an address of quiet dignity, the Japanese lieutenant gave us the official news, saying, "I will be a true friend to you from now on." Some of us began to realize that he had perhaps always been a true friend to us, more of one than we had ever thought.

Down went his beloved "Rising Sun," and up went our "Stars and Stripes," made from material Lieutenant Asaka had given us. Alongside it fluttered the "Union Jack," long concealed by our British cousins. We had our own American formations, our own bugle calls, and our own commands given in English. The [Japanese] guards were relieved and we took over their rifles. Some of the guards hurriedly left for parts unknown, for they feared reprisals for their brutalities at the mine. Only Lieutenant Asaka and that kindly man, the interpreter Yamanouchi, stayed on. The civilian population was friendly, due, I think, to Asaka's quiet presence and force.

American planes dropped food, clothing, medicines, and the advice "not to eat too much." The starving Japanese helped us collect the supplies, stealing nothing. Ever among us, unarmed, without his samurai sword, was Lieutenant

Asaka. His heart must have been breaking, his mind filled with uncertainty as to the fate of his beloved emperor, his own future blasted and perhaps hopeless. Still dignified, erect and calm, he returned our salutes better than we gave them. One doubts if a man ever passed him without first rendering the honors.

Captain Fleming told me that once when Asaka and he were talking, as soldiers will, they got to comparing wounds. Asaka, rolling up his shirt, showed him a row of machine gun bullet scars across his stomach, enough to have killed several ordinary men. He had gotten them while at the head of his troops from the Chinese Communists in the Great Bend of the Yellow River, in Shensi. Then he later showed some others his bayonet scars and ruefully muttered, "Marine Raiders, left me for dead. My men came in later and took me away." Perhaps it was in the Solomons, but I am not sure. Now we knew, at last, why he had been assigned to prisoner of war guard duty. It may not be amiss to add that he lost over twenty pounds in weight during his eleven months at Hanowa, and he had come there a slender, wiry man.

For nearly a month we loafed in our barracks, waiting to be released. Then came a midnight departure, with a long walk in the rain and mud to the railway station. The whole town seemed to see us off, lighting our way with miner's headlamps. (These men all had to be at work by six-thirty the next morning.) Lieutenant Asaka rode on the train with us; there were no other Japanese except for the train crew.

The next morning we arrived at Shinagawa. Armed American soldiers and sailors were in the harbor, and we saw strange and weird-looking landing craft, all new to us.

We had all hated Asaka. Here, at last, among our own armed forces, was the chance to take revenge on him. Yet you know what happened without my telling you. I last saw him on the station platform shaking hands with a crowd of ex-prisoners, now free and happy, and yet he was still the officer and commander, erect and unsmiling.

As I said earlier, I do not understand the Japanese. I

ought to hate this man with an intense, burning hate. I can recall only too vividly the beatings from his guards. But only eight of our men died in the dreadful winter, one from a mining accident and seven from starvation and diseases. I was later to find out that our camp had the lowest percentage of deaths of all camps in the empire.

We passed the incredible might of the American fleet in Yokohama harbor. Alongside of me at the rail, two Marines, Master Technical Sergeants I. L. Buster and C. L. Bjork, were talking about Asaka, for he still dominated our thoughts. Said one, "When we have the Japanese for our allies in the next war, I would not mind serving under that fellow's command."

Let such as this epitaph be always in our memories.

Epilogue to "The Story of Lieutenant Asaka"

In 1947, while I was serving at the Marine Corps recruit depot in San Diego, California, Captain (now Major) Fleming wrote me a long letter from Japan, where he had gone as a War Crimes Commission witness, and mentioned that Lieutenant Asaka had been tried and sentenced to be hanged for cruelties to prisoners. He said that the sentence had been passed by the court in the Yokosuka area set up for the trials of such offenders.

I found out in a hurry that Asaka's defense counsel was Judge Joseph G. Featherstone of New York City, appointed by President Truman for this duty. I sent a cablegram of some length, and it held up the execution. This manuscript was airmailed out to Judge Featherstone. He made good use of it—the lieutenant's sentence was reduced on first appeal to twelve years' imprisonment; on second appeal to a higher authority to six years; and then finally, on the third and highest appeal, to release.

I told the judge that Asaka, being proud as Lucifer, would probably never acknowledge any help from me, and

I was right. But his family sent me, through Judge Featherstone, effusive letters of thanks.

Apparently this entire manuscript reached the attention
of Maj. Gen. William F. Marquat, U.S. Army, General
MacArthur's chief of staff for supply—G-4. General Marquat had been my battery commander when I was in the army
some twenty-five years before, and a personal letter I sent
to him might have had some effect. I did not receive a
reply from the general, but the results speak for themselves.

I must have been the sole defense witness for Lieutenant
Asaka. An enraged Army Department of Criminal Investigation went into action to find out why I had defended him;
efforts were made to have fellow prisoners testify that I
was a collaborator; several times I was interrogated in San
Diego by their representatives. Finally they let me alone.
Knowing what I know now, and the trouble it caused me, I
would do the same thing over again, and gladly.

Here is Lieutenant Asaka's speech on the occasion of
Japan's surrender. (The speech [literal in its translation] was
delivered to us, his former prisoners, on 20 August 1945
through his interpreter.)

Peace, peace comes to the world again. It is a great
pleasure to say something to you. To announce it for
all of you, now. The Japanese Empire acknowledges
the terms of suspension of hostilities as given by the
American Government. Even these nations do not still
reach the best agreement of a truce.

As a true friend, from now on, I am going to do my
best in the future for the convenience of your own life
in this camp, because if able to get friendly relations
between them the Japanese has decided her own policy for your own nation.

Therefore, I hope you will keep a comfortable
daily life by the orders of your own officers, from
today, while you are standing here. All of you surely
will get much gladness in returning to your lovely
country. At this time one of my wishes is for you and

your life henceforth to grow up happier and better than before, by the honor of your country. In order to guard your life, I have been endeavoring in ability, therefore you will please cooperate with me in anything more than usual, I hope.

I close this statement, letting you honor, again, the peace. The peace already has come.

4

THE STORY OF DOCTOR WADE

Lieutenant Commander Ernest C. Wade, Medical Corps, United States Navy, died obscurely. I found out a few details here and there; suffice to say that planes of his own beloved land bombed and sank the prison ship carrying him to Japan. Some say there was only one survivor, others say more. The main fact we know is that he is dead.

For nearly three and a half years we had been what we ironically called ourselves, "guests of the emperor." Hardly a day passed, and this is the plain, simple truth, that some of us prisoners did not break the ceaseless talk of food, food, food to muse briefly upon Doctor Wade.

When the news of surrender came, it was followed by a month of glorious *ya si me*. With freedom from the accursed copper mine, and with that manna from heaven, K rations, dropped to us from American planes, we spoke more often of him. We spoke not only of his deeds—we were all talked out on that subject during the long dreary years of imprisonment—but asked each other only, "Did Doctor Wade get through?"

After a train trip to Shinagawa, processing on the USS *Relief*, a voyage to Yokohama on the USS *Girard* (an auxiliary personnel attack ship), and a day or so aboard the big transport USS *Hyde*, came a plane ride from Japan to Guam. There I heard the news I so hated to hear. I looked squarely at a hard, tough Marine mess sergeant, T.Sgt.

(Technical Sergeant) Leon B. Ellis, 2/4, (2d Battalion, 4th Marine Regiment) whose eyes glowed gauntly in his hollow face. I saw tears. I sat down on a white coral rock and, in that brilliant sunshine, glanced up at the fluttering "Stars and Stripes," now misty through my own tears. I saw another Marine from H/2/4, (Company H), Sgt. Claude H. Harrell, not far away, weeping unashamedly.

A pause followed; I looked up to see the flag again. The mess sergeant spoke, more to himself, "He would have liked to have seen that flag, too." There must be something to mental telepathy, I thought.

I am sure some of us think of Doctor Wade every day. I will never forget him. Engraved in my mind, indelibly inscribed in my heart, is the memory of one of the bravest acts I ever saw. This man performed it, and it probably never occurred to him that it was heroic. It was simply *his duty.*

He was the battalion surgeon in the 2d Battalion of the 4th Marines. I had known him well in Shanghai as a kindly physician, a skilled surgeon, a splendid gentleman, and a navy officer of high standards. I got to know him much better in Bataan and Corregidor, and even in the Old Bilibid Prison.

On at least two separate occasions he was awarded the Silver Star for rushing forward to save wounded men under bombing and shellfire. He got there ahead of other Marines, soldiers, and sailors. Some of them received the same award.

He was a tall, lean, wiry man; his face was strong with a look of benign repose; his hair was blond, and his eyes were the blue of the sky. His most striking physical asset was a pair of long legs. I guess this is why he could run faster over those rocks and ravines of Corregidor than other men equally brave.

Of course, his work as a battalion surgeon in war was of a high standard. It was appreciated, but we thought little about it. It was taken for granted. Other navy doctors were doing the same. It is just part of the tradition of the navy's medical service.

Men get the Medal of Honor, the Navy Cross, the Silver Star, and the Bronze Star in proportion to what they do on the battlefield. Sometimes they get it for saving lives, but most often it is awarded for killing men. Under the stress of "kill or be killed," some men rise to the occasion. Among the most commonplace virtues a soldier has to offer, his battlefield courage, their comrades remember some deeds more than others. There is a ceremony afterward, a bit of bright ribbon and gleaming metal, cunningly wrought, handshaking and photographers, blaring bugles and marching troops, and another name is added to the records of a long line of heroes. But often another kind of ceremony far away from the din of arms occurs. A delegated officer, resplendent and with quiet dignity, gives the cherished medal in hushed restraint and quiet to the winner's next of kin, for the hero is dead. This is how they will give out Doctor Wade's Silver Stars.

Two Silver Stars—and one is glory enough for any man! I was there when Col. S. L. Howard, commanding officer of the 4th Marine Regiment, gave him the paper, for no medals were available on beleaguered and besieged Corregidor. The "Old Man" shook his hand and glanced nervously at the sky, for enemy bombers were overhead. We looked warily over our shoulders at the Bataan shore, for Japanese artillery was shelling the North Mine Dock; the ceremony was over. We all walked leisurely back to our shelters, for we feared our comrades would see that we were scared, and resumed our waiting for the next working-over the ravine would get from the high explosives of the Japanese.

Just another man decorated, some thought. And there may have been others who wondered whether Doctor Wade would live to wear his decorations in the States.

After the Allied surrender to the Japanese, after the tension was gone, the "peace that passeth all understanding" was ours at last. Of the dreadful days to come most of us were blissfully unaware.

The conqueror seemed kind and friendly. Around Malinta Tunnel [the Allies' main bunker on Corregidor], to which spot we had been marched, we were allowed to break open our own stores and gorge our hungry bellies. We talked with friendly Japanese officers who spoke excellent English; we traded haircuts with Japanese soldiers. We knew, of course, that we would soon be transported to prisoner of war camps, but we worried little. We were in the hands of civilized men such as we were, and we were alive! How soon we were to be terribly disillusioned!

The disillusionment came suddenly, on the early morning of the third day. "Fall in in column of fours; hurry up about it; these Japanese mean business," rang out the shouts of our officers. We looked and saw that they did. Gone were the smiles and the sharing of American canned fruit; all we could see were snarls, ferocious looks, and menacing naked bayonets.

Most soldiers who are issued a bayonet hardly think about it except as a nuisance and a piece of useless gear. I had read a phrase once, and liked to repeat it: "The breastworks of the American Civil War made the bayonet as dead as a dodo." Our bayonet was twelve inches long, its handle four more, and it weighed a pound. It was of dulled blue steel, an unlovely thing, and unloved. But the Japanese bayonet is a beauty of gleaming steel, longer than ours is by several inches, with a point upturned in a cruel curve. Their officers glory in their samurai swords, but the troops worshiped their bayonets with a fanatical devotion. These bayonets were now brought most forcibly to our attention; for the next three years and more we were never allowed to forget them.

"Don't stop for water, they just stuck a fellow," was the word passed. We looked at the moving column up ahead, and there, as that column divided itself like a swift, rushing stream around a rock in its bed, we saw a pitiful, crumpled figure lying in the road, his bright blood reflected against the shining sun.

"Let the chow alone, they just got another!" was barked at me as I was stuffing my shirt with C rations from a roadside dump. I looked up, and there was a man in the ranks passing by, supported by a comrade and trailing a few drops of red in the gray dust. I sprang into the ranks and took no more rations.

The march was short, some three miles or so to Kindley Field, along the rubble and the shell holes of the road blasted from the living rock. Here and there as we marched we saw our dead—the men all killed three days before. Some lay behind rocks, some behind a fold in the ground, some lay sprawled in the open, and some, like horrid over-ripe fallen fruit, lay beneath straggling trees whose leaves had dried to a gray-green in that pitiless sun.

In the tropics a dead man turns red, like a boiled lobster, on the first day; the second day he turns black as coal, but there is no gleam in his blackness; the third day he begins to turn a pea-green shade, and then comes that awful, pene-trating, all-pervading, clinging smell that he who has known it will never forget. On the fourth day he turns to an all-over pea-green color and begins to swell. (Some of us shall never like French green peas again, for they remind us of our dead.)

All of these dead men were in more or less a kneeling position, facing in the direction of the foe, and some still clutched rifles in their hands. Alongside me trudged G.Sgt. (Gunnery Sergeant) Armand J. Sealey, Company D, 1st Bat-talion, 4th Marines, a man of much rifle range work and many target matches. Professional instincts got the better of horror, and he said, "You know, that sitting position we spent so much time on, I never thought was any good. Here we see the real thing—all these men fired in battle from the kneeling position."

We passed the battered water tower where Supply Sergeant Haskell of our regiment had died in the darkness, throwing grenades at the foe beneath him. There was still a body there lying on its face, with the arms hanging down along the walls. The clutching fingers were outlined blackish-green against the alabaster white of the walls. We wondered who the dead man was. We could not see his face because it was turned away from us at a crazy angle.

But there were no Japanese dead along the route; they had already been given their honorable burial. Reverent hands had sawed off each right arm and cremated it. The ashes of these arms were placed in little white pine boxes on the mine dock, awaiting shipment to the homeland where they would be enshrined. The bodies were loaded on barges to be cremated or otherwise disposed of in Manila.

Now we had come to Kindley Field, a postage stamp size of an airport badly battered by shell and bomb. Here we were dismissed from our ranks. On and on along that dusty, rocky road crawled the long snake of marching men, and when it had ended there were some 14,500 men crowded together plus some 2,500 officers—whites, Filipinos, Chinese, and now and then an American Negro.

The only shelter from the blazing sun, reflected against the glaring white of the landing strip of concréte and the still whiter sands of the seashore, was a huge building covered with torn sheets of corrugated iron, its gaunt ribs showing where bomb and shell had ripped the covering away, and marked with a large sign, 92ND C. A. GARAGE. Few of us ever knew or cared about the name Kindley Field; that place, then and forever after, to us was simply the "92nd Garage."

Those who arrived first headed for the Garage while the later arrivals milled aimlessly. Around us were busy little Japanese soldiers stringing barbed wire and erecting poles and scrap canvas over machine gun nests whose barrels were trained ominously on the camp. And in and around us were more of the same little Japanese soldiers with their dreadful bayonets.

Over us was the burning sun of the dry season, its heat made more intense by the glare reflected from the concrete strip and the white sand. The heat rays came back to us from the gray-white, battle-scarred hills. There was a great scurrying to and fro for driftwood, broken steel rods, anything at all with which to erect a shelter tent if you were lucky enough to have one. The men simply had to try to escape that blazing inferno of heat. The crowded, huddled place began to take on the life of a gigantic hobo jungle.

Most of the men had so hurriedly "fallen in" that they had no water. Some had food. Some few had eaten breakfast. And then the dreadful reality began to dawn on us with a sort of numbing shock—there was no water!

In the days of my somewhat spotty pious youth, I had often been forced to listen to a certain type of sermon that began with, "O, ye backslidden creatures of hell, repent, repent! Where will ye spend eternity? In heaven or in hell?" This was followed by a description of just what eternity meant, eon upon eon of years, infinite, everlasting, never-ending. Then followed the meaty picture of fire and brimstone punctuated by cries of "And this for all eternity, too!" The good man who strove to bring my childish mind into the paths of rectitude had somewhat the right idea, but he should have first suffered thirst and then tried to describe it.

And still the burning sun glared on.

Thirst benumbs the senses. It makes one helpless. The all-consuming desire for water overshadows everything else. Added to this, in our case, was the abrupt transition from the last three days of plenty to the shock of just what it meant to be a prisoner of the Japanese. We sat back; helpless, stunned, beaten, and bewildered men.

Now, men began to die.

Filipinos, in their futile dependence on the lordly white man, pleadingly asked, "Have you some water, Joe?" Joe had no water, and merely sat down and shrugged his shoulders. It seemed that all the doctors and medical corpsmen were up in the Malinta Tunnel hospital caring for the wounded.

I observed Quartermaster Clerk Frank Ferguson of our regiment, with head hung down between gaunt shoulders and face partially covered with a loose bandage. I knew that he had been wounded leading a forlorn-hope bayonet charge in the gray dawn of the last day of fighting. I also recalled that he had gotten a Silver Star some time before. His wounds were of the type that needed daily attention, but he had no water and no doctor to dress them.

Then I began to notice stretcher parties carrying men to

the 92nd Garage. I wondered, arose, and walked that way. Surely the stretcher-bearer trail led to doctors, and they must have water. Blessed, divine water!

In the Garage, men had roped off areas and tagged these ropes with their unit names in a last, futile huddling for protection. The same instinct perhaps, I thought, that makes them huddle together under shellfire and allow a single burst to kill several men.

In a bombed and shell-torn partition, with life-giving shade, was a little group. A rope separated the usual crowd of idlers from it. A crudely lettered sign read SICK BAY. On the ground lay another sign, COLONELS ONLY, trampled underfoot.

I saw Doctor Wade, stethoscope around his neck, kneeling over a still figure on a stretcher. He arose, dropped his head to his chest, and shook it slowly from side to side. A stretcher party picked up its burden and headed for the main gate. I knew who they were carrying; I had known that now lifeless clay for many years. First Sergeant Schmidtmann, the personnel sergeant major from Headquarters Company, 4th Marine Regiment, lay dead on that piece of canvas. Doctor Wade now bent over the next case, taking care of a gasping man.

This was no place for me to ask for water, so I walked away.

And so I came to find out that Doctor Wade had been able to carry his medical kit with him from Malinta to the Garage; that he had organized stretcher parties and obtained volunteer assistants. Somehow, some way, he had by sign language induced the guards to permit the desperately sick to be carried to the hospital, where medical service and water awaited them.

Later that afternoon there were water parties. We heard that Doctor Wade had arranged for them. Perhaps some other officers helped him, but from then on the legend of Doctor Wade grew and grew.

Some said that he had even made the arrangements for burial parties, and he had taken out the first dismal burden.

You know how things sometimes get a little bit enlarged in the telling; it shows, however, what the other fellows thought of him.

Doctor Wade was the only physician working around that sick bay except for Doctor Hogshire of the US Navy, who helped him get things started. The latter was early overcome by heat prostration and had to be carried away himself, but he helped a great deal. There could not have been another doctor in that camp, for had there been, he would have been there with Doctor Wade.

How many lives were saved that day by this navy doctor I do not know. Who can tell? There was an opportunity for leadership and for service. Doctor Wade arose to them both. This was his supreme moment. For this he had been trained as a physician. The emergency he met not only with quiet, sublime courage, but also with force and intelligence. He produced results.

The next day the area was swarming with doctors and medical personnel, for the Japanese had sent them down from the hospital. The crisis was over. Do you think Doctor Wade took a well-deserved rest? Should he not have taken a few hours' sleep in order that his matchless skill might be saved to preserve more lives? The simple, sober truth is that he kept on, without sleep, for seventy-two more hours, doing the same thing he had been doing the first day.

Frank Ferguson waited until the next day when the crisis was over, and only then did he take up Doctor Wade's time. The physician asked, "Why did you not come here sooner?" Ferguson grinned and made no reply. I like to think Doctor Wade understood. It is men like Ferguson who make our Marine Corps what it is. Thanks to Doctor Wade's skill, his once-festered face and bayoneted chest today bear hardly a scar.

Doctor Wade went on to the Old Bilibid Hospital. While he was head surgeon there, many men, broken in spirit and body, knew his kindly care. His fame spread among all of the [POW] camps. Perhaps it puffed up a bit in the telling, like a snowball rolling downhill.

I last saw him there in the early fall of 1944, on my way to a prison ship and Japan. He did not seem to be too badly starved. I know he was happy, doing the work he loved, bringing the broken bodies and dim minds back to a semblance of health and sanity before they were sent out to the work camps again.

Perhaps someday the Navy Department will get around to sending his family a Silver Star, or, rather, presenting it to his next of kin. There will be lofty speeches, restrained tears, and quiet dignity. We are all familiar with these things.

But in the old, ruined city of Manila there should still be standing some part of the thick walls of the Old Bilibid Prison. And down on Kindley Field, unless the Japanese tore it up for its steel, is that battered shell of the 92nd Garage. When I think of them, I think of Doctor Wade. He needs no further decoration, for these are his honors.

In the town where I was born is a church, the Grace Episcopal Church, located at the corner of High and Church Street in Petersburg, Virginia, with lovely stained glass windows.

As a restless youngster during the "Ye backslidden creatures of hell, repent, repent!" sermons, I used to wriggle and squirm around to look at the visage of an angel, its face strong and kind, its hair of a fair hue, its eyes as blue as the sky. The window is the third one on the left, in the nave. The face of the six-foot-high angel is exactly like that of Doctor Wade. Truly the old artist that made it wrought well.

I visited that old church not so long ago. I looked for my angel. It was there, and the shaft of yellow light diffused its glow through the Gothic arch. My angel's face grew misty from the uncontrollable tears that welled up in my eyes. I was looking at the face of Doctor Wade.

5

THE STORY OF JOE PEARLSTEIN

First Sergeant Joseph Pearlstein, Headquarters Company, 2d Battalion, 4th Marines, is no more. Joe was a Corregidor Marine. We heard he died in the fall of 1942, in Moji, the gateway port of Japan to China and Manchuria, while being shipped with other prisoners of war from Cabanatuan.

We idly inquired "How?" and got the laconic reply, "Starvation, of course," from the old quartermaster sergeant of Marines, Albert S. Lemon, who had been with him. We all had seen the same thing so many, many times that it was an old story to those of us who were recently released "guests of the emperor." No further comment was necessary and we returned to our duties.

We knew all about it, we thought.

The talk among these men reverted to the usual topics of booze, women, and tall tales of far-off foreign lands. Lies, of course, but lies with enough truth in them to always be entertaining.

The old battalion sergeant major reflected. In the early days of imprisonment, as hunger began to gnaw at bellies and brains, he had observed that the men's talk changed from women and liquor to liquor alone; as the dreadful gnawing hunger ate more out of their bellies and brains, food and food alone was the topic of conversation. For long years they thought of nothing but food.

He recalled the endless recipes and the arguments over them; he remembered the time Doctor Dan had put Quartermaster Sergeant M. K. Martin and Radio Sergeant C. L. Bjork in the "psycho" ward of his hospital in Japan for writing down every recipe they could lay their hands on; he had labored hard to restore them to sanity. He thought back to when Japan had surrendered and the storehouses were opened. With these supplies and with the food dropped from American planes, in a short time they began to talk of liquor and eventually of sex. Then he knew that their tortured minds had made it back from the dim world of half-insanity; that the shadows were gone, that they were well, and that life was, again, good. He breathed a short prayer, blessing *ni ju ku san*, for the Japanese always used the honorable prefix of "mister" when referring to the B-29 [bomber]. He was grateful for the atomic bomb.

The sergeant major bought a round of drinks and cleared his throat. The gang around the table grew silent and looked up expectantly, for it is only common sense to listen politely to the man doing the treating.

"You fellows think you know all about Joe Pearlstein and how he died. I was not there in Moji with him, but I can add quite a bit. I guess I knew him better than any of you, for I was his sergeant major.

"Joe was Orthodox. He would not eat pork, ham, or anything that had no backbone or scales, and a whole lot of other things. There is a book in the Bible called 'Leviticus,' and it tells you what the Jews cannot eat. You all remember the occasional spoonful of squid we got now and then? Joe used to give his portion away. If he had eaten it, he might be alive here today. But, Joe was true to his principles, in his quiet way. Whether mistaken or not, under the conditions he was facing, you have to respect him for that.

"We like the Jews we have in the Marine Corps. It takes a certain amount of guts to enlist anyway, for you sign up 'for general service only.' Maybe you later can get assigned to some specialist job, but you are not sure. Some folk think that Jews are not good fighting men, but that is only because

they do not know them. All of us who have served with
them know better.

"Before this war we had only thirty-eight sergeants
major of the line. It was the hardest rank of all to make.
Come to think of it, at least six of them were Jews, like First
Lieutenant Irving 'Jackie' Fine; Captain Horace Larn;
CWO [Chief Warrant Officer] Marvin Goode, killed in action on Guam; all first-rate men. Since we got out of jail, we
have heard all about CWO 'Slug' Marvin, his medals, and
how he came to die.

"Joe joined us in the summer of 1941 in Shanghai. A veteran of World War I, he had been seagoing, on a Nicaragua
expedition, and had finally drifted into a soft post exchange
steward's job; then he got into the quartermaster and made
staff sergeant. By some freak accident he made first sergeant instead of supply sergeant; we often wondered how on
earth he had done it, but no one ever asked him.

"He served along with me now and then; he did not interest me. Not knowing him well, I did not like him.

"You all know how he looked. He wore a poor, ill-fitting
issue uniform, he had a shambling walk, and that awful look
of helpless bewilderment on his face. Fumbling is perhaps
the best word to picture him, fumbling and pathetic.

"Here he was, a brand new first sergeant, given to us to
take over a company in the Second Battalion, when things
were tough and the war clouds were gathering over Shanghai. It takes the average smart 'first soldier' about six
months to learn the answers; our battalion office figured we
would have to show Joe everything and do most of it for
him. I know that this is a sergeant major's job and what he
gets paid to do, but I was spoiled and lazy. First Sergeant
Albert W. 'Liver Lip' Gordon had just left; we had First
Sergeant Edward W. 'The Champ' Browne, Sergeant Major
Wayne K. 'Dusty' Miller, and Sergeant Major Richard
'Bozo' Duncan for our first sergeants. They were the best
'top kicks' a Marine could want."

"Yes, they surely were, and now they are all dead," inter-
jected Field Music [bandsman] Pvt. John Corley. The ser-

geant major was irritated, but he reflected that this mere boy
had won the first Silver Star in the regiment for carrying
a wounded Signal Corps officer, a Second Lieutenant Mc-
Carthy, to safety at the risk of his own life, mixing up in
something that was not his concern, for the man he saved
came from the army. "Three drowned on [Japanese] prison
ships, and old 'Liver Lip' died in the Solomons,"[9] continued
the boy. The others around the table frowned, for a lowly
Music does not ordinarily speak in the presence of his
seniors, especially when one of them is buying the drinks.

"Another round, Mister Bartender, on me," said the sergeant major, and the audience settled back in respectful attention.

"We talked over Joe with the 'Old Man,' Lieutenant
Colonel H. R. Anderson, the command officer of Second
Battalion, who was later killed in action, and with Major
L. B. 'Chesty' Puller, the battalion executive officer. They
sympathized and helped to the extent of switching 'The
Champ' [Browne] to Company E, a big outfit, while Joe
went to the little Headquarters Company in his place. It was
a special duty company and their officers were just down the
ladder from ours.

"It gradually dawned on us that we did not have to help
him. Fumbling and helpless as he looked, a scarecrow on
the parade ground, he kept up his paperwork. His men did
not seem to come up for mast punishment as much as they
did in the other outfits. At first, 'Chesty' used to tear his hair
out over him. You know he always said that a good parade
ground Marine always turned into a good field Marine. I
guess he found out that Joe was good long before any of the
rest of us did.

"Then we went to the islands and the war. Headquarters
Company swelled up to a big one; Joe looked as fumbling
and helpless as ever, but despite increased work his stuff always came in on time and was of a high standard. The bat-

9. Sergeant Major Gordon committed suicide at Camp Pendleton, California, in 1944, we later learned.

talion sometimes asked 'Dusty,' 'The Champ,' and 'Bozo' for a bit too much, or a bit too early, and arguments resulted. They were very strong characters, and often told me where to go, but, I could always bully Joe and he never talked back. When you feel superior to another guy, you like him.

"You know how the supplies broke down early on, and we went on half rations, or less? Drawing our chow together in the mess lines, we made the amazing discovery that Joe was Orthodox. He then became very popular, for he gave away his pork, ham, and bacon, little enough that it was. He had to keep a sort of book for his newfound friends, to keep them straight on when they were to get his chow.

"Here is a trivial incident, but one that shows Joe for what he was. The island [Corregidor] had been under heavy bombing; now there was a lull, and when we would hear the call of 'Motors in the west,' we could not know. The company had to draw clothes. It was a mile climb from James Ravine to Middleside, where the clothing storeroom was located. One would have thought they could have had Corporal Julian Jordan, a battalion truck driver and a very brave man, deliver the clothes by truck, risking only one man's life, but you know how wars are.

"Joe fell in with his men, some seven or eight kids. The young Marine is too ignorant to think about danger; the old-timer reflects and sometimes hesitates. I was not in for clothes, I was an old-timer, I reflected, and I told Joe I did not want any clothes. He could tear up the slip and I would get along on what clothes I had saved from the time they bombed Middleside. At least forty men were in for clothes, and most of them must have felt the same as I did. You can't blame them, for the heavy bombing we had gotten was less than an hour old.

"Joe could have turned the detail over to Corporal 'Whitey' Morvan, the young property corporal, who was there. Joe was not in for clothes, but he took those fellows up there. He was the first sergeant, and it was his job, he thought. The atmosphere of the quartermaster storeroom was thick with restrained tension; they had only three inches of concrete on the roof; bombs had killed men there that morning.

"They got their clothes and Joe led them back. There was not much cover on that route either. Shortly after they got back, the [Japanese] planes came over. The whole area was a hell of bombs and steel fragments shooting around from the exploding ammunition dumps, which they set on fire.

"Later that month they gave me a reserve position on the Upper Belt Line Road, to protect the beach trenches with overhead fire when the [enemy] landing came. It was some eight hundred yards long, exposed and open. Along it were twenty-one ammunition dumps, all artillery shells, with not even a single tarpaulin to cover them. We shuddered to think of just what one little incendiary bomb would do among those three-inch, seventy-five, and one-fifty-five millimeter shells. To man that line we had Filipino mess attendants, re-called from sixteen-year reserve, bandsmen and dog robbers from the Headquarters Battery of the 91st Scouts, and my-self—with three Marines—First Sergeant Joe Pearlstein, Sergeant Larsen of the pay office, and Corporal 'Whitey' Morvan.

"I was allowed to pick the Marines—at least they gave me that much of a break—so I chose them. The 'Old Man' [Lt. Col. H. R. Anderson] had offered me a line gunnery sergeant, but I still picked Joe. He gave me a quiet nod of approval when he assigned Joe to us.

"I really resented the job. I had the regular battalion job at headquarters, and this was extra duty. It was really an of-ficer's assignment. I supposed I should have felt flattered at the confidence the 'Old Man' placed in me, but I was not. I was sore. And besides, it was darned dangerous. No one likes to get shaken loose from a bombproof shelter at any time, and Corregidor was one awful place to be out in the open. So positions were assigned, foxholes were dug, and we stood by to man them when the Japanese slammed down a barrage. Those people were only forty-one hundred yards across the North Channel; a barrage was likely to be the prelude to a landing.

"There are lots of people who get nervous when somebody shoots at them; me, for instance. When Joe was told of his new job, he visibly shook. I tried to hide my fear, for I was more afraid of Joe's finding it out than I was of those shells. 'Whitey' and young Larsen knew, for they were veterans by now to shellfire and bombings. I like to think I put it over on Joe. After his first fright, he looked at me with that silly, dumb, trusting look he had while he was being given the dope."

The glasses were empty, the bartender looked up expectantly, but no one noticed him. The sergeant major continued his yarn.

"One night we all went up there to deepen our foxholes. The Japanese bombers came over, and we cowered and shook in those little foxholes. To our surprise, there was not the usual horrid scream of falling bombs followed by the dull *crump, crump, crump* of explosions. There was a gentle sighing noise, like the wind in the forest, followed by a series of faint *pops*. We had, for the first time, been bombed with magnesium incendiaries. By a miracle, only the ammunition dump where Joe was digging had been badly hit. He and Filipino Scouts soon put out the fire. I ran down there, found Joe wounded slightly from the burst of a one-fifty-five shell, ordered him below for treatment, and hurried to the flank to see if any more damage had been done. Later, we learned that Joe did not go down to see Doctor Wade until his fire was completely out.

"In the last few days of the horrible nightmare on the island, the battalion headquarters was moved to the Middleside Tunnel, as was Joe's company command post. Corporal Julian Jordan, as nonchalant and fearless as ever, drove his little truck with the company's papers and baggage while Joe and the rest of us trudged up the hill to the new position in the darkness. The 'Old Man' should have relieved us of that reserve position, but he probably had too much else on his mind to think about; we never thought they would order us into it again, now that we were located a mile away from the rest of the battalion.

"On the day before the final landing came, and with it the end of Corregidor, the Japanese put down the heaviest barrage that James Ravine had ever received, even worse than the one we had taken on the emperor's birthday. It was a feint to fix us in position while the landing was made on the First Battalion at Monkey Point the next night. We had just one telephone line that was not blown out by the shellfire; it rang, and Captain Lloyd E. Wagner, our adjutant, answered.

"His face was very grave. He looked at Joe and myself. 'The exec orders that position be manned down in the ravine. Good-bye and good luck,' he said, as he held out his hand. Captain Wagner of the Marine Corps Reserve is dead now, one of the really good ones.

"We ran out of the tunnel, stumbling over the rocks. I was the faster, for Joe's feet hurt him, and I had to slow down. As we neared the edge of the terrible barrage, and through the inferno of flashes, we were shocked to see nothing left but bare tree trunks; all of the camouflage was destroyed. We saw the fires and heard the bang and shrieking whine of the burning one-five-five ammo dumps.

"We flattened ourselves on the ground to avoid a burst, for by now we were on the edge of that hell. Flashes, noise, dust, and flying gravel were in our faces. Then no more came, and the barrage had ended. Amid that great peace and calm, except for the burning ammo dump off to our flank, and a long way off, we picked ourselves up. Joe's mouth was trembling like a scared rabbit's. I looked at him with scorn because, as I have said, I could always bully him.

"He said, 'It's a hell of a war, but the only war we've got,' and laughed. The tremble was gone; his face was bright and clear. The reaction after great danger set in on me, and I nearly collapsed. He supported me, saying, 'Take it easy, we're all right now.' We sat down on the ground, his arm around my shoulders, and I shook and chattered my teeth in hysteria.

"Joe had found himself. If ever a man had conquered fear, he had done it.

"A few hours later came surrender. From that time on our

positions were reversed. He was the strong man upon whom
I leaned.

"The 'Old Man' told me to get a roster of the battalion
for him. I was too dazed and dispirited to do a thing, but Joe
got it for me and I got the credit. It is also typical of me-
thodical Joe that he carried his service records away with
him, and gave each of his men his own record. It is doubtful if another first sergeant in the Fourth Marine Regiment
was able to do this. Some of these fellows still have their
record books and highly prize them as souvenirs.

"In Cabanatuan, I got amoebic and bacillic dysentery together, and moved out near the heads in the rear of the
'nipa' barracks to die. Joe was sick, too, but he came out
there and forced me to eat. You know how it is when the
bacillic dysentery has you down; you simply cannot eat, and
soon you die. Joe's gentle patience got a few mouthfuls of
hateful rice down my unwilling throat. Most of the men who
lay in that grass in back of the heads died, as you well know.

"Then Joe brought an army medical captain out to see
me, Captain Lee Schirmer. That dear man, may the gods
bless him, from somewhere, somehow, had gotten the miracle drug, sulfathiazole. Seven pills put me back on my feet;
I began to recover and was as hungry as a wolf. I weighed
only ninety-five pounds, so Joe hovered around me, taking
good care to see that I got food to eat.

"You remember how it was nearly a month before we got
any meat, and then it was only a tiny pig for some fifteen
hundred starving men? We all received maybe a teaspoon of
chopped pork, with some moldy flour, to make about two
ounces of gravy per man. How good it tasted! Joe, being Orthodox, was offered several pesos for his, and at that time a
peso could buy quite a lot. Instead, he gave his share to me.

"Then Joe began to dry up; his ribs showed. His big, dull
eyes stared out from hollow sockets. He grew morose and
kept to himself, for by now I was able to get my own chow
and wash myself. He would hardly speak, even to the 'Old
Swede,' First Sergeant Earl O. Carlson, his best friend.
'Swede' died with him in Moji, you know, from the usual

thing. Joe used to sit out in the grass all alone; his head-shaking and trembling jaw came back, only it was worse than ever. His body was covered with ulcers and he began to stink.

"The naval officer in charge of the barracks, appointed from the prisoners, did not know Joe and did not like him. No one could blame him, for Joe gave one the creeps. In October, when they made up the Manchuria detail, Joe was on it. He could have gotten out of it by seeing the doctors, but he no longer cared about anything. The 'Old Swede' volunteered to go along with this detail, to take care of Joe. We all thought the 'Swede' crazy, for he had served in Peking; he certainly knew how cold it was going to be in Manchuria.

"So we never saw Joe again. But I like to think back to that time when we nearly got ours from that barrage, and his laughing remark, 'It's a hell of a war, but the only war we've got!' He was a man."

The end had come to the sergeant major's tale. The group looked at him, whose eyes were suspiciously misty. All were silent. The eager bartender moved in with his, "What will it be, gents?"

"My round this time, the same," said the Field Music. But the sergeant major got up and walked slowly away.

6

THE STORY OF
LT. COL. MASAO MORI

His name is Lt. Col. Masao Mori; I do not recall his particular branch of the service; all I remember is that he was an officer of the Imperial Japanese Army, and in the early days of our imprisonment he was the camp commandant at Cabanatuan. I personally hope he is dead; if he still lives, I hope the War Crimes Commission gets hold of him.[10]

In these days of victory they are trying men as war criminals; we read in the papers how Gen. Tomoyuki Yamashita himself, the conqueror of Malaya, mounted the gallows in the dim hours between midnight and dawn in a Los Baños prisoner of war enclosure in the Philippines. A pair of smaller fry were his companions in death. The army drew a decent veil over the more morbid details of his execution.

I once read that Lord Wellington, the Iron Duke, at the Battle of Waterloo, when shown a chance to train his cannon at the Emperor Napoleon, disdainfully replied amid the din and clash of arms, "It is not the business of commanders to be firing off heavy ordnance at one another."

In World War I, both Germans and Allies shunned bombing each other's headquarters, like rival beauties passing each other on Broadway. But this was different; the clock

---

10. In 1951 a Marine master sergeant in the maintenance department at Parris Island, S.C., told me that he had been in charge of Lieutenant Colonel Mori's hanging on Iwo Jima. That was good news!

was turned back to the Dark Ages; the spirits of Alaric, Attila, and Genseric seemed to rise from their graves. Headquarters were freely bombed, culminating in that attack in the worst taste of all, the bombing of Pearl Harbor the day after payday! Nothing seemed sacred anymore. But we suppose the Japanese, who copy everything, could say that this violation of military etiquette was no worse than George Washington's attack on the drunken Hessians at Princeton on Christmas night. It all depends on who is getting attacked, you know.

The pendulum swings slowly. Ten years from now we might be ashamed of what we have done. But there are some of us who still wish that Lieutenant Colonel Mori had dangled at the end of a rope as the gallows-mate of General Yamashita.

I am none too sure that he is alive, for I have last heard of him in the early spring of 1943, when he was promoted from a major to his present rank. But one rather thinks he survived; one suspects him to be on the payroll of the forces of occupation, if any former officers of the Imperial Japanese Army are so permitted. For Lieutenant Colonel Mori was a cultured gentleman with winning ways and a disarming charm. Some men, more skilled in character reading, might describe him as ingratiating. If he is in the land of the living, I fear that he is held in great respect by our officers and his advice and counsel on affairs are eagerly listened to by other Japanese. No doubt he mixes a charming cocktail and serves it even more charmingly, for he is a perfect host.

But some of us in the lower ranks do not feel the same way about him as do some of those in the higher ranks; we think you could get plenty of volunteers for the odious office of hangman, from the privates, if Lieutenant Colonel Mori were the victim. In fact, a few of the Texas boys have been heard to say that if they could have his person in their custody for about a week, there would be no need for a hanging at all.

Old Lieutenant Flynn of the 31st Infantry used to have plenty to say about what he would do to Lieutenant Colonel

Mori if he had the chance. He told us of an old Greek book called *Plutarch's Lives* he had once read, for "Old Dobe" was a scholar of sorts. He related to us the awful "Death of the Boats" from *Artaxerxes*, and said he would like to see how long Lieutenant Colonel Mori could last through it. No one ever pulled the wool over Lieutenant Flynn's eyes.

I have recorded elsewhere that I do not understand the Japanese, and in the case of the lieutenant colonel, I will also put myself on record as saying that I do not understand my fellow Americans, for most of the officers seemed to like Lieutenant Colonel Mori. Some of them tried hard to show others the errors of their ways by pointing out what Lieutenant Colonel Mori was doing for them, but such arguments were useless. When a man has his mind made up, you make him an enemy by showing him, clearly and logically, his error. After several attempts on my part to besmirch the character of Lieutenant Colonel Mori, I gave it up and discussed him no more with my fellow prisoners.

One first heard his name in the city of Cabanatuan, Nueva Ecija Province, some twenty kilometers from our destination, Prison Camp Number Three. After a journey by rail from the Old Bilibid Prison in Manila, with some 120 men packed à la sardine–style in a pint-sized boxcar of a narrow gauge railroad line, we rested in the evening on the ground beneath the floor of the local schoolhouse. This was in early June 1942 in the sweltering heat at the end of the dry season. The season was coming to an end, and with it came the chance of welcomed showers after the sun had set. Only one man had died in that boxcar on the way up, but we had seen so much of death that little was thought of it. The comment probably ran, "He just couldn't take it. Maybe he is better off than we are." And the chaplain, Captain Talbot, a Jesuit priest and a man of profound learning, said, "Now that he has ceased to know, he knows it all." But we worried little about our dead, for we were more concerned with the coming of morning and that mess kit of rice and canteen full of water. When day broke, our Japanese guards took us off in groups of one hundred each to begin the twenty-kilometer march to our new prison camp.

Our prisoner officers were summoned before the interpreter; grave-faced they came back to give us the news. Our coastal artillery officer, 1st Lt. R. T. Pullen, USA, whom I had known on Corregidor and was to know again in Japan, told us, "Any man who falls out will be shot. All sick prisoners will report to the Japanese doctor. Published by, then, Major Mori, the camp commandant." It was highly dangerous, we thought, to go before any Japanese doctor from what we had already seen of their work; hardly a man thought himself unable to make the march, so nearly all of the men fell in at the command. The pace was absurdly slow, with frequent rest stops. Most of us were hard and tough, and most were young; dysentery, pellagra, beriberi, scurvy, malaria, and malnutrition had hardly laid their blighting hands upon us then, for we were mostly Corregidor men and had not suffered the sickness and starvation of the Bataan forces, caused by the breakdown of their supply lines. My principal ailment then was numerous ulcers, from the "Guam blisters" I had contracted on Corregidor, and surely I had none on the soles of my feet. To trained infantrymen the march was a picnic. And American trucks filled with loot from Bataan and driven by impressed American drivers followed our column with the omnipresent armed sentry in each vehicle.

Men did fall out, and they were picked up and put in the trucks. No one was shot. And such was the beginning of the Major Mori legend.

But in the same squad with me marched Master Gunnery Sergeant George B. Case, a veteran of World War I and the 2d Division of those days, a companion in the same battalion of the 4th Marines in Bataan and on Corregidor. He had come through unwounded but with a severe case of unchecked malaria. I could see that the heat was beginning to affect old George. He was often urged to fall out; others had done so and no one had been shot. Case refused, saying, "Maybe not yet, but who can tell what will happen to those fellows on the trucks after we get in? The Japanese are an unpredictable race." George Case refused to take a chance, and on his arrival in camp he went out of his head. A Japanese officer thought Case's clutching grasp to support himself on "Old Pick," a Marine quartermaster sergeant named Pickering, was an attempt to start a fight, and he ordered his guards to use their rifle butts and slug him down. It might not have hurt a healthy man very badly, but for Master Gunnery Sergeant George B. Case it was fatal.

One hour later he was dead, for we had no American doctors with us. We buried him that afternoon. "Old Pick" gave him his blanket, with the letters USMC on it, for a burial shroud. That blanket could have been sold for ten pesos then, and that could have bought a great deal of food. But Old Pick had been his close friend. (On the way to Japan, two and a half years later, Old Pick's prison ship was sunk by American bombs and torpedoes. Most of those the Japanese did not machine gun to death or kill with hand grenades tossed into the holds of the stricken ship were drowned. I shall never see Old Pick again.) But it was so nice of him to have given George that blanket to be buried in, the kind act of a true Marine.

Lieutenant Colonel Mori, I give you the benefit of the Scotch verdict of "Not proven" in George Case's death, in the tribunal of my considered judgment, as I thought it over in the long years of imprisonment that were to come. But others said, "George asked for it, and he was dumb. He should have gone before those Jap doctors and never had tried to make the march. He should have dropped out and gotten into a truck. Lieutenant Colonel Mori never shot anyone for that, you know. He is a good Jap." So ran the talk, and the legend of Lieutenant Colonel Mori grew apace.

Cabanatuan Number Three Camp, compared to what I ran into later, might have been called a pleasant place, of sorts. We had less than one hundred men die there in four months before they moved us to Camp Number One, eight kilometers away. The only work details were those for camp maintenance, and on the outside details to collect wood we could buy all sorts of food from eager Filipinos whose prices were, then, not too high. We soon ruined those prices in our frantic efforts to outbid each other, as our selfishness was always too much the rule with us in prison. Mori had issued orders against such outside trading, and his guards were supposed to search all incoming work parties at the gate. Violations were open and flagrant, but few were punished. We thought that Lieutenant General Homma, headquartered in Manila, had issued these orders and that Major Mori had done his part in publishing them and had humanely overlooked infractions. Men spoke well of him.

In the Old Bilibid Prison we had been given a look at some printed orders that read, For every man who escaped, ten men would be shot to death. General Homma signed these orders. (Not long ago I read that General Homma died before an American firing squad. A just nemesis had finally caught up with him.) But one could not really vilify the Japanese for this order, for there was very little the Japanese did that could not be matched with well-authenticated American documents. It may be recalled that our own Maj. Gen. J. Franklin Bell in "the days of the empire" published an order to the effect that for every sentry shot by an Insurrecto while walking post, two Filipino prisoners would die. Perhaps shooting ten men for an escape attempt and two for the killing of a sentry, in trying to rid their native land of hated invaders, is just the same thing, but the same iron spirit underlies them both.

We had just been formed into "shooting squads" of ten men each, but not by name, when the first escape was made. Four young privates of the army's coast artillery, lads originally from Fort Drum, just walked away. How this happened I do not know, for there were plenty of Japanese sentries posted around the camp. None of us ever got a chance to talk to these poor youngsters afterward. At nine o'clock that evening they were brought in after a six-hour absence. Major Mori's myrmidons trussed them up in a most effective fashion. They were tied to wooden posts, the supports of a shed in the motor pool area, on the south side of the building. Bareheaded they were, and between the calf of their legs and the back of their thigh was lashed a piece of timber two inches by four inches in size. Their hands and ankles touched, drawn tightly together by a piece of line. Here they knelt on ground covered with jagged gravel. Of their anguish and pain, their knees in the sharp stones probably hurt them the least, for that cruel timber was a diabolical torture. And some men told afterward of how the sentries would, now and then, throw a handful of dirt in their mouths when the men begged for water.

The prison "grapevine" said they had been caught after they had asked, or demanded, of a frightened Filipino *tao* some food and water. Discovery would have meant death for the man and his family, so he turned them in. Some say the motive of greed for the reward offered by the Japanese for an escaped prisoner was the real reason. From what I know of the natives under the occupation, I do not like to believe this, but it may have been true.

Until three o'clock in the afternoon of the next day these four men writhed in the pitiless sun with, I repeat, a handful of dirt thrown in their mouths from time to time when they begged for water. We all saw them that terrible day, and we all wondered who would be the forty to die with them. But a grave for only the four was dug, just outside the gate on the way to the swift-flowing Cabanatuan River. At three o'clock they were untied and dragged, for they could not walk for some little time, before a drumhead court-martial.

We watched the proceedings from a short distance away. A Japanese officer or two, a handful of noncommissioned officers, were the tribunal of death. It may have lasted half an hour. We saw them start down the path to the open grave, awaiting its prey, the sentries guarding these doomed young men. Behind them followed the firing squad. Some of us turned away for we could look on no longer, but though we ceased to look, it seemed to us that these four young boys walked with the eager steps of bridegrooms on their way to the nuptial altar. For after such torture, death was a welcome release.

Sitting in the nipa-thatched barracks, I could hear the comments of those who watched their deaths. "They are tying their hands! They are blindfolding them. No, they refused it! They are standing them up in the grave! They are putting lighted cigarettes in their mouths, but the big fellow, Private Gordon, spit his out! Right in their faces, too! Their heads are high. They have lots of guts!"

I heard the scattered rifle volley, ragged and torn. Then came more cries of wonderment. "The big fellow got up again!" A few more scattered shots came, to be followed with a "He's down at last!" Then there was the sound of four mercy shots, one after the other. Outside the barracks were comments. "The big guy cursed them to their faces to do their damnedest!" It was over.

The next day we were officially put into "shooting squads" and warned. For several days we worried over the fate of the unknown forty, and how we would be chosen. But no one was shot for the escape. The tale went the rounds that the day of the shooting Mori had ordered the torture, hoping this punishment would appease the general and that no one would be shot. There was a further tale that General Homma let Lieutenant Colonel Mori start back for Cabanatuan without a definite decision as to the fate of the four soldiers, but when the major reached his camp the messengers of death had preceded him. Whether Mori himself made up this pleasing story we cannot know; with his winning ways, he is a most plausible man. And so most of the officer prisoners thought him to be a fine fellow.

As a result of scanty rice, a tiny ration of waste vegetables, practically no medicines, and overcrowded conditions, malnutrition and dysentery set in. There was now a camp commissary, established by the grace of Major Mori. In the beginning of our imprisonment, many prisoners had money and some of the "haves" shared with the "have-nots." At once the black market raised its ugly head; not only in food, but also in lifesaving sulfa drugs that changed hands for precious pesos.

I like to think of jovial, fat, retired chief boatswain's mate

"Cal" Coolidge, who had been like a St. Boniface with his Luzon Bar. The tale was told that he had bought sulfa drugs on the black market and given them freely to the dying to help save lives. But I hate to think of a sergeant named Monk, in our own Marine regiment, whose conduct was a disgrace to humanity, known to drive a truck outside of the camp under the guard of a corrupt Japanese sentry. In Manila and in towns along the way he would buy drugs cheaply; in the camp he would sell sulfa pills for two and a half pesos each. The commissary prices were much higher than those in the towns; whether our Major Mori shared in the marked-up prices, I cannot say. Most of my fellow prisoners would indignantly assure me that he did not.

Across the road from where we were imprisoned was the guards' camp, where food and medicines were in considerable abundance. Some lucky prisoners were assigned to work there, and they grew sleek and fat. If any of these menials became sick, their considerate captors gave them medication. Our mouths watered at the tales of stalks of ripe bananas laid out on each mess table of the Japanese. Some of our doctors frantically begged Major Mori for sulfa drugs to help save the lives of those men down with bacillic dysentery, and were told, with well-simulated regret, that he just did not have any. Yet certain men who waited on Japanese tables or who worked in the Japanese hospital had sulfa drugs for sale at very high prices.

If one were nearly dying and could be so certified by the Japanese doctors, they would have him moved across the road to what was called the isolation hospital. Here food was better, but there were few, if any, sulfa drugs. Oh, Major Mori, could you not have spared just a few of those precious sulfa pills? Had you done so, the pretty cemetery you allowed us to fix up might not have had so many graves!

Major Mori was well aware that bacillic dysentery was rampant. There was also amoebic dysentery, which kills slowly, and sometimes does not kill at all. A man who contracted bacillic dysentery would be suddenly seized with cramps and violent bouts of diarrhea; sometimes he bled, for his bugs were hungry, too. He would get so weak and helpless that he could not keep his bedding clean as he lay on the bamboo slats of the nipa [thatched barracks] nor could he squirm in his agony without jostling fellow sleepers, so crowded were we all. As a result, there was much cursing and snarling at the sick, for it was necessary to have someone on whom to vent one's spite. You dared not do it to the Japanese, for they would shoot you for "insulting the honor of the Japanese army." If you insulted a well man you might have a fight on your hands, but a desperately sick man could not hit back. Most of the bacillic cases moved out in back of the barracks, near the heads, and lay in the grass. The rainy season was now upon us, but we hardly knew, nor did we care very much. Some of our comrades drew food for the sick and carried it out to them, urging them to eat, for after a while, with bacillic dysentery, one loses his appetite. And there were some men who brought out food, urging it upon the dying, but secretly hoping the sufferer would not eat it and would tell his Good Samaritan to take it. And all around the camp hovered those human vultures offering two *dobe* brown cigarettes for a mess kit of rice. This was the beginning of the "dog eat dog" world.

A few sulfa drugs trickled legally into the camp and the number of deaths slowed down. The camp isolation hospital, a place of the crudest sort, had already been set up. All cases brought there were carried across the camp on stretchers after the Japanese doctors had given their approval. The food, to some degree, was much better there, but before a man died in this place, if the doctors were aware of it in time, they were allowed to go to Camp Number One some eight kilometers away. We were told how much better this place was than our own, but later we learned the terrible truth. Almost all of the men sent to Camp Number One died there. Major Mori was a smart man, for, as senior to the other camp's commandant, he kept his death rate figure down at the other officer's expense. To most Camp Number Three prisoners, however, one could not say anything against Major Mori, for it was pointed out that Camp Number One had a death rate of nearly thirty men per day for long months; and it took Major Mori to stop this high death rate by assuming command and securing Red Cross food and medicines. But, all other prison camps in the Philippines received this food and these drugs at the same time.

Less than a hundred of us died in those four months at Camp Number Three. But some five hundred or more contracted the edema or "wet" type of beriberi, with symptoms all too plainly visible. Scurvy was also rampant, and a long line of men, often hundreds of them, waited to see doctors, hoping to get something to cure the sores in their mouths. A few cheap limes and lime leaves from trees that grew just outside the camp were issued to those who could show visible oral sores. The scourge was curbed but not stopped. Major Mori, we thank you for the limes, for they saved lives.

You had us bury our dead nicely, with fitting ceremony. Dog tags were stuck in dead mouths before rigor mortis set in; dog tags were tied around dead necks, for each man had been issued two of them. The name, rank, serial number, and date of death were written down on a piece of paper and buried inside a beer bottle placed in the grave. (Of course, you and your men drank the beer, Major Mori, not us. It was even whispered that you sometimes invited our senior prisoner officers to your quarters for a meal and a bottle; at this time you deplored conditions and the little you were able to do for your prisoners.)

As our burial parties wended their way to the graveyard with their dismal burdens, the work was light, for hardly a man lying dead on his stretcher weighed as much as a hundred pounds. We could see, ahead of us, the bright blossoms of the wildflowers that we had been allowed to plant where our comrades slept in their eternal rest. But to our right side, just before we reached the final resting place, there was a nameless grave with no whitewashed crosses, where no flowers were allowed to grow. Here lay the bodies of the four young men you tortured, Major Mori, before merciful execution came. The neglect of this grave I cannot reproach you for, Major, for I have read in the newspapers that General Yamashita, the conqueror of Singapore, and his two companions in death, with their necks stretched tight by the gallows rope, also sleep their eternal rest in a weed-covered grave.

There were no more escapes from Camp Number Three, nor were there more executions. We used to tell our shooting partners, "If you must escape, for God's sake let us know before you take off so we can go with you."

Now came the time, in October 1942, to close down Camp Number Three, for we were all to go to Camp Number One. We had heard evil things about Camp Number One, that it was a place of malaria, of many shootings, of dysentery, despondency, and suicides. Those sick with visible symptoms of "wet" beriberi were to ride in trucks; there was the endless making and remaking of the coveted list by our doctors, for there were only a few trucks, and you, Major Mori, gentleman that you were, respected the plight of fellow gentlemen and had most of these trucks carry the prisoner officers' baggage. Vigilant doctors would have placed a large number of these men in a hospital had they been the prisoners of any Allied power, perhaps even of the Germans or Italians. Yet we thank Masao Mori for these trucks that were once our own. The Japanese tried to make the war pay for the war.

We even took along two or three cerebral malaria cases, guarding them carefully ourselves, for these men did not know an American from a Japanese and might come to harm if not watched. One big fellow was violent and dangerous; two long years later, when some of us left the islands forever, we heard he was still confined in the insane ward at Cabanatuan. You who may read this have probably never heard of cerebral malaria; I hope you never see it. Even we Marines who had served in Nicaragua, Haiti, San Domingo, and other such malarial pestholes had never before heard of it, for our malaria patients always received quinine. When one contracts malignant quartan malaria and there is no quinine, cerebral malaria comes upon you.

Perhaps, Major Mori, as you claimed, you could not get quinine for our sick, but your guards always seemed to have it for sale to our black market kings!

A month or two before the move to Camp Number One, Major Mori had been commanding both camps, but whether the incident I am about to describe occurred under his regime I am not certain because I am not sure of the exact date he took over Camp Number One. In this camp, two army lieutenant colonels and a navy lieutenant approached the "dead line" of the barbed wire, intent on crawling under the fence in the latrine ditch to escape. The inside sentry, a prisoner armed with a club, an army private, ordered them back, for their escape might result in the shooting of thirty men. The outside Japanese sentry heard the argument and covered them with his rifle while he called for the guard. They were confined. We heard of a week's unending torture before merciful death ended their agonies. The lieutenant colonels, both older men and probably beaten more, had to be dragged to the place of execution and were bayoneted several times along the way. The younger lieutenant was able to walk and to face his firing squad defiantly on his feet. Major Mori, I would have to have more definite information on dates, not supplied to me by the Japanese army in those days, before I could accuse you of this killing, but it bears your imprint!

Camp Number One we discovered to be as evil as rumor had told us, but the death rate had gone down to around twenty-eight men per day. We were formed into three groups besides the hospital patients; we called our graveyard "Group Four," and for our eight thousand–odd prisoners, it was the largest group of all. There was still an occasional execution, always preceeded by one or more full days of torture. Perhaps, Major Mori, your men think of death as no punishment at all, but only a welcome release from a heavy burden; hence the torture before departure from this veil of tears!

To "wet" beriberi was now added the dry type. It had been coming on slowly in Camp Number Three, and here in

Number One it came to its full flowering. Hundreds of men stayed awake all night with "screaming feet"; many were afflicted with the progressive numbness of their limbs, starting in their extremities, and here we coined the phrase "beriberi shuffle." After a month and a half of this, in came those wonderful Red Cross foods and medicines. The lame walked, the blind began to see, and the death rate, except for an execution once in a while, dropped to a man per month. Men blessed your name, Major Mori!

I used to see you walking among the prisoners, unguarded by sentries and perfectly sure of your safety, wearing your new collar tabs of a lieutenant colonel. It was said by many men that your work in stopping that awful death rate had come to the attention of your superiors; the Imperial Army Headquarters was so pleased with your efficiency. You had a certain type of democratic camaraderie about you, and you liked to come upon a prisoner and talk with him. I remember you well—stocky, pleasant, and affable with your little military mustache. Your English was halting, but you were desirous of improving it. I liked the way you inquired directly about our welfare.

Among the ranks who spoke well of you, I distinctly remember one very senior officer, Lt. Col. Curtis Beecher, commanding officer, 1st Battalion, 4th Marine Regiment, who had a little house he shared with a few of his prisoner staff. But alongside of us on those bamboo slats, his orderly slept at night, a fat young private first class named Aschenbrunner who weighted nearly 220 pounds. He slunk in after dark and departed before daylight, for he was ashamed of his portly size among us living skeletons. But even the file spoke well of Lieutenant Colonel Mori!

After a month or so of the Red Cross food and medicines, you departed for an unknown destination. We regretted your departure, for your successor was old and weak. The Farm you had started became a thing of hell and horror, for the old and weak major could not control his men, even if he had wanted to do so. Some of his executions smelled none too good, for he sometimes dispensed with the trouble of a drumhead court-martial. Dulled as we were to such doleful affairs, we gave them but little attention and comment.

Some of us are still unregenerate soreheads with very bitter memories. There are always people who, no matter how much you do for them, are never appreciative. These men can never forget, Lieutenant Colonel Mori, that day four young privates of the coast artillery—those Fort Drum lads—had to be dragged to their drumhead court-martial, for they could not walk. We recall how, a half hour later, they marched like men to their deaths, defiant to the last.

Note: I have been informed that this story of Lieutenant Colonel Mori started the investigation that ultimately led to his trial and subsequent hanging on the island of Iwo Jima in 1951.

7

THE STORY OF LIEUTENANT COLONEL ANDERSON

We Marines are often accused of thinking too much of our own corps to the disparagement of the other branches of the armed forces. This is quite true. We even hear some of the men around us claiming we are now the principal branch of the navy, and that the name of the latter should be changed to "Marine Corps Transportation Division" if the proposed merger of the services goes through.

Let us say that the end justifies the means. The career of Lt. Col. Herman R. Anderson, United States Marine Corps, will lose nothing in the retelling, and it might even help mold the seventeen- and eighteen-year-olds we are now getting to train them into Marines as brave as those who took the Pacific Islands, those Marines who were consumed with a burning ambition to close with and kill the hated enemy. Our recruit depots teach not only basic weapons and battlefield tactics, they teach what is perhaps of equal importance—a fierce pride in being a Marine. When we really get to know a top-notch young officer of the army's combat forces, our veteran noncommissioned officers may grudgingly admit that he might make good material for a Marine officer, after he had been through the officer's boot camp, the Basic School. This is praise of the highest order.

Lieutenant Colonel Anderson came from Ohio; he was appointed an officer in 1917 and served continuously from then on. His life was that of the usual Marine officer, with navy yard duty, seagoing duty on both battleship and air-craft carrier, foreign service in far-flung outposts, atten-dance at schools (for our officers must be reeducated now and then in the latest ways of killing people), and no doubt he had a couple of little "banana wars" under his belt. Among the officers he was known as "Red," but in his last command, the 2d Battalion of the 4th Marines, his men al-ways affectionately and simply called him the "Old Man." Just the "Old Man" and nothing else.

Any Marine officer having a command, regardless of his age, is automatically the "Old Man." All company com-manders enjoy this title, but in Lt. Col. "Red" Anderson's command, he was the only "Old Man." The skippers [com-pany commanders] were variously called "Shifty," "Old Bard," "Big Hutch," and "Big Ben." Respectively, they were Capt. Austin C. Shofner, Headquarters Company; Maj. J. V. Bradley, Jr., Company E; Capt. Clyde R. Huddleston, Com-pany F; and Capt. B. L. McMakin, Company H. This title was used in reverence and respect, for Lieutenant Colonel Anderson had that rare quality of being able to command some very hard men, along with some others who thought they were hard, and they loved him with a type of love rarely given to a battalion commander.

In the spring of 1941, Lieutenant Colonel Anderson came down from Peking in the north to Shanghai on the China coast to take command of the 2d Battalion. Wearing civilian clothes and smoking his pipe, he came to the gate of his new command to take over from his friend, the out-going battalion commander, Lt. Col. Donald "Donald Duck" Curtis. The guard was mostly new Marines who had never known "Red." When he asked to see the battalion commander, he was given an escort of a private first class, as all civilians were, and taken to Headquarters Company.

On the way, his easy and captivating manners disarmed his young escort. When the supposed civilian asked the ca-sual, "How is duty here?" (the age-old question all Marines ask in a new post of the old-timers), he got an earful. With machine gun rapidity came out, "It's no good here. We can't wear civilian clothes, and the curfew will not allow us out on the street after midnight. All the decent cabarets with White Russian girls are out of bounds. The MPs would lock up their own mothers. Liberty is lousy. We seldom get it, because we can meet ourselves coming off and going on at nearly every guard mount and stand-by platoon." All of this was punctuated with vehement adjectives, ugly little four-letter words, explosive, salty, and not of a nature that would appear well in print.

Thanking his guide for taking him to the colonel's office, the "Old Man" bade him a friendly "See you again, my boy," and went in to confer with "Donald Duck."

Later, on the way out, the sergeant of the guard at the gate recognized the new colonel and called out a loud "TEN-SHUN!" A quiet "Carry on," and the "Old Man" shook hands with an old friend following this. His garrulous informant stood by speechless, for Marines are not supposed to talk, as he had, to their lieutenant colonels, much less use such adjectives as this young man had used. As Lieutenant Colonel Anderson left the gate, his left eye closed in a deliberate wink at the red-faced private, and in that instant he had made a friend, a loyal subordinate, and a better Marine. The story came out and made the rounds of the regiment amid gales of laughter, and in the 2d Battalion there was proud reflection on the new battalion commander.

A trivial thing, and to the uninitiated, a triviality, but of such trivialities are made the soul of a good Marine battalion.

After some months came the clouds of war, swiftly and suddenly. We had always been a good battalion before the "Old Man" took over, and it would not be telling the truth to say we were any better, for one could hardly improve on "Donald Duck." Let it be said for the record that as far as efficiency was concerned, Colonel Anderson did not suffer in comparison to his predecessor.

Hurriedly we were sent to the Philippines and within a week after our arrival what we knew was coming had come; at Olongapo we suffered our first casualties in our baptism of fire. We had no aviation with which to fight the Japanese planes. There was no concealing from the men their desperate situation, but we could take comfort in the fact that we were certainly well commanded. It is typical of the "Old Man" that when we left Olongapo for Mariveles he was in the last echelon, the post of danger.

The 4th Marine Regiment went to Corregidor Island, and later, some of the men went to hard-pressed little outlying forts, grim and rocky islets, to relieve the coast artillery of the duty of beach defense, for they had enough to do in manning their larger guns. We were under enemy bombing on the island of Corregidor almost at once; men were killed and wounded, and soon came enemy fire from their 105mm guns. Our ammunition dumps were on fire and our installations were smashed and pulverized. Under the spur of necessity the Marines of the battalion worked night and day on our beach defenses, and perhaps we did it more for the sake of the "Old Man" than on account of the desperate military urgency of which we were only too familiar. The "Old Man" contracted malaria, that scourge of the islands, but he kept right on going, shaking and chattering with his chills.

One day enemy bombs hit in James Ravine right near his command post. Urgent cries of "First aid, wounded men!" came to his ears. The air raid was still on, and burning ammunition dumps of artillery shells set on fire by the bombs began to fill the air with the shriek and whine of flying steel splinters. Daredevil volunteers, navy hospital corpsmen and Marines, raced in with stretchers to rescue the wounded. And there, amid the smoke and yellow-colored picric acid fumes from the explosives was the "Old Man," taking charge of the situation. As a battalion commander he should have remained under shelter and let his Marines clear the wounded from danger. But our "Old Man" went out, among the first to arrive, and the U.S. Army gave him their Silver Star. Our pride in him was immense, and we looked on our other battalions with condescension.

On the ninth of April 1942, Bataan had fallen. By 2 P.M. of that fateful day the Japanese had their 105mm guns firing into our back door, with a channel of only forty-one hundred yards at its narrowest point separating us from them. Like Singapore, built to be defended from seaward attack but taken from the rear, so would be the fate of Corregidor.

In a short time, perhaps as many as 290 cannon, from 105mm to 150mm, and those terrible uprooters of heavy steel and concrete forts, the 240mm guns, were delivering a continuous volume of fire, so heavy that at times it seemed as fast as a machine gun. Added to this was day and night aerial bombing, and you can get some inkling of just what we were undergoing. In a modern war, open tactics prevent many men from knowing the attrition of casualties and the nerve-racking experience of "drumfire" and constant bombing. Fewer men know what it is like to have several out of many hundred burning ammunition dumps sending out flying splinters of red-hot steel at the same time. We Marines knew what was going on. On our tiny island fort we grimly awaited the end, which we knew could not be too far off.

There is a necessary, theatrical bravery for a combat commander to show his men the first time he comes under enemy fire. The young Napoleon showed it in the affair at the bridge of Lodi, during his first campaign in command of an army. Ever since, soldiers have thrilled to the tale of how the general rushed into the enemy fire of grape and canister; how the longer-legged Colonel Lannes outran him, and the inspired infantry followed their leaders and took the bridge. In a tone of stern reproof, the boy army leader turned to his companion and reprimanded him: "It is not proper for junior officers to precede seniors without authority. Do you fully comprehend, GENERAL Lannes?" And we all know the story of how Gen. Robert E. Lee, during the Wilderness fight, tried to lead a bogged-down Texas brigade into battle. The men of that brigade took hold of "Traveler's" bridle and forced their beloved general to the rear while the rallied brigade surged forward.

Let any commander of troops be lucky enough to show his personal courage the first time he comes under fire, and be lucky enough to survive, and his reputation is secure.

After that his men take it as a personal reflection on themselves if he continues to risk his life. The "Old Man" had been doing it all along and there were mutterings about it. But knowing we were doomed, we also took a fierce pride in his regular inspections of our defenses. He seemed to bear a charmed life. It was pathetic to see young privates beg him not to expose himself to enemy fire.

By now our battalion had over sixteen hundred men in it, a motley collection of sailors from beached or sunken ships, Filipino Air Corps cadets who had no planes, and Filipinos of the Insular Navy, the Constabulary, the National Army, and the Scouts along with American army soldiers who had managed to get out of Bataan when it collapsed. To all these officers and men Colonel Anderson was affectionately known as the "Old Man." All knew him by sight, and many personally, for enemy shellfire seemed to mean nothing to him in his daily inspection rounds of positions on the South Shore and the North Channel. He was still sick with malaria, but his indomitable spirit carried him on.

Platoon Sergeant Davis, Company F, had his defense group out digging defense lines at a place known as Morrison Hill. Captain Ames, 60th Coast Artillery, of the Chicago Battery, whose bravery we had learned to respect, had his men near Davis on the same duty, for only one of his guns could now fire. The "dogfaces" were getting ready for the enemy landing they knew was not far off. Ames said to Davis, "When they come up Morrison Hill, I am going to get my ten before they get me." This remark was not theatrical, for Ames was a man seldom given to talking at all.

When Sergeant Davis was telling this to a group around the battalion command post, Mess Sergeant Leon B. Ellis, from our battalion's Headquarters Company, said, "Hell, the 'Old Man' has been telling me that all along." Whether Ellis was entirely truthful is open to doubt, but his remark shows the fierce possessive pride those Marines took in their colonel. The sergeant major[11] followed with the inevitable

11. CWO C. R. Jackson, USMC.

remark, "That young man would make a good Marine officer. 'Chicago' Battery men have never run from a gun pit yet." And Maj. Joe Heil, the battalion executive officer, grinned his approval. (Both Sergeant Davis and Joe Heil are dead now. I hope that Captain Ames made it, but I don't know.)

Some years before this war, the Philippine Department had a Maj. Gen. Frank Parker, USA, commanding it, of whom the army personnel used to tell stories about his unseemly efforts to get publicity in the Manila newspaper. Some of us in the battalion were there at the time, and we remember reading in the newspapers, when he was taking over the command, a story he told about himself in World War I when he commanded a famous regiment in a famous division—the 26th Infantry, 1st Army Division. He stated that after each battle, "It was pathetic to hear the wounded in the dressing stations asking, 'Did the colonel come through?' " or something to that effect. Maybe the story is entirely true, but some men made uncouth remarks about the press relations officer being overzealous in his loyalty to the chief.

Perhaps our wounded never asked the same question about Colonel Anderson, but all along the beach defenses, the men—seeing his tall figure leave his car to walk slowly along amid shellfire and bombings, hearing his cheery, "Keep your chins up, men!"—used to ask one another where the "Old Man" was if he did not show up on time, "I wonder if they got the colonel today?" If you should doubt this, ask any of the few survivors of his battalion. It would be best to be tactful in your approach, for some of these men might misunderstand your motives and trouble would ensue.

The final enemy assault, so long expected, came upon the 1st Battalion's position at Monkey Point. Lieutenant Colonel Beecher's Marines put up a darned good fight, along with the Reserve Battalion. We cannot be sure of these figures, but we like to tell the young recruits they inflicted some six thousand casualties on the enemy. All of the searchlights had been shot out but one, nearly all of our cannon had been put out of action, and most of the shelters in this area had been blasted to bits.

James Ravine, where the "Old Man" was, had a heavy barrage put down as a feint to cover the landing, so his battalion could only stand by, with grim determination, to resist another landing if and when it came. By morning, Lt. Gen. Jonathan M. Wainwright, USA, decided that further resistance was useless; the Japanese had gotten several tanks onto the island, and their infantry had a foothold around Monkey Point.

So Lieutenant General Wainwright—having the responsibility on his hands of the 4th Marine Regiment, reinforced with navy sailors and others; the four coast artillery regiments, two of them Filipino; some one thousand or so engineer, quartermaster, and service troops, all out in the defense; and in addition, seven thousand or more noncombatant service and headquarters troops and civilians all jammed together in the Malinta Tunnel as their last refuge—surrendered us all to prevent a victorious enemy, whom further resistance might have inflamed to murderous ferocity, from killing the whole garrison.

The "Old Man" went into captivity and it was several months before I saw him again, after our removal from the island of Corregidor. He was mighty thin from starvation, and in the days to come I watched him grow thinner with a tightening of the heartstrings. He always came around to talk to his beloved Marines, to tell them that we were sure to win in the end, and to the very last he labored to keep our morale up. It brought a lump to our throats to see that tall, gaunt figure, still erect and with that charming smile, now almost a living skeleton.

And in time to come, he took that last, fateful voyage on a Japanese prison ship. Bombed and torpedoed, she was sunk by our own forces. Colonel Anderson was not among the survivors. This was the tragedy of it all, for him to be killed by the American might he so confidently assured us was to come. I, who knew him so well, like to think that when the awful moment came, he was cheered by the thought that the lives of a few broken prisoners were of little value in the balance scales compared to the loss to the enemy of a fine, new, fifteen-thousand-ton freighter.

As I said before, if you are imprudent enough to smile your disbelief when we boast about our "Old Man," certain violence may follow.

The "Old Man" often showed his battlefield courage, but of all the yarns that his Marines related about him, I like this one best, for it shows his fine moral courage. I know it to be the plain, simple, bitter truth.

Just before he went to his last roll call in the waters of the Yellow Sea, one of his noncommissioned officers, an old-timer, got the first real break of his imprisonment, a job in the Japanese galley. To steal from this place could mean death if the offender were caught, or at the very least, torture and a severe beating. This Marine had a rice sack doubled around his waist for an apron, and he cut a hole in the inside fold, next to his body. In this apron he slipped two little four-ounce coffee tins and was able to fill them with sliced, boiled corn and dried, salted fish. Just two little four-ounce coffee cans of food—to a starving man they would taste like the ambrosia of the gods!

As soon as it was dark, this Marine took those cans to his beloved colonel. Telling him he was now in a position to get these little cans filled for him daily, he pressed them upon the colonel.

"You know, you might be killed or tortured if they caught you doing this? Thank you very much, but I have gotten along all right so far on what they have given me. This extra food might make me sick. Eat it yourself, for you need it more than I do," said the colonel. It was dark, but he must have smiled and winked that left eye as he shook his head. It was useless to argue the point once the colonel had made his decision. Under cover of a building, where no one would see him, the inventive thief wolfed down the food.

I heard recently, that when the records get sifted over, the Navy Department might see its way to giving the "Old

Man" a posthumous decoration, and it would be very good, for we would like to be able to speak of Lt. Col. Herman R. Anderson, United States Marine Corps, Navy Cross and Silver Star, who once commanded us.

Maybe in his hometown they will put up a memorial tablet of stone, with something about him written on a bronze plaque, with his awards in suitable carved relief. It would look very nice, and people would say nice things for a while, and by the time they had forgotten him the bronze would have a wonderful patina of age.

But if some of us had anything to do with the carving of that stone and bronze, we would put a little something extra on it. We would like to think that up in the Valhalla of all good Marines, the "Old Man" would look down and give us his smile and confidential wink when he saw the monument unveiled.

That little something extra would be just—TWO LITTLE COFFEE CANS!

8

THE STORY OF YAMANOUCHI

His name is Shoshichi Yamanouchi. His address, which I took the trouble to get from Captain Fleming on the train ride from Hanowa to Shinagawa, is Sasamori-cho, Hirosaki, Aomori Ken, Japan. In case this story should see the light of print, some of you who were there may read it, and I think you might care to drop him a card. It would make him happy.

He was good to you. His superiors on your behalf beat him more than once, as you are well aware. He is a kindly man.

In the beginning of our imprisonment there were some five hundred of us, prisoners of war from the Bataan and Corregidor campaigns in the days of 1941–42. We were now in an out-of-the-way place located some four hundred miles northwest of Tokyo, called Hanowa. Tucked away in the incredibly jagged mountains, Messrs. Mitsubishi had a copper mine there. We worked in it.

We had been there for a month or so, all lean and wiry men and very tough. Perhaps emaciated would best describe our appearance, and we were tough, for we were still alive. Most of us had survived the Death March of Bataan, starvation and beatings through the long years, and a nightmare trip aboard a prison "hell" ship from the Philippines to Japan. We were still alive under a progressive type of starvation, for the Japanese had begun to feel the effects of the naval blockade, and to feel it badly. In the matter of food, they put themselves first and their prisoners afterward. This was only simple, cold logic.

When we first arrived, our camp commandant was a rosy-cheeked young second lieutenant of some infantry regiment of the Imperial Japanese Army, hard and strict, as is proper for those who wear the samurai sword and carry a commission under his august majesty, descended from the Sun Goddess, Amaratsuru, the emperor Hirohito. Yet the lieutenant had his good points. Let us say that he looked on us as draft animals. To make a profit on his balance sheets, the beasts had to have care and food if they were to be kept alive. We were useful in getting out the copper to be used in the killing off of the hated Americans whose advance, like an incoming tide, was relentlessly closing in on the doomed empire.

In every one of the prison camps there was an interpreter. The one attached to our camp was a slender man, rather on the tall side, with sloping shoulders and a petulant look always on his face. His face was further marred by an ill-concealed leer of low, animal cunning. It was said of him that he had been some missionary's houseboy; perhaps he had been required to serve foreign masters, he, a member of the master race! Now the master race was on top, as was meet and fitting; as far as we prisoners were concerned, we were in their power.

We avoided the interpreter as best we could, for his slaps stung cruelly. The Japanese soldiers are always slapping one another; the sick get slapped by their doctors before they are asked what is wrong with them; they get slapped during the medical examination; and they get another slapping after they are prescribed for. It is just one of the little grains of sand that make up the final concrete of that weird product, the Imperial Japanese Army. Most Japanese slap with a stiff-arm motion and you get plenty of warning. Whether you are standing at rigid attention or are down on your knees, chin drawn tightly in, arms stiff along your sides, you could still roll with the punch, for most of us knew some of the rudiments of boxing. But this interpreter seemed to be wise to this trick, for he slapped with a loose arm motion and with the speed of a striking cobra. His slaps stung. Long ago we had gotten over the indignity of being slapped, but his slaps really hurt. And he was hated accordingly.

Those men foolish enough to get involved with black market transactions with him (for some men still had concealed watches and fountain pens) got the short end of the deal, if their treasures were not confiscated outright. A good fountain pen might bring a quarter pound of precious, necessary salt from this fellow. For a watch, he could dig up a few capsules of quinine to help ease a sufferer shaking from malaria chills.

After a month of this man and his commander, we received a new commandant and interpreter. We stood at stiff attention in massed *bango*, the formation the Japanese military and civilians loved so dearly, for they hold it so often, and we observed our new master. Hard of face, inscrutable, unsmiling, he stood at a more rigid position of attention than his charges. The professional soldier element among the prisoners gave him a grudging approval, for they knew only too well his type. Was it not Frederick the Great who said, "The good soldier fears the swords of his officers more than the bullets of the enemy"?

Looking at this man, one dimly realized the why of the fanatical bravery of the long ago, almost forgotten charges of the Japanese in the Bataan jungles. One knew the reason now why the tiny handful of Japanese prisoners taken alive used to say with a fatalistic shrug, "When Japanese take Bataan, not long now, officer take big sword, you kneel down, he go swish, you finished."

The nonprofessional group, those youngsters who had so eagerly or reluctantly gone to the colors in 1940 and early 1941, who had sailed for the islands in ignorant bliss, untrained and undisciplined, wide-eyed at the sight of new, strange, and exotic lands, shivered with apprehension. They were battle-hardened veterans now, but the long years behind barbed-wire stockades had given them that tragic, beaten look one knows so well from the pictures of concentration camps in another land and another continent.

And then we saw Yamanouchi. We chuckled to ourselves behind frozen faces. No soldier was he, nor would he ever be. He was clad in the ordinary regulation cotton uniform of a two-star private of the Imperial Army. Around his waist sagged the ammunition belt, with attached water canteen and bayonet that no Japanese soldier was ever without. We have often seen his type in our own forces, strange fish caught up in the net of the draft, the "sad sacks" of the services. If you had dressed Yamanouchi in a fine, tailored uniform adorned with glittering accoutrements and then left him to his own devices for a few moments, he would have looked like a hopeless, frustrated mess. All armies have such men, but the Japanese army seemed to have fewer of them than other nations. The contrast between him and the soldierly Lieutenant Asaka was so marked that it made poor Yamanouchi look all the more ludicrous.

After the preliminary *"Kiotski, kashara naga! Ya si me!"* (we were duly impressed by the rigid, grave salute First Lieutenant Asaka gave as he slowly faced from one flank to the other), our new "supreme being" addressed us in Japanese. (We were later to learn that he spoke English well, but seldom condescended to use it in speaking to any of us.) A lengthy, sonorous sentence, a pause, and the interpreter translated. His English, at best, was quaint; perhaps weird would be the better word to describe it. His face would light up and his eyes glowed with a hopeful desire to make us understand him. The curt, brutal phrases of discipline were softened in his halting efforts, for an army coast artillery lieutenant, Richard T. Pullen, a fellow prisoner, who understood Japanese, later told me so. I thought that he used the phrase, repeated after each warning, "You must be punished," with a shudder to his gentle nature. He seemed pleased to see us, and when we got to know him better, we thought he was glad to have the opportunity to soften our lot, when and if he could do so.

As the soldierly officer and the unsoldierly man each

passed us in his turn, we formed snap judgments about them. "A tough officer, but just and fair," was the opinion of the professionals. "Hell on wheels, 'ware rock and shoals," thought the youngsters. We knew where we stood with Asaka, and what more can a soldier ask? But, Yamanouchi made all of us think of such stock army phrases as "lack of capabilities in any other field, hence to be assigned to permanent latrine duty," or "habits and traits incompatible with the military service, and recommended for discharge under the provisions of Section VIII, Army Regulations so and so." If there was ever a perfect "blue discharge" [undesirable] man, Yamanouchi certainly looked the part.

Yet we all knew him as a kindly man, even by our own standards. No one would voice his thoughts about this, for fear of the scorn of his friends. He who ventured a good word for the Japanese was foolhardy indeed. But we all knew that we had at long last found a friend, and only the gods knew how badly we needed one.

Speculation was rife about him. Like felons in the "big house" who study the most minute and trivial traits of the dull, gross, and ignorant people assigned to guard them, so we, too, studied those who had charge of us. We were in jail, too, but with these important differences: the criminal has some idea of when he is getting out, unless he is a lifer; he is never hungry; he receives medical attention. We had no idea when our time would be up; our gnawing craving for food gave us all our own peculiar type of "stir bugs"; and when we were sick there was but little medicine. But at least we had the immense advantage of not being cooped up with degenerate beasts, as would have been the case in one of our own penitentiaries, and this thought was cheering.

Word soon got around that the interpreter had been a teacher of English in a high school, was the father of two small children, and was a Christian. This last title I cannot with certainty state, but if so, he must have imbibed the words of St. Paul, "And let us consider one another to provoke unto love and good works."

Too many of us who had served in the Orient dismissed

the humble missionary and his works with some degree of scorn—who has not heard the term "rice Christian"? Perhaps Yamanouchi was born with "love and good works" in his soul, but if some unknown humble "toiler in the vineyard of the Lord" implanted those words in his heart, we 550 men, less the eight who did not survive, might occasionally give a thought of gratitude to the Christian missionaries for men like Yamanouchi.

We had to salute and bow to all the Japanese guards, and to Lieutenant Asaka we had to give a special type of military servitude. Woe be unto the unfortunate prisoner who should forget to salute as he passed the guardhouse, a Japanese noncommissioned officer, or any one of the small permanent detachment. Yet few, if any, ever took the trouble to salute Yamanouchi. Those who did were rewarded with a gesture, fumbling and apologetic, and often a mumbled "Thank you" in English, for he was always the soul of courtesy.

His duty was solely to interpret, not to alleviate. In the Imperial Army a slapping on the spot summarily punishes Japanese army temerity, like other petty military offenses. Even the civilians slap one another, such is the ingrained militarism of their race. A more serious offense calls for a beating, and we all knew the effects of such behavior on sadistic minds. The worthy who combined in his person the jobs of police, property, and mess sergeant, one Sanhai, had his good points, but he also looked on us, we feared, as draft animals to be kept in good shape. He was eternally screaming, *"Bioki me, dame dame, yama shigoto joto!"*—which meant, "You sick men, you are no good; go back to the mountain to work, in a hurry!" We frequently realized that the Japanese could not always control the excessive zeal of their subordinates, and in his fanatical efforts for *yama shigoto* this man probably went beyond Lieutenant Asaka's desires. When he began to slap men in his sadistic rage, he often impaired the efficiency of the draft animals for ordinary work.

Yamanouchi often had cause to interpret for this formidable character. His heart frequently exceeded his head, and he made suggestions where it was imprudent to do so. Being guilty of the military offense of temerity, he was beaten. We laughed heartily at the sight and remarked, "The poor old interpreter just got beaten up again," for cruelty begets cruelty.

Yamanouchi frequently climbed the *yama* and came around to see us working in the mine. We never asked him to make the work easier, we only asked for more food. And he always promised to do what he could for us.

A cynical remark had a passing vogue: "Yamanouchi is the most promising private in the Imperial Japanese Army; he will promise you anything!" And yet, how many of us dared to ask the Japanese for anything? The interpreter we did not fear.

On such trips to the copper mine we tried to discuss the war with him. One imagines he knew very little, so ignorant were the Japanese of the true state of affairs. "Maybe very long war, maybe ten years more. I do not like war!" he would say so sadly as he tried to parry our questions. Another current saying had its dismal run: "My frans, I do not like war! Eleanor does not like war! Yamanouchi does not like war!" mocking President Roosevelt's fireside chats, followed with bitter, insane laughter.

Yamanouchi had one vice that we knew about—he liked to smoke. Cigarettes were issued to both the military and the civilians, but none too often to us. We guessed that Yamanouchi received about ten "hard rolls" each week, yet he often gave a cigarette or two to a group of men with gracious courtesy. Our craving for the Lady Nicotine was so intensely degrading that we often watched a workman, who was smoking with greedy eyes hollow and dully glazed, hoping for the precious "short." Sometimes it was kindly given, but more often it was contemptuously thrown down on the ground, burned almost to ashes, while the "master race" laughed at the strange antics of the lowly beast that greedily snatched it up. We all know how a begging setter looks; let a man light up a smoke and his companions eyed him in the same wistful way. It was seldom that Yamanouchi ever smoked in front of us, for he knew how we craved tobacco. Whenever he did, he freely offered from his own small share.

Yamanouchi got a few days of furlough and he returned with some large red apples. Apples, priceless, precious to men to whom the eternal diet of rice, millet, or barley had caused the taste of such fruit to almost be forgotten. He gave one to each of the officers, who were gentlemen and men of Yamanouchi's own class, even though they came from half a world away. Some of the apples he gave to certain listless living skeletons. The burning desire for tobacco caused some of them to get in the hands of the big dealers; I can recall hearing a cry through the barracks of "A big red apple for two bowls of rice, one now and one on Sunday!" I wonder what would have happened to the kindly Yamanouchi if the guards had found out that he had given precious apples to despised prisoners of war?

In the beginning the prisoners were required to turn in all letters, all books, and all printed or written material, even Bibles, and all photographs for "censoring." Time dragged by, and they were not returned to us. I had made a list of the property I had lost in the islands, typed by a friend in a bombproof shelter while enemy shells were falling, and it was witnessed by several Marine officers. It was made out beneath the light of a sputtering candle, and if I could keep that precious paper, upon my release it might be worth one thousand dollars, for it had the "Old Man's" signature to attest to it. I spoke to our prisoner sergeant major, Chief Yeoman T. L. Lietz, and I was taken to the interpreter. Yamanouchi was carefully told what was wanted, and listened carefully. Finally he said, "I will give the papers back to you, but you must not tell anyone." Think of that, a mere two-star private taking a chance fraught with such danger, for it was Lieutenant Asaka's ironclad order to hold those papers until in his sweet pleasure he got around to looking them over. The man kept his word and the papers were cunningly concealed. After my release as a prisoner of war, I received seven hundred dollars for my lost property by reason of those papers.

The dreadful winter wore on. I do not like to remember it. It may best be summed up in the following episode: A US Navy chief boatswain's mate was given the opportunity to write a ten-word card to his wife, one of those rigidly censored prisoner of war letters we so seldom had the chance to send home. When he turned his card in to Captain Fleming, the latter showed it to me, for I was helping him precensor the cards. There were just three words on it, only three words, and nothing more. "I AM ALIVE."

The difficult art of expressing a great deal in a few words was brought to its highest peak of development by the ancient Spartans, and derived its name from the name of their country, Laconia. Philip the Great of Macedonia once threatened invasion, writing, "If I invade your land, I shall ravage it with fire and sword." The reply of the ephors and council is a truly laconic classic, for they attached to the missive a sheet of papyrus with one word. "If."

The Spartans were free, intelligent, educated Greeks. This man was not free; hunger and misery had dulled his intelligence, and one could not consider him any too well educated. But these three little words, truly laconic, grim, and to the point, had a world of pregnancy in their meaning. How well that message expressed our condition, how well it described that terrible winter! I handed the card back to Captain Fleming without comment, for there was nothing I could add to it.

The Japanese had a strange custom of continuing to print certain editions of their English-language newspaper during the course of the war. They used to give us these sheets, printed in Manila, when the tide of war was flooding in their favor. After Axis defeats at El Alamein and Stalingrad we saw them no more. We could only guess why. But now, in February 1945, a package of U.S. Army stationery arrived in camp wrapped in a *Japan Advertiser*. It gave full details of the battle of Manila and other world news. It told of [an Allied] task force proceeding to attack the Bonins, and of

the conquest of the Philippines by our armed might. The
prisoner sergeant major's duties often carried him into Yamanouchi's office. Summoned to get the stationery, he
found the place empty. He had a chance to read the important news and he took it. In a short time we all knew about
it. It was our first true glimpse of the outside world in nearly
a year. Did Yamanouchi deliberately leave that newspaper
out for those precious few, fleeting moments? I can only
wonder.

What a world of good that glimpse of the outside world
did for us, through the almost impenetrable curtain that had
been drawn around us! I recall a phrase in that paper explaining the fall of the Philippines to the Japanese people:
"It is now blood and guts against oil and steel." That one
phrase gives the foremost reason why Japan lost her war.

Yamanouchi's weird English was always a source of
laughter. When Lieutenant Asaka and his guards were on
the rampage about salutes, the interpreter had to translate
the speeches. "You must always remember the salution. The
salution, how important it is to us Japanese!" Yet we who
laugh at him might reflect on how his own people laughed
at us in our halting efforts to use the Japanese tongue.

One of the highlights of Yamanouchi's efforts to help us
came when Asaka permitted a dispatch from American
headquarters to be read to us. The gist of it was that, by an
act of Congress, no person could be promoted while serving as a prisoner of war. We had received copies of this dispatch a year before in the Philippines. Now Yamanouchi
came into our barracks, his eyes shining with transfigured
light. In halting phrases, using "r's" for "l's," with much
hissing and intakes of breath, he slowly read us the glorious
news. We are sure he hardly understood it, for it was in the
dry, technical language of the War Department, but he was
so happy in being allowed to give us "news from your
America" that we refrained from laughing our bitter laugh.
We listened, we bowed respectfully, and he bowed in return.

In that spring came a furious digging of air raid shelters
by the Japanese, but we dug none. By now we had learned

much of the language. Friendly workmen (for when you work alongside a man underground, he gives you a grudging friendship, even if he is the enemy) told us a bit, a fragment here, now and then. Pieced together, we had a fair picture. Now came the air raid sirens, a period of indifferent waiting, and then the "all clear." "Indifferent waiting" is the term, for you think it will never happen to you, but always to the other fellow. Yamanouchi used to tell us now and then of the havoc being wrought in the big Japanese cities by our planes, ending with, "Your Mister B-29s they kill so many people." (The Japanese always referred to this bomber as "Mister" B-29—*ni ju ku san*—no other plane was so honored.) "It is too bad," he would say, "I don't like war." And that night the current remark about "My frans, I do not like war! Eleanor does not like war! Yamanouchi does not like war also!" would resound through the barracks.

With the coming of the cherry blossoms, pressure was placed on the sick to return to the copper mine. As the lovely blossoms whitened on the innumerable trees and the beautiful deep pink azaleas blushed in bright color on every hillside, Yamanouchi himself suggested to us that it was better to be at the *yama* than in the barracks. His suggestion was couched in a different way than that of the camp commandant, for he said, "When the Mister B-29s come, more better you be underground."

Kindly, diplomatic Doctors Dan Golenternek and John E. Lamy echoed this advice as they gently shook the tree of the "quarters" list.

Suddenly there came the news that Japan had surrendered, and in the midst of our delirium of joy, Yamanouchi came among us. Tactfully he suggested that there be no noise, for he was not sure of what the civilians might do. "The Lieutenant Asaka take good care of you, for the honor of the Japanese army, but you must be quiet," he told us.

Now we made much of the interpreter; he talked glowingly of returning to his beloved books and his English classes at the high school; addresses were exchanged; he wistfully asked us to write to him. Many gave him testimonials in case the occupying forces might get tough with those known to have done duty in the prisoner of war camps.

When the American planes dropped food, clothing, and medicines to us, he was given all he could eat, a bundle of clothing, and a good supply of medicine. No doubt Captain Fleming and the two doctors saw to that, for Yamanouchi was by then almost as thin as we were. One supposes that, when he went off at the last, he was loaded down with a supply of chewing gum for his little ones, and for a lot of little ones other than his own up Aomori way, in the far north of Honshu Island.

Whether he made that last walk with us in the rain and the mud down to the railroad station in Hanowa, I do not recall. My mind was too full of other things than to think of a Japanese soldier. But I do like to think of a motto he printed for us and stuck up, all over the barracks and in the mine. (He was always giving us moral sermons on stealing and cleanliness, probably by Lieutenant Asaka's orders.) As the signs faded out in the rains and snow, his hands would lovingly touch them up again.

And here it is: "False Security is a Great Foe. True Happiness Comes From the Heart and Makes Him Glorious." We used to laugh at it. But, thinking of his simple sincerity, some of us do not laugh.

9

THE STORY OF NEGRO BELL

I never knew much about him, for he was very quiet and a self-effacing man. I could tell that he was very old. His skin was a dark chocolate brown, his face gentle and kindly. His hair was a gray, woolly thatch, and his wise, shrewd old eyes peered up at everyone above the eyeglasses perched low on his nose.

The appearance of the old fellow summoned images of characters from *Uncle Tom's Cabin*, and I recalled the words of Stephen Foster's song, "Old Black Joe." But the war gave him an equality unknown in those years back home, for we were all prisoners of the Japanese behind barbed wire and under the vigilant stare of sentries of the Imperial Army. His first name I never knew; his last name was Bell. And so, to all of us, he was simply "Negro" Bell.

Old 1st Lt. John Paul Flynn, late of the 3d Battalion, 31st Regular Army Infantry, answered some of my queries when I had ceased thinking, for brief moments, of food, food, food, or how to work up a good set of symptoms to try out on the doctors in an attempt to beat The Farm. "Old Dobe" had served long years in that regiment in the islands before war gave him a battlefield commission and a bad head wound. A profoundly self-educated man and a shrewd judge of his fellow soldiers, in other circumstances he might have been a scholar. His dry wit and enormous fund of anecdotes made him a sort of oracle at whose feet we sat, hoping to get him to talk.

Usually Negro Bell sat by himself, his white sailor's cap pulled down over his ears, looking up over his glasses. His walrus mustache was stained from tobacco, for he chewed the weed incessantly. Somewhere he had gotten a blue flannel double-breasted coat with brass buttons, now faded and torn. Around his middle was a Japanese army issue "G-string," his legs were bare, and so were his feet. With knees drawn up to his chin, he looked just like a solemn old owl. He was still limping from a broken thighbone, the result of imprudently taking a sick man's place on The Farm work detail.

I generally respected Negro Bell's privacy, for it was said that he had a native wife and two little boys in the Manila area and had not heard from them for over two years, since our Bataan days.

Lieutenant Flynn told me that Negro Bell had been retired just before World War I as a thirty-year soldier, for they used to be allowed double time for foreign service up to the year 1912. He had been an employee of the army quartermaster ever since, and had a little ranch just outside of Manila. His wife and son helped him work it after his army duties were over for the day.

I thought of his existence as a pleasant one, humble, with a happy blend of the urban and pastoral, if I thought about him at all. Manila was a good place in which to live; one arose early with the sun, and a day's work was done before the noon hour. A light lunch was followed by a two-hour siesta, and then the fag ends of your office work were attended to. You could close your place at about three o'clock and head home.

Hardly an American labored, for most of them supervised the work of the natives. In the days when I knew the old Cavite Navy Yard, only one white employee was officially classified as a laborer, a Mr. Louie Cox. He was really in charge of a section of the lumberyard. Having lost a Corregidor job for obscure reasons, he had appealed to the

Labor Board, headed by a Mr. Tom Carpenter, of the Cavite yard.

Over drinks in the Nutshell Bar, the unofficial headquarters of the Labor Board, located just outside the yard's main gate, his case was pondered, for he was well known and liked. With no vacancies existing for a leading man or a quarterman, he agreed to be carried on the rolls as a "laborer," and this enabled him to support his native wife, his children, and his stable of fighting cocks besides being able to buy his share of drinks in the Nutshell. It was hoped that in due time his status would be elevated.

Among such *dolce far niente* men, American Negroes were quite rare. The few I saw were never thought of as such, for they were most capable and well liked. In referring to them, the word "Negro" was generally prefixed to their names. [There was old "Negro" Hill, he who had been Admiral Dewey's chief quartermaster on the USS *Olympia*'s bridge at the Battle of Manila Bay before he became a Boniface of sorts in Cavite, selling bottles of hard liquor with his general notions at Hill's Bazaar.] The word "Negro" was used merely as a handy reference. We usually called them Mister Hill or Mister Bell to their faces, until familiarity and friendship had mellowed the formalities. Old Bell probably handled his simple duties in the quartermaster with great care and diligence; he drew his pay on top of his pension as a retired soldier, and he lived in something like affluence.

In the Philippines, among the poor and the humble, and even reaching into the middle classes, there is no racial discrimination. There never was any, and I hope there never will be. I liked the way Gen. Douglas MacArthur wrote to the War Department during the Bataan campaign to put the pay of the Filipino soldier on an equal basis, instead of half, with the handful of white men who were helping "Juan de la Cruz" defend his homeland. "The blood of the dead crimsons the battlefield the same dull stain," or something like that, went his appeal, for the Great Man had a gift of lofty rhetoric.

The genial warmth of the tropic sun appealed to Old Bell, this descendant of African slaves; he and the kindly Filipino people liked one another. So as I have said, he came to acquire a wife in his later years, he begot himself a son, and his life was good.

Then came the invasion. Most of those civilians in the Manila area who escaped death were swept up into the concentration camp known as Santo Tomás, the seat of an ancient university, for the early Spanish conquistadors were fond of learning. Here they could live with their families, here they would have to work only at housekeeping tasks. Inducements were offered to them to come in as "guests of the emperor." (Later they were to know what starvation meant when the ugly, scaly head of "dog eat dog" reared itself among them, but even to the end they had the consolation of being together with those they loved.)

A small handful of hardy civilians, however, joined the armed forces. I have not much idea of their exact number, but I recall around 250 later locked up in Cabanatuan; I think most of them who survived the campaign and Death March went there for imprisonment. These men were skilled in the repair of big guns, in the building of rock tunnels, in the repairing of shell-torn roads under fire, and in the handling of the quartermaster's stores.

Many of them were employed by the Pacific Naval Base contractor and worked at a furious speed against time to further fortify the Corregidor rock or build the Bataan underground shelters along Mariveles Bay. Some of them, engineers, were given commissions in the Philippine National Army, but most of them remained as they were. Under the Law of Nations, as it was understood, if they were captured with the armed forces and were not duly enlisted, they were liable to summary execution if found with weapons in their hands. There is not a fine distinction in the minds of a victorious enemy between a civilian caught firing a machine gun, a civilian serving a fourteen-inch rifle with its crew, or a civilian working with engineers repairing a bomb-wrecked casement.

There were stranded merchant marine sailors, men of diverse nations, not all at war with the Axis. There were merchants and salesmen, sellers of American machinery and automobiles. But of the Americans not made officers by the general, the vast majority had seen service in the army and navy, had been discharged to accept employment in the islands, or, like Negro Bell, had lingered on to go out on the thirty-year retirement plan. The army folk called them "old dobes"; "bamboo Americans" was the navy epithet; but they themselves rather liked the Manila newspaper term of "Sunshiners." Sometimes they were called "tin roofs" and it was said they had "missed too many boats." But, by the almighty gods, we combat men admired their guts. Most of them neither knew nor cared that they were on anyone's payroll; there was a war on and they were helping as best they could to help stem the invader. Negro Bell was of this group.

The gallant 60th Regiment of coast artillery, composed of antiaircraft gunners whom we Marines admired and envied, was well served by some of these skilled ordnance mechanics. Many a damaged three-inch gun that the Japanese thought out of action raised its long snout from its pit to knock down an enemy bomber, thanks to these "old dobes." We heard that Negro Bell had attached himself to this outfit.

When Bataan fell, some of these men were able to join their comrades on Corregidor. The merchant marine element among them was foremost in the work of handling small craft overloaded with men and stores in the face of the onrushing Japanese. The navy remembers them with gratitude.

Old Bell had served obscurely on the Rock, for he was never a man to talk. And so, in the spring of 1943, I came to know him in the dysentery ward of the Cabanatuan military prison hospital.

The Filipino army, in its belated efforts to train before the islands were invaded, had constructed a camp for a division some eight miles east of the city of Cabanatuan in the province of Nueva Ecija, in rice paddy country. The place was never finished, but there was a well, some pipelines, and about a hundred flimsy barracks, most made of rough *tanghili* lumber with woven grass mats of *swali* for walls and thatched roofs of nipa palm. The buildings were largely of the same dreary, monotonous structure, 50 by 120 feet, with dirt floors and a raised sleeping space on either side of the middle aisle, covered with bamboo slats. Some four feet higher was a second sleeping deck, exactly like the one below it. Beneath the roof peak was an overhead catwalk. (If the barracks were not too crowded, this area could be used for baggage, but seldom was this the case.) The supporting *tanghili* timbers served to divide the berthing space into bays, five to a side, twenty to a building. One supposes that the little Filipino soldiers were packed five to a bay, which meant that the barracks normally held one hundred men. But when the Japanese packed us bigger Americans five to a bay, we were tighter than sardines in a can. (One barracks, of which I am too painfully aware, slept seven men to a bay, with the human overflow on both the catwalk and the damp ground underneath, some 170 prisoners of war!)

There were a few headquarters buildings, mess shacks, or storerooms of somewhat similar construction, but with the addition of wooden floors for the offices. There were no trees in the area, for the surrounding area had been stripped to become rice-producing land. For some years the mud walls of the rice paddies had been leveled, the land had lain fallow, then had grown up with the tall cogon grass in places just outside the immediate vicinity of our barracks. Around the entire camp was a double fence of barbed wire, and internally this same type of barbed-wire fence separated our camp into large divisions. One of these divisions was designated the hospital, with about half of its area isolated by the same barbed wire for the dysentery section.

In the beginning, some thousands of prisoners had died of dysentery aggravated by starvation. A headquarters-type building with a wooden floor was set aside for those men thought to be dying. It was known as the Zero Ward because those men assigned to it were thought to have no chance of recovery. Its alumni should be able to form a very exclusive club today, if they are of a mind to do so, for not many of its inmates survived. (I am a graduate of this ward, one of the few who came out alive!) We had the comparative luxury of crude, homemade bunks and mattresses stuffed with cogon grass, but those men who slept on the bamboo slats of the other barracks did not envy us. There was peace and quiet of a certain type in the dysentery area, for the Japanese feared the place greatly. They seldom visited it, and when they did, they wore protective masks and rubber gloves. But the American doctors, who were prisoners, feared it not. Two surgeons handled each ward, with a medical corpsman, if they had one, attached. The patients took care of their own maintenance and were segregated from the rest of the hospital population by prisoner guards positioned along the barbed wire fence on one side. On the other three sides were the Japanese sentries and their guardhouses.

By this time the death rate had dropped to about two men per month, for the Red Cross packages of food and medicines had begun to arrive. (Executions on the working side of the camp were not counted in figuring into the death rate.)

Negro Bell was in one of the dysentery wards, sleeping, sardinelike, among men from all sections of the States. He was a very resourceful man, for he seemed to have knives, pliers, nails, string, needles, bits of cloth for patching his worn khaki, and, most remarkable of all, a raincoat and a pair of rubber boots. How he managed to obtain these articles I discovered later.

In the rain and mud, that raincoat and those rubber boots kept him alive. They were the envy of every prisoner. But more important, Old Bell always seemed to have money. The berth space alongside Old Bell was therefore highly desirable, even if one came from the Deep South where colored men shuddered at Jim Crow laws, got off the sidewalk for their betters, and even said "sir" to poor white trash. To a large number of people he was "Mister" Bell, for stark hunger had significantly lowered the barriers of racial pride

among these soldiers, sailors, and Marines, mostly new-
comers to the islands. But the title was never necessary, for
Mister Bell would always share with those who had nothing.
Gladly would he hone a man's mess gear knife into the semblance of a razor with which he could shave, for this old
man was skilled with his hands.

At the time I entered the dysentery ward, there seemed to
be a divergence of opinion among the medical staff about
this disease. The effects and cure of the bacillic type of
dysentery were no mystery; it came on quickly, and unless
you received sulfa drugs, you died quickly. But there was
endless argument among the prisoners concerning the
amoebic type of dysentery. Some of us had been on the other
side of the barbed wire in the hospital with the beriberi
shuffle. The Red Cross food, little though it was, had begun
to work its cure; men were being returned to the working
section of the camp and to the terrors of The Farm.

Our doctor had warned all of us to be on our guard
against the amoebic bug, for it was sure to give anyone, in
time, a brain or a liver ulcer. I was a bit worried over my internal bleeding, so specimens were taken. I remember very,
very well the day I stood by the microscope technician and
he asked me, very gravely, for my full name, rank, and serial number. Then, like the Voice of Doom, came the
dreaded sentence, "I am sorry to have to tell you that your
specimen shows traces of amoebic dysentery." A prisoner
guard, kept handy for just such occasions, took immediate
charge of me, for I was now numbered among the unclean.
Before I was marched away, I saw our doctor, Lt. Col. Warren A. Wilson, bent over his the microscope, muttering the
words, and "unencysted, highly vegetative." I shuddered
with fear.

My emaciated appearance and beriberi shuffle caused
me to be sent to the dreaded Zero Ward. After a few days,
when I failed to die, I was moved to another ward in the
dysentery area, and so I came to be berthed alongside Negro
Bell. He allayed my fears, in answering my questions.

"Why, I have had it for forty years or more, ever since

I've been in the islands, I guess. The white gentleman doctors have medicine for it. They even cure most of them that have it. Those they do not cure, their bugs come to some sort of agreement with them. Mine is a little worse right now than before the war, 'cause I ain't gettin' the proper food to keep them contented. They sort of chew a bit in my intestines, for they are hungry, too. But I don't worry about it, for my bugs got plenty of sense. If they kill this old nigger, where they going to be at? Uncle Sam will be back here before long and then I'll have plenty of chow for my bugs, and medicines to keep them from having too many children. Why, listen to me, any man that has come as far as you have they can't kill. When the time comes for you to die, you will be like my old uncle back in Alabama. They had to cut out his liver when the undertaker was laying him out, and beat it to death with a club!"

The old man chuckled at his sally of wit, for it made me laugh, too. And I had not laughed for so long that I had nearly forgotten how.

This discourse on dysentery was the longest speech I ever heard Negro Bell make. Thereafter he lapsed into monosyllables. A year later Dr. Albert A. Weinstein, a captain in the army's Medical Corps and a former university teacher of medicine, gave me the same description, but in more technical language, as befitted a physician of his skill. But I always thought of Old Bell's homely definition of chronic amoebic dysentery as the best I ever heard.

In the Philippine Islands, the women have certain qualities that command considerable admiration. They are the financial brains of the family. The laboring and farming class of men give their pay to their wives. Their "better halves" then allow them something back for a game of "monte," a twenty-centavo daily ticket, perhaps, on the *jueteng* (the numbers racket is entrenched there, too), and a bit more to wager on the Sunday afternoon cockfights. While the husband toils for his family, his wife often sets up a small retail stand in front of their house to add to their meager income. Between washing, cooking, raising a family, running this tiny store, and waiting on her lord, she finds time to do a bit of that lovely handicraft for which this pleasant land is noted. Even in the upper classes it is doubtful that a big financial deal would be attempted without the approval of the wife. And Negro Bell had a Filipino wife.

After a while, some of us noticed that Negro Bell used to sit out at the crude latrine at regular hours and for long intervals, staring at a woman working a carabao (water buffalo) on a ranch across the road some two hundred yards or more away. Along the barbed-wire fence marched the brisk, alert Japanese sentries; at each end of it, some eight hundred yards apart were their guardhouses, with the Japanese soldiers sitting stiff-backed on a wooden bench. We could see their roadblock, always stopping and searching the passing *caromatas*, *calesas*, and *caratelas*, drawn by tiny ponies little larger than police dogs; or making the lumbering bull carts, the *caratones*, drawn by carabaos, pull off to the side of the road while their *caradores* submitted resignedly to insults and indignities. We idly watched those sentries in their open thefts and brutalities. Now and then some Filipinos were tied up to stakes and left out in the sun and rain, for what offenses we knew not. Now and then we saw some marched away in bonds in the direction of Cabanatuan City; their fate we could only guess. "The Co-Asiatic Prosperity," the "New Freedom" so graciously bestowed by Japan—this was their *independencia*.

Possibly it was First Lieutenant Flynn who first guessed what the woman was doing. Few prisoners ever realized what was going on, for Negro Bell talked little to anyone. The shrewd Flynn kept the secret, for its disclosure would have meant certain death. Bell had organized his own personal, private underground; hence his collection of tools, his boots and raincoat, and his money.

Now and then I saw the woman being assisted by a young boy—a *tao*. I guessed it to be her son who helped her in tilling the field. There was the husband and father, two hundred yards away, the sentries, and the barbed wire always between them. There was torture and death for the slightest mistake, for the wartime guards had little use for due process; suspicion is tantamount to guilt and immediate conviction. Old Bell had always shared the food he bought in the commissary with those who had no money; occasionally a sufferer's pain was relieved with strange medicines, surely not of any Red Cross origin. But he kept his precious boots and raincoat jealously for himself, for he, too, wanted very much to live.

How in the world his wife and son, such as they were, managed to get the stuff through that barbed wire and past those sentries was never discovered. An individual sentry could be bribed, as was well known, but we could never trust the Japanese. Men had been tortured and executed for bribing sentries and getting things through the wire. I remember the fate of seven army soldiers who had bribed their way through that wire to buy outside food from the local Filipinos. The guard had unexpectedly been changed before they came back. After a week of torture we heard that they were shot because the Japanese thought they would die anyway from their beatings, with no food and no water. The farther one stayed away from the "dead-line" of that barbed wire, the better for all concerned.

In September 1943 the hospital area was closed down and moved across the road into the working area. Outgoing work details had greatly reduced the strength of our camp, and the guards were pulling in the barbed wire to make the camp smaller. Old Bell's ward was moved from the northeast corner of the camp to the southwest corner, and a smaller barbed-wire enclosure was set up for the dysentery wards, now reduced to a half dozen patients. Some two hundred yards to the south was the Cabanatuan Road, with its main guardhouse and permanent roadblock.

For some time the few of us who suspected Bell's secret did not see the familiar figures of the woman and the young man. Negro Bell no longer had food and medicines to share with others; he visibly pined and withered. The familiar lines of "Old Black Joe" again came to mind, the "I'se coming, I'se coming, for mah haid is bending low," for here was a dreadful, living example. The old man still used to go to the latrine at regular hours and sit there for long periods, but he did not see the ones he longed for.

The camp had, among several undergrounds of little importance, one really large one, and of this one, the less said, the better. Suffice to say that most of its big shots did not seem to be starving. We heard a rumor that Negro Bell had procured a plump duck through it, and that the very senior officer, one Lieutenant Colonel Mack, formerly of the inspector general's department and a former West Pointer, had muscled in on the civilians who had started it and shared part of Bell's bird, for he had a surfeit of corned beef and Red Cross food. Perhaps Bell gave part of his duck away freely, but then the "have-nots" used to tell ugly tales of the "haves," and the belly of that very senior officer might well have graced a portly colonel of the army's Quartermaster Corps in time of peace. Some say he died aboard a prison ship a year later. No doubt he did some good with his underground activities, but some men will shed no tears over his reported fate, for prison life sears and scars.

Finally a woman and a young man were seen quietly working in a new rice paddy just across the road, never glancing at our camp. First Lieutenant Flynn noticed them; he arose from his usual "dobe" squat to limp over to Old Bell. The latter got up from his bed of hard bamboo slats and ragged blanket to shuffle off to the latrine. There he sat for several hours. Next morning he was known to have given out a few pesos here and there, and he was seen placing a commissary order with the officer in charge, for hard cash. A few days later I assumed that he and his "bugs" had resumed their mutual tolerance of one another. Doctor Weinstein had said he would live to see release. Doctor Dan Golenternek, who was there also, remarked, "The old fellow is too tough to kill."

The Japanese guard at the roadblock became stricter, and there were now more Filipinos tied up and beaten than before. Prices rose sharply and terribly; inflation was rampant across the land. The occupation pesos that we called

"Mickey Mouse" could buy very little. "Old Dobe" Flynn's pay of thirty pesos a month, less what the old man spent for his chewing tobacco and regularly sent each month over to First Sergeant McNulty on the working side to buy tobacco for the survivors of Company L, bought but a fraction of what it had before. Flynn worried over his "boys"; Bell grew visibly depressed, squatting in his owl-like position wearing his "G-string" and matching coat of blue with its brass buttons, silent and morose.

It was remarked that he no longer chewed tobacco. Negro Bell placed no more commissary orders, but occasionally he and a few other living skeletons were seen hovering around a stove they had made from a battered five-gallon gasoline can, with punched in sides and bottom, burning ashes from the galley fires, for that charcoal gave off no telltale smoke. In their homemade tin cans, laboriously fashioned from cast-off sheet metal, simmered native vegetables, *opo*, *cinquemas*, *telilun*, and the trunk of a papaya tree cut into sections like fish steaks. These surely did not come from our camp.

For a while I idly watched the woman and the young man, but after a time they were seen no more. Negro Bell applied to the underground for information, but before an answer could arrive, the prisoner members were seized and placed incommunicado by the enraged guards. We heard that a Russian woman link in Manila was under sentence of death; Father Talbot, an army captain chaplain who before the war was a Jesuit Ph.D. who had taught at Georgetown University, asked his tiny prisoner congregation to pray for "a certain dear benefactor in Manila who is in terrible danger."

I saw, for a day, the very senior officer, Lieutenant Colonel Mack, peering at the Japanese guardhouse where the underground members were confined. Visibly shaken, and white as he was, he and his belly were quivering behind the lumber pile. The next day he was taken to join his companions in torture. And the tale ran around the camp that when the Japanese guards came for him and searched his little shack, a former storehouse, they took away over five hundred cans of Red Cross corned beef that had been cunningly concealed beneath the floor, and several thousand pesos from his portly person. I never saw him again, but some, alive today, recalled him as a fellow passenger on that ill-fated prison ship and spoke of witnessing his drowning.

Old Bell haunted the latrine. Between scanty meals in the chow line, he practically lived there. He never saw what he was looking for again. Now his "bugs" seemed to get hungry; he moved from the latrine to his bamboo-slatted bed. Captain Weinstein sat up at night to watch him; Doctor Dan took care of him during the day. He died in his sleep. Captain Weinstein told us the next morning, "He heard the gentle voices calling. Your 'Old Black Joe' is dead." And some of us cried openly, like women.

It was not considered remarkable that some of the dysentery patients from the southern states asked to be allowed to carry Old Bell out to "group four" on his stretcher to that last resting place on The Farm. But the Japanese refused to allow a burial detail from the isolation area. After working hours, four men came from the other side of the fence with an officer prisoner. The four men were tired after a hard day's work at The Farm and were cursing bitterly about their luck in being selected for a burial detail. They cursed doubly when they found their burden was a colored man; besides, the day was Sunday, and they had received no *ya si me* at all that week.

Doctors Weinstein and Dan wrote Old Bell up as being sixty-six years old; that the cause of his death was "chronic amoebic dysentery, with severe erosions, extending over a long period of years, aggravated by malnutrition and senility." But I do not believe they knew the whole story.

First Lieutenant Flynn probably had a better diagnosis of the cause of death, for he was heard to say, "Mister Bell died of a broken heart."

10

THE STORY OF
KOENIG AND CORLEY

On the twenty-ninth day of December 1941, the 4th Marine Regiment, less detachments left behind on Bataan, lay in Middleside Barracks, of Fort Mills, Corregidor Island, the harbor defense of Manila Bay. The regiment was waiting for the U.S. Army to assign it to sectors for beach defense duty.

Off to the northeast, we could see the smoke of the burning Cavite Navy Yard; to the north there was the black plume of a smoldering French liner *Aramis*, bomb-gutted and run aground in the shallows of the bay. The yard had seen a lot of our Marines killed, while the liner had been the scene of death for two of our men. The Filipino Army was withdrawing from the southeast and the north to unite their 1st and 2d Corps and form the final Bataan defense lines. Manila was to be occupied in a few days by the advancing Yellow Horde.

We knew what bombing was, for we had already received our baptism of fire in Olongapo, Cavite, and Mariveles. We thought Corregidor to be impregnable; the workmen around the dock, when we had landed there two nights before, had boastfully told us so. We were reassured to hear, "We have not yet been bombed; our antiaircraft guns will blast them from the skies. They will never dare attempt it."

We were packed in the huge Middleside Barracks, some sixteen hundred or more of us, along with men of two army coast artillery regiments, antiaircraft, and headquarters troops. Most of these soldiers were elsewhere at their battle stations, but we guessed over three hundred to be in the barracks with us. The talk ran, "The barracks is perfectly safe with over thirty inches of concrete on the roof and on all ceilings. The Japanese have no bomb that will penetrate it." This comforting assurance was said to have come from the army quartermaster himself, or so ran the talk.

Our regimental commander, Col. S. L. Howard, was a prudent man. He was taking no chances, so all hands were duly told what to do in case of an air raid. There was no shelter other than the barracks available to us, so we were assigned cover on its lower deck. In the meantime, we were making ourselves shipshape by sweeping down, fore and aft, and doing such other chores as we do at cleaning stations aboard ship, for the Marine is a cleanly animal. Our officers are a bit fussy about such things, and we growled as we worked, as Marines do the world over.

In the new galleys, strange and unfamiliar, our mess sergeant had been late getting out the breakfast meal. The colonel would be around at nine o'clock to inspect; it was almost that time now. Astute company commanders had therefore cleared the upper two decks of all idlers, so that the work of the cleaning details might not be undone, for the "Old Man" himself was coming around for a "look-see." It was best that all hands, and even Soochow, the regiment's mascot, had everything spick-and-span. Some of the army staff would be with the colonel to look at these strange sea-soldiers, and we Marines had a reputation to maintain.

Many of us were lolling around the arcade of the lower deck or were just outside the barracks, basking in the bright sunshine at the start of the dry season. Suddenly the word was passed, "Air raid! Air raid! Air raid!" In a matter of seconds it came; the loud bark and crack of 3-inch and .50-caliber guns ushered in the terrible *swish, swish, swish* and *crump, crump, crump* of falling and exploding bombs, followed by the droning whine and zoom of enemy planes pulling out of their dives. Several bombs penetrated the roof of the barracks and exploded on the top deck; several more went through all three floors and burst in the galley and washroom areas. "Twenty-seven bombers were in the first wave, and we think we downed two," ran the cry, and there were cheers from many. But where the bombs had hit the kitchen and showers, there was the yellow, acrid smoke of picric acid explosive, confusion, and cries of "First Aid!" And there was also heard the so-called "battle cry of the Marine Corps," of "Corpsman! Corpsman!"

The thirty inches of overhead concrete were only three! Someone had misinformed us! The brave hospital corpsmen and stretcher parties took care of the wounded, and while they were engaged came the second wave. More bombs erupted in huge craters just in front of the barracks and on the parade grounds. In the passageway, at the back of the barracks, just under the hill, we heard dull crashes—smaller bombs with instantaneous fuses burst on the roof and top deck. We knew there were similar scenes being repeated all over the island. We cowered and huddled together, afraid the bulkheads were going to cave in and bury us all beneath the crashing concrete.

For nearly three hours this air attack went on before the welcomed "All Clear" was sounded. Then the first sergeants called the roll of their respective companies, for it behooved us to know who had been wounded or killed. After all the missing had been checked, Headquarters Company of the 2d Battalion reported PFC Fred Koenig, familiarly called "Bones" because of his lean and hungry look, missing, while Company E could not find Field Music John Corley. There were indignant mutters. "The so-and-sos ran out on it, the dirty bums! That Bones Koenig, what else could you expect of a deadbeat athlete, always jockstrapping in Shanghai to duck out of guard duty! And that kid Music! Just shows how useless and undependable field musics are! What darned good are they?"

The debris began to get cleaned up, the wounded were sent by truck to the Malinta Hospital, and the dead were taken to the post cemetery. We glanced nervously now and

then at the sky, for we hoped that no more air raids would
come that day. Reports from other places began to trickle in,
and we heard of thirty-odd men killed with a battery commander in what they thought was a good bombproof. The
post was promptly repaired and named Battery Hamilton
after the dead Captain Hamilton.

Around two o'clock in the afternoon our lost sheep
strayed in. In answer to questioning, sharp and severe, they
blandly replied that they had been in Malinta Hospital helping the wounded. The army doctors were short of first-aid
men and had kept them there. They were rather vague about
why they were in that area, nearly a mile and a half away,
and successfully evaded that searching question. For the
time being their absence was overlooked. The "top soldiers"
gave them a stiff tongue lashing about wandering around the
island. Since there was no paperwork to write up on the two
miscreants, the affair might have been considered closed,
for there was more important work to do than worry about
"Bones" and "The Music."

Colonel Howard had put pressure on the high command
to take his men out of that death trap, so that his regiment
could get into its beach defenses. The 1st Battalion went to
the other side of Malinta Hill, in the Monkey Point area of
the pollywog-shaped island, the 2d and 3d Battalions occupied the fringe of the pollywog's head; from the South Shore
through Cheney and James Ravines for the 2d, while the 3d
continued on through the North Shore, Battery Point, the
North Mine Dock, Bottomside Town, and the South Mine
Dock. Headquarters Company of the regiment, with service
troops, was scattered here and there with the command post
located in Queen Tunnel, next door to Malinta.

"Music" Corley went about his daily runner duties, duti-
fully trudging on foot between James Ravine and the South
Shore; "Bones" Koenig performed his chores with the Intelligence Section of the 2d Battalion, down near James
Ravine. Their absence during the bombing was well-nigh
forgotten, and might have continued to be had it not been
for a certain first sergeant of the 2d Battalion, 1st Sgt. Earl

O. Carlson, known as "Old Swede." He was an extra "top-kick," having been picked up when we received our share of the disbanded Olongapo garrison. Until a suitable job was found for him, he was in charge of the Marine Military Police in Malinta Tunnel. Here he encountered a senior non-commissioned officer named Snyder who had been the sergeant major of the 60th Coast Artillery at Middleside Barracks the day we had been bombed so heavily. Now he was a newly commissioned warrant officer, over whose desk flowed all recommendations for medals and awards.

"The Marines must be a pretty hard bunch. Just what does a man have to do to get a medal or commendation, kill a couple of hundred Japs? The old limey army used to give out their Victoria Cross when a soldier saved an officer's life under fire at the risk of his own. Two of your Marines saved an officer's life during that big bombing on the twenty-ninth of last month; took him down to Malinta, and then helped bring in the wounded at the mouth of the tunnel during the whole affair while bombs were falling like rain. You people pay no attention to it." And Mr. Snyder shook his head at the vagaries of these strange men, half sailor and half soldier.

The "Old Swede," a battle-hardened veteran of World War I, was an inquiring man, and he soon learned the whole story. During a lull in the bombings he strolled over to James Ravine. Here he talked earnestly with the adjutant, a Captain Wagner, and the sergeant major, duly impressing these important men. His good deed for the day done, the "Old Swede" worked his way cautiously back to Malinta, for the journey was hazardous.

As soon as he could take time off, Captain Wagner himself went over to Malinta. Inquiring in the hospital lateral, he was conducted to one Second Lieutenant McCauley (I hope I have the right name), of the Signal Corps Reserve. The young man was laid up in dry dock for major overhaul and repair; there were numerous bomb splinters in his body and his shattered leg was supported in a traction rig. The formalities of introduction over, Captain Wagner took out a pencil and notebook, recorded what the lieutenant had to say, had it typed by an obliging corpsman of the navy, and brought it back to be duly signed.

I got a very good look at it later and, in full, it read something like this:

"When that first stick of five-hundred-pound bombs fell, I was on the hill behind the barracks, in the open, and was hit by numerous fragments of one of those bombs. My leg was shattered, badly bleeding, and I yelled 'First Aid,' but hardly expected any help, for I heard the cries of those wounded Marines below. Out of the smoke appeared these two fellows; the bigger one, whom you tell me is named Koenig, gave me a lighted cigarette and told me to take it easy. He and the very young one, whom you call Corley, applied a tourniquet and a rough splint. All the time they were doing this, bombs were dropping all around us. They were not only brave, but they went about their business in an intelligent manner. They knew what they were doing. Then they told me they were going to get a truck and that they would be back. I never expected to see them again, for lying on my back, I could hear and see another large wave of enemy planes coming over; the antiaircraft guns began shooting, bombs would soon be dropping, and they might reasonably be expected to take cover below.

"Mr. Smith, a civilian employee of the Ordnance Section who is now a captain right here in the tunnel, came down the hill, saw me, and ran back up to his quarters to get me a blanket. While he was gone, these two Marines returned with a stretcher. They had already put me in a bomb crater and took cover there themselves while they looked over my tourniquet, adjusted it, and checked my splint. Bombs hit all around, but we were not struck, just sprayed with dirt. Then they picked me up, carried me off to a truck, had me tell them the way to Malinta Hospital, and got in the back with me, with some other Marine for a driver.

"A quarter of a mile or so along the route, a bomb hit nearby while a diving plane sprayed the road with machine gun fire. I could hear the splinters whine and felt the shock as these splinters and bullets hit the truck. The driver stopped the vehicle and started to get out, looking for cover. One of these two Marines in the back, who I guess was Koenig, cocked his rifle, leveled it at the driver, and said, 'You ——————————, if you don't drive this wounded lieutenant to the hospital, I'll kill you where you are!' The driver started the truck again and we made it to the hospital with bombs dropping all along the route. As we went through Bottomside, even lying on my back, with the tailgate of the truck hanging down where a big splinter had knocked it, I could see machine shops smashed and burning and the whole area a mess.

"These boys got me to the doctors, who complimented them on the good job they had done. They were told that they had saved my life. I tried to get their names, but they had gone. I heard later that they had done a further good job of unloading the wounded outside the tunnel for the next few hours, and I was not surprised. I owe my life to those Marines."

The captain and the second lieutenant parted company, never to see one another again. Captain Wagner was to die in a prison ship on the way to Japan; whether the second lieutenant lived, I do not know.

Before Captain Wagner left the tunnel, Captain Smith, Ordnance Corps Reserve, was duly interviewed. I heard that he said, "I have been trying to find out who those Marines were for some time. Lieutenant McCauley told me that they had done a first-class job on him; in view of the continued machine gunning and bombing, he never expected them to come back. I rushed up the hill to my quarters to get a blanket; when I returned to take care of McCauley and get a truck, they were gone. From the trail of blood, I could figure out what had happened. I will be only too glad to make a statement. I saw those Marines for just a second, but I am sure that I could identify them. To take a truck down that road under such conditions seems gallantry in action above and beyond the call of duty. It strikes me as Medal of Honor stuff. I want to come over to James Ravine and see them in person."

Captain Smith was as good as his word. The sergeant

major produced the mystified Marines; they were positively identified. The battalion commander, Lieutenant Colonel Anderson, shook their hands and gave them his confidential wink.

The sergeant major was told to "write them up to the regiment for meritorious conduct, concurring with contents of basic communication." There were many other gallant deeds done on the twenty-ninth day of December and in the days that followed to be considered; by the time the Personnel Section, Awards Division, of the Headquarters and Harbor Defense put it through, the recommendation was only for the Silver Star.

If only someone along the line had thought to insert in the letter and endorsements the words, "This act of gallantry was above and beyond the call of duty, at imminent risk of their lives," for such phrases were there for all to read, duly recorded in both officer witnesses' statements! Alas, probably no one noted Lieutenant McCauley's additional statement, "Intelligent application of first aid, in applying the tourniquet and splint, while bombs exploded all around, showering us with dirt."

Such was the narrow margin that separated a Medal of Honor winner from a holder of the Silver Star. The award was duly radioed to Washington, D.C., and is there as a matter of record. The statements appended to the letter and the endorsements were probably lost when Corregidor was surrendered.

There was a fitting ceremony in James Ravine; Colonel Howard himself braved bombs and shells to be there with some of his staff. Koenig and Corley fidgeted and blushed, and went back to their duties as soon as they decently could. The colonel lingered on to tell the group at the mouth of the bombproof that he was "damned glad to know he had men like that in his regiment; it is an honor to command them." Then he hurried on, for there was a second lieutenant of Marines due to get his Silver Star for locating a battery of Japanese guns on the Cavite shore; he had remained in the open, under fire, to direct the army's heavy cannon against that battery, and silenced it.

"Bones" Koenig went on to scale the heights in heroism. Quiet and modest, I suspect he took charge in his intelligence outpost under shellfire while certain of his seniors cowered and shook, and "Bones" duly reported over the phone where the flashes of enemy fire were located.

A few nights before the surrender, James Ravine received one of its worst shellings. The adjutant and the sergeant major, crouching behind their sandbag revetment, observed the bursts. "I wonder what old 'Bones' is up to now?" remarked Captain Wagner, for the intelligence outpost located on the other side of the hill was being heavily bombarded. And just then occurred a remarkable thing, for, as these Marines spoke about Koenig, he appeared on the path around the turn carrying a Filipino Air Corps Cadet named Gonzalez, whose arm was tied up with a tourniquet just below the shoulder.

Doctor Wade and Pharmacist's Mate 1st Class Bray grabbed the boy, took him into the dressing station, gave him merciful morphine, and amputated the arm at once. It had been hanging by only a few shreds of skin. A tourniquet skillfully and intelligently applied while shells were ripping up the landscape had saved his life. Koenig sat quietly, white-faced, and now and then gave a little gasp. When the stump had been skillfully dressed and the Filipino cadet slept his merciful drugged sleep, Doctor Wade came out of his dressing station to talk to Koenig and to shake a brave Marine's hand. "Bones" rose shakily to his feet, saying, "Please, sir, look me over, for I've been hit in the hip."

Doctor Wade and Bray sewed him up, and Koenig talked them out of having him sent to the hospital. He claimed that the trip under that shellfire was too dangerous; and, after a while when the barrage had ceased, he was heard to remark, "Well, I guess I had better be seeing about getting back to the outpost."

The orderly clerk was ordered by the colonel to "tell the sergeant major to write 'Bones' Koenig up for the Distinguished Service Cross. Put it in those exact words, and maybe the army will give it to him this time," for the "Old Man" had always been pretty sore about that Silver Star award; he thought Koenig and Corley should have had more.

But the sergeant major and his Filipinos had gone up to man their reserve line just after Koenig had come in. It was early dawn before they came back. The sergeant major was told of the "Old Man's" order, but there were many other things to be done that day.

It was noted that Koenig had dragged the wounded boy around the long way, on the path that encircled the shoulder of the hill. Up and over and down the hill was the shortest route, several times so, but "Bones" knew the wounded lad could never have survived such a trip through the dense jungle, thorned creepers, and through much barbed wire. The shoulder road was under continuous fire of hideous intensity. Inquiry revealed that Koenig had been hit by a shell splinter just after he had left his outpost, but he knew the lad would have died from shock had he not hurried him down to Doctor Wade. Corpsman Bray always said he reached there in the nick of time.

The adjutant and his sergeant major moved up to Middleside Tunnel the night after Koenig's exploit. By a flickering candle stuck in a wine bottle, the orderly clerk, Sgt. Wendell N. Garden, typed out the recommendation for the army's Distinguished Service Cross in clear, unmistakable English that told what Koenig had done. The sergeant major and adjutant checked it, sent it down to James Ravine for the "Old Man" to sign, and it was forwarded to regiment. Two days later came surrender, and a gallant deed was unrecorded. I do not recall the Filipino boy's full name; I hope he survived. And, until I can see a roster of the survivors of the 4th Marines, I cannot say if Koenig is dead or not.[12]

Poor Corley did not finish the war in such a blaze of glory. A month or so after he received his Silver Star, while he trudged on his route from James Ravine to the South Shore, he had occasion to duck into the Malinta Tunnel, for the way was under shellfire. There were some seven thousand

12. Koenig survived the war. Today he lives in Oceanside, California.

headquarters troops, service personnel, and civilians in that place, crowded and pushing one another around. It was against all orders in the regiment for a Marine to go in there, but it was a matter of life or death for little Corley. He could use the Main Tunnel Route along the tracks, come out on the backside where there was a defilade from the enemy shellfire, and worm his way around to Major Bradley's command post on the South Shore.

The "Music" got pushed into the way of a small electric locomotive that was hauling supplies, and his leg was badly crushed. He spent nearly two months in the hospital, and he came out just before the surrender to shoulder a rifle in the South Shore trenches, for Major Bradley had lost men by shellfire and this Marine's services were needed. Even with his limp he could help repel a landing with his rifle, for he was known as a good shot.

The sergeant major, Mess Sergeant Ellis, Quartermaster Sergeant Lemon, and others, saw "Music" Corley in the San Diego Naval Hospital, where they were all being "drydocked" after their release. Behind Corley's back they told all who would listen about his saving the wounded lieutenant's life. The pretty nurses made much of him, and his embarrassed blushes caused raucous laughter on the part of the mess sergeant, a rather rugged character.

They all got together in a bar for a drinking bout and made sport of the Field Music of the Marine Corps as a class. Corley was told that "field musics" and second lieutenants are the most useless people in the Corps. "Isn't it just like a damned 'music' to violate orders and go into the Malinta Tunnel, hoping to rubberneck at pretty nurses or maybe see the general himself? Then he gets hurt by a dinky little electric train!" And the mess sergeant added, "What damned good are 'musics' anyway?"

But this time Corley did not blush, for he knew this to be inverse praise. He bought the drinks.

11

THE STORY OF THE OLD SWEDE—
1ST SGT. EARL O. CARLSON, USMC

"Greater love hath no man than this, that a man lay down his life for his friends" [St. John, chapter 15, verse 13]. I had often heard this quotation, but I never thought to see a living illustration of it until I came to know the full story of Joe Pearlstein and the "Old Swede." Of course, the "Old Swede" never figured he was laying down his life for anyone, for I'm sure he wanted to live as much as those of us who came back alive, but it just worked out that way. There was more nobility in his character than I thought, or that he, himself, ever knew.

The "Old Swede" always vigorously denied he was a Christian, but toward the last, when the shadow of the grim reaper hovered impatiently over him, he probably denied it with blasphemous profanity. I have no doubt that his lips were always unrepentant, but I know that in his inward heart, near the end, while still rejecting the "faith of his fathers," he practiced their precepts. When the tremendous sound of the last trumpet shall usher in the Day of Judgment, when the sheep shall be separated from the goats, we may indulge in a charitable hope that the manner in which he came to lay down his life (it was all he had to give) may tip the balance of the scales in his favor and counteract his "life of sin."

The "Old Swede" was addicted to drink, when he could get it, and his relationship with the gentler sex was not a proper example to set before young Marines. He often aired his agnostic's views, though he claimed, while in his cups, to be a devout Mohammedan.

He came from old American stock, a seventh generation Swede and a descendant of those hardy Scandinavians who first settled our state of Delaware. His ancestors, moving westward under the pioneer urge, finally came to anchor in the Dakotas, and here he was born. In his youth he toiled on his father's farm, from there he went on to college.

Big and strong, his muscles swelling under his jacket, he answered the blare of the bugles in those days of 1917, when his country was calling for volunteers. In the very beginning of that war he may have been imbued with patriotic fervor. Had anyone commended him for it, he would have denied it with fine scorn. The "Old Swede" was of that stuff of which professional Marines are made.

His name, the ancestry of which he was so proud, and his gift for mimicry in the heavy dialect of the Minnesota Americans of Scandinavian ancestry soon caused him to be called the "Swede." I know that he did not like the nickname, but his name and appearance, with his tales of "Yohn Yohnson," as I have already said, made it a natural. He submitted to the inevitable with his unfailing good nature, but in his later days he would always buy anyone a drink if they addressed him by his first name.

He saw much frontline action in the 116th Infantry of the army's 1st Division. In this famous unit of the old regulars, where being a noncommissioned officer required at least two "hash marks" for most men, he rose to the heights of first sergeant. He had the advantage of having had much better schooling than the others; in his later days, as a Marine Corps "first soldier," his paperwork was a thing of beauty and a joy forever, though at the very last his sergeant major had to put the prod on him to get it in on time.

It is written in the records that his old division suffered over 100 percent casualties; as a result, otherwise despised recruits were able to get the prized chevrons. It is well to remember today that when you see the three stripes up and three down with the diamond between them, it means some skipper thought the wearer to be the very best man in his company of two hundred odd, and had him made in that rank, and that subsequent company commanders concurred and retained the "topkick" in his position. It may not denote moral character of the plaster saint variety, but it does indicate military character of the type that combines force, dependability, and loyalty.

The "Swede" had become addicted to the bottle early in life. In the days before there was prohibition in the land, the hardy "squareheads" were often adversely commented upon because of their preference for grain alcohol rather than the more varied beverages of their effete neighbors, but this preference showed their farsightedness. They were twenty years ahead of their time. Perhaps the blood of far-off Viking ancestors was stirring in his veins, but the "Swede" belonged to a division in which plenty of men were getting killed and wounded. Soldiers are very prone to drink, anyway, and if they indulge in the cup that cheers in their brief respite between the business of "kill or be killed," and in the rear areas, who can call them sinners?

Those of us who knew the "Swede" may recall the ugly little hole in his forehead. The tale is told that at a terrible place called Cantigny, which was quite messy for all concerned, a piece of red hot shell splinter smote him mightily. His trench mortar platoon commander thought him dead, and his death was regretted because he had proven himself a valuable young sergeant. Littered back to a battalion dressing station, unconscious, in this backwash of battle he was given but a glance, tagged with the red "gunshot wound" label, and laid among the dead. The doctors and hospital corpsmen were rather busy that day with some very pressing cases. Some time later the "Swede" came to; with horror he realized he was lying among that by-product of the battlefield, other twenty-year-old dead, and rose unsteadily to his feet.

In those unenlightened days, before blood plasma was in use and when morphine was rare, all hospital corpsmen carried a full quart of cognac for treatment of shock. The "Swede" grabbed the nearest container, drank rapidly, and soon had made a "dead soldier" of it. It must not have been full, for even the "Swede" could not have stood up under it, great as was his capacity for alcohol. Before the surprised medical men could recover from their shock, the sergeant seized a canteen and was on his way back to the sound of gunfire up front.

He was received in his platoon with acclamations of joy, still with his wound tag, that red badge of courage, dangling from his blouse. It is said that he fought with desperate courage and was outstanding among other brave men, until the effects of the second canteen, taken at seasonable intervals, became too painfully visible. He was gently chided for this breach of military discipline, for the regulations prohibit those other than authorized medical personnel from carrying shock preventative with them to the battlefield. For this reason he did not receive the Distinguished Service Cross. Perhaps it was for the best, for the winner of that bauble received for it two dollars in additional pay each month. In the long years to come that sum would have bought quite a lot of rum and could have tipped the scales against the "Swede." He was always philosophical about this affair.

Outside of this one distressful fall from a state of grace, he managed to keep his indiscretions from the notice of his officers, for the "Swede" was cursed with the ability to carry far more liquor than was good for him. (Soon after this incident he became a "top.")

Some ten months after the armistice his division returned to the States, received fitting honors, and its members dispersed to the four winds. In his native town his war record, his good manners, his education, and his industry caused him to prosper. As a successful civilian, he thought he was through with the war business. But Prohibition had come into the land, and a craving for whisky began to hum in his soul. The Marine Corps beckoned with its bright posters of far-off tropic lands; there were "banana wars" then in San

Domingo, Haiti, and Nicaragua, and there were the glamors of seagoing life or the China station. And, of course, there was the fact that the "Swede" was a professional soldier at heart. Even in his later days he would always stand up for colors, while others at the first warning note ducked under shelter "to get out of the rain."

The Marine Corps quickly made him a sergeant, for the "Swede," being a good soldier, overcame the handicap of being known as a man who had previoU.S. Army service. The Marines are a jealous group that likes to promote first those they have nurtured and raised themselves. We well remember one officer, Capt. Marvin W. Scott, portly and redfaced, who was referred to by the more ribald element, behind his back, as the "Bull" and sometimes as the "Bartender." It was said by some that the Marine Corps had ruined a good police sergeant when they had given him a commission. Behind his gruff exterior he had a soft heart for the erring and wayward. He often said, however, that he did not care to have ex-army men in his command, for unless a situation was covered in detail by orders, they would sit down and do nothing in an emergency.

We Marines serve with such a variety of weapons in such diverse units that we have a little knowledge of many, but real mastery of none. In the army of those days, one put in a whole three-year enlistment in a machine gun company, for instance, and became quite learned in that weapon. So when an "ex-dogface" showed up in a machine gun unit, his superior abilities could not be hidden well, and some Marines resented them. The wise ex-soldier soon learned to keep his mouth shut about the army, at least until he had attained his second pay grade. Our wiser officers realized that our best recruiting ground was the line of the army and welcomed them gladly. The Marine Corps offered travel, adventure, and, to the professionally inclined, the "banana wars," while the army in those days had no similar inducements.

The "Swede" got along famously, and they made him a first sergeant in faraway Peking in a much shorter time than those who had served solely in the Marine Corps could ordinarily attain. He had, before this time, a bit of seagoing and the tropics under his belt; now in the Far East he was getting a bit too much of the Demon Rum, but his body was young and strong then. He could carry his liquor.

He used to deliver pontifical talks to the younger Marines, and he always had an audience, for his hand was never slow on the draw when it came to signing a chit for the drinks. He always paid his bills, too, for he knew the value of sound credit. Too often Marines say, "The first turn of the homegoing propeller, and mask [hide] the chits!" No one was ever able to say that of the "Swede."

He soon acquired a girl named Nellie in an attempt to secure an illusion of domestic bliss. She was a lovely Chinese girl with her roots in the mire, for, of her many virtues, alas, chastity could by no means be considered her outstanding one. The Marines, who give the girlfriends they encounter on the beaches of foreign shores such hideous names as "Roach," "Murphy," "The Joker," "Regulation," "Greasy Grace," "Hot Pants Rosie," or "Kitty the Shakes" (these ladies we recall among the "Flower Streets and Willow Lanes" of old Peking), referred to "Swede's" girl as "Dirty Neck," but the "Swede" always called her his "Nellie."

There was severe criticism of the "Swede" when he bought his "Nellie" a fur coat. The dubious honor of being the first Marine sergeant to buy a fur coat for his girl belonged to Sgt. W.F.A. Trax, who earned the hatred of every "squaw man" in North China for doing so. The other "squaw men" were importuned by their ladies for coats of karakul, Persian lamb, or even Russian sable, and there was trouble in the *hutungs* [Chinese for "alleys," and Marine slang for the red light district east of Hatamen Street where the squaw men lived]. These two Marines had really started something; the custom soon spread along the ports of the China coast; in Tientsin the soldiers of the 15th Infantry complained about this Marine custom of spoiling "squaws" with kindness of this sort. By 1940, when I was again in Shanghai, no cabaret queen of the Majestic or Little Club would listen to any "shack deal" without the preliminaries of a fur coat. In fact, many of the sly minxes had several such garments, for all girls liked "scalps" to display as proof of how they had "trimmed their suckers."

The noncommissioned officers elected the "Swede" the president of their club, with a hundred dollars on open book for "entertainment purposes." One of his profound sayings in the club has long been quoted as good advice for the young Marines on China Station: "The man who shacks up with a White Russian has generally one or more of these three things happen to him—he gets a court-martial, a social disease, or gets married." The truth of this statement is all too evident to one who has personally observed his fellow Marines in the Orient.

The "Swede" perhaps took his club duties a bit too seriously to the despair of "Nellie," who was forced to seek her recreation among the younger Marines. They abused his hospitality and drank his beer when he was away at the club, but he never seemed to find it out. Poor Nellie, in later years we heard the lass died before a firing squad, along with a character we Marines called "Sweechow," the Chinese term for "sleepy," for he had an eye affliction that required him to raise his head to see. It seems they were detected selling that curse of the Orient, heroin, cunningly concealed in blown-out duck eggshells. [From 1920 to 1936, Sweechow had a small bar located about two hundred yards west of the Marine barracks at the foot of the Tartar Wall by the pumping station. Nellie and Sweechow died together at the Temple of Heaven Bridge.]

But we should not blame the "Swede" too much for living a life of sin. Half of the six-hundred-man garrison, at the very least, was living without benefit of clergy. The restraining influence of religion was absent, for the post had no chaplain; and the doctor was said to tacitly approve, for "squaw men" or "shack masters" seldom appeared on the sick list for "misconduct, not in the line of duty."

The "Swede" returned to Nicaragua where the Marines were chasing the elusive rebel Sandino. There were elec-

Col. Samuel L. Howard, right, inspects the beach defenses on Corregidor with Lt. Col. Herman R. Anderson, left, commander of 2d Battalion, 4th Marines, and Maj. Gen. George F. Moore, USA, center, overall commander of the Corregidor defenses. (Department of Defense Photo (USMC) Phi-9)

Cavite Navy Yard, 10 June 1940. The yard is located on the island at the bottom and the Sangley Point installations at the top of the photograph. Note the PBYs in the harbor. (National Archives)

Lt. Col. Herman R. Anderson stands on the beach at Corregidor with the assembled officers of 2d Battalion, 4th Marines and several Filipino officers. Note the thick layers of oil on the beaches from ships sunk in Manila Bay. (Department of Defense Photo (USMC) 58736)

The commander of the Japanese guard in Shanghai bids farewell to Col. Howard and the 4th Marines. (National Archives)

Cpl. Jackson, 1930
(Author's Collection)

Lt. Col. Curtis T.
Beecher and his runner
pause during one of
his daily inspections of
1st Battalion defenses.
(Department of
Defense Photo
(USMC) 58735)

Charles Ream Jackson
Petersburg, Virginia
Charlie, Jack
(United States Military
Academy, *Howitzer,*
Class of 1919)

Sgt. Maj. Jackson,
USMC, retired, 1970
(Courtesy of the Jackson
family)

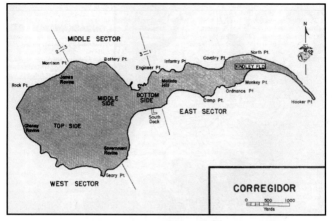

Map of Corregidor (Courtesy of the Marine Corps History and Museums Division)

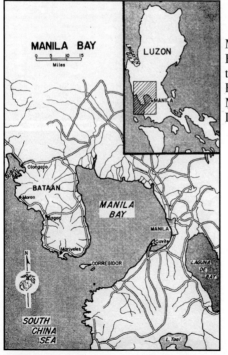

Map of Manila Bay (Courtesy of the Marine Corps History and Museums Division)

Marine 1st Sgt., 1940 (Author's Collection)

Pvt. Jackson in Panama, 1928 (Author's Collection)

A Marine platoon sergeant of the 4th Marines instructs Filipino cadets in the use of the Lewis machine gun. (Department of Defense Photo (USMC) 115.07A)

Douglas MacArthur and General Wainwright (U.S. Army)

A member of the 4th Marines guarding Sochow Road, 1940 (Author's Collection)

4th Marines standing guard, Shanghai, 1940 (Author's Collection)

Beach defenses after the surrender of Corregidor. Note the captured defenders standing in the trench line. (National Archives)

United States execution of a Japanese war criminal, 1946 (National Archives)

tions to be "supervised"; there was banditry rampant in the hills, and there were jobs for the professional Marine. It was just another "banana war," and when a Marine or two was killed every so often, the news hardly ever made the papers. The admiral formed a pair of new Marine units, forty men on each destroyer, to rush the sea-soldiers to threatened points. The "Swede" was made the skipper of one of these detachments aboard the USS *Sturdevant*, for they were short of officers, and he left for the hills.

When he reported aboard and was assigned a berth in the chief's quarters, the "Swede" found some fourteen hundred dollars beneath some shelf paper in his locker. A chief petty officer—a man of strange habits, for he carefully saved and concealed his money—had recently had that locker. He had died, his body had been consigned to the deep, his personal effects had been duly inventoried, and his sole surviving relative had been notified. The superstitious sailors had shunned that berth and locker, but the "Swede" cared not for death, for he had so often looked upon it while serving in France. And it mattered little where they assigned him, as long as he was comfortable.

He did what to him was the only natural thing to do—he took that money at once to the ship's executive officer. The genteel poverty of a sister in faraway Denmark was relieved by this sizable bequest, the "Swede" was much acclaimed, even by the secretary of the navy, and pieces appeared in the papers about the "most honest Marine."

In time he came to do duty at Quantico, Virginia, and that was his downfall. The nearest legal dispenser of hard liquor was in Fredericksburg, some twenty-eight miles away, and the powers that be frowned on such for the Marines in their charge. Beer and wine in reason, yes, but distilled spirits for the men? Decidedly not! So the "Swede" became unduly intimate with that creator of strife and disorder, purveyed by lawbreakers, corn whiskey. One likes to think that he would have held up under good liquor. The disciples of John Barleycorn always have said, "Good liquor never hurt anyone."

It has been observed that professional Marines, when they reach their late thirties, begin to reflect seriously upon their drinking habits. The wise slow down and acquire the virtues of temperance. They are in the majority. A much smaller number stop entirely. Still tinier handfuls continue at full speed ahead to the ultimate breakdown of splendid bodies and bright minds. The "Swede" continued his drinking career under forced draft.

To some it seems the tragedy of the Marine Corps that the very young so quickly lose their boyhood and acquire, in about two years, the vices and mentalities of thirty-year-old men. Many who put long years in the Corps never seem to get much older, either in gray matter or looks. Venerable sergeants major, elderly quartermaster sergeants, venerable and elderly in years alone unless they have the curb of "holy deadlock" put upon them in time, too often, alas, consort with the young and spirited in shocking familiarity, for Marines do not have the class distinctions between the enlisted ranks so rigidly enforced by the peacetime army.

The "Swede" had never married, and he could still carry his load in the most approved type of military jag, but his constant state of alcoholic glow began to cause his officers much concern. There were then some thirty-eight sergeants major of the line. It was a coveted rank, carrying dignity and privileges, and it paid about fifty dollars more a month. The 260-some first sergeants waited for some sergeant major to die or retire before they could hope to be chosen from so many for the prized position. The "Swede" had been a couple of years overdue for his promotion, but the new lists did not show his name, and his juniors began to climb over him. I suspect that his drinking was the cause of his omission from the promotion list. He was never heard to say a word in envy of others, yet he must have felt it keenly, and his forced draft drinking took a sharp increase in speed. Men began to say he took a quart to bed with him to drink. No longer were his services as first sergeant eagerly desired. A reduction by a court-martial might have put some sense in the "Swede," but he was still well liked. He had become the exception among first sergeants, in that his subsequent skippers retained him in his rank after he had begun to slip. But they started him now on his Odyssey.

In short order several West Coast stations knew him. He went to Alaska and back to the States again and was soon "shanghaied" to, of all places, Shanghai, China, in the spring of 1941, with the war clouds gathering.

His now mixed reputation had preceded him, and he could not shake himself of his failing. Colonel Howard sent him from pillar to post, hoping that he might fit in somewhere, for by now he was one of the traditions of the Corps with an acquired fame as a Marine Corps "character."

His friends were alarmed at his physical downfall. Of his moral fall from grace they cared little, for some of them were more heathen than the Chinese who catered to their vices. It was thought best to procure for him a temporary wife of a grasping nature who could cut down sharply on the amount of money the "Swede" was throwing away on John Barleycorn.

A woman, the separated relict of a tough platoon sergeant of the 1st Battalion who had recently departed for home side, offered possibilities in her restraining influence. So the "Swede" was steered into an alliance with "Annie the Gold Digger" in the pleasing hope that she might divert a large part of his funds from "Four-Eyed Jim's Slop Chute." The exchange rate for American dollars was too favorable, Jim's was located directly across Ferry Road from the "Swede's" billet, and the plan did not work out as expected.

Little Annie proudly added a fur coat to her collection of scalps (she had never, however, been able to get one from her platoon sergeant, that man with the wisdom of the serpent), for the "Swede" was always kind to his women. "Swede" still had a nostalgic fondness for the memory of his dead Nellie, his love of some fourteen years ago. She had a sweet face, and he said Annie even looked something like her. Come to think of it, as Annie flaunted her shame in her gray Persian lamb down Bubbling Well Road while her "shack master" fought the booze in both the billet and Jim's place, there was a resemblance to that little girl with the sweet and wistful face who had faced the firing squad in the fall of 1934.

Despite all this minx could wheedle from the "Swede," he spent too many nights and days in the congenial atmosphere of Four-Eyed Jim's. And then old Jim was cunning in his ways of slipping bottles into a billet.

The first really serious shock we got as to just how far the "Swede" had slipped came when he permitted a pair of Chinese hold-up men to stick him up in Jim's one afternoon as he sat alone in the place. For a Marine to be held up by a bandit was well nigh unthinkable. We remember with pride the days of 1921 and 1926 when the Marines were placed on mail guard. No hold-up was ever attempted, for the criminal element knew those sea-soldiers would shoot to kill. And here was the "Swede," a first sergeant of Marines, a veteran of several wars, stuck up and robbed by a pair of contemptible Chinese bandits!

The garrison in Cavite had to be increased, and this was a good chance to withdraw part of the Shanghai force before the jaws of the death trap of war should close. The sick, lame and lazy together with the grossly overweight were thither dispatched. Such is the good old military custom from time immemorial when one is ordered to transfer a draft. Our regimental sergeant major, a gentleman named Curry, had long ears—some thought a bit too long—and he must have had all the details of the "Swede's" recent embarrassment. So the "Old Swede," for he was called that by now, was picked for the detail. Colonel Howard would not stand for having a board called upon him to determine his fitness to hold his rank under charges of "chronic drunkenness, extending over a period of several months, but not of such a nature to warrant severe disciplinary action for a specific term." It certainly would have been difficult to convict him before a court-martial, for it would have taken a doctor's certificate to the effect that the "subject named man was found to be under the influence of intoxicating liquor, the result of his own misconduct, and unfit for the proper performance of duty" for the doctors in our regiment, while officers of the navy, were kindly men who all knew and liked the "Old Swede." Sergeant Major Curry, we heard, suggested a board instead. When his recommendation was turned down, he submitted "Swede's" name for Cavite and it was quickly approved.

Later we heard of his trip to the islands with much laughter, but for some of us who knew and liked him, with sad head-shakings. Let it be noted that in Cavite he was "shanghaied" again, and when we seven hundred–odd Marines left Shanghai and arrived in Olongapo a week before the war came, there we found the "Old Swede." In disgrace he was, a first sergeant doing a thirty-day restriction, relieved of all duties. A very capable and perhaps kind Marine officer, Maj. Stuart W. King, USMC, had snapped him at long last out of his alcoholic stupor. He had done something that should have been done long years before by other officers, mistakenly kind, for Major King had not only deprived the "Old Swede" temporarily of his duties, but the punishment had even been entered in his record book, giving him his first black mark in all his years of service! The "Old Swede" felt the sting keenly and had stopped drinking entirely. He was making valiant efforts to come back to the man he had once been, but his body, so long sodden with liquor, responded slowly. It was too much to ask of long-suffering, abused nature. Even under the stress and excitement of war, the once keen brain, alcohol-soaked for so many years, took time to come back. There was so little time for any of us; so fast were the sands of our hourglass running.

They put the "Old Swede" back in his old battalion where no one wanted him. He never ran from bombs and shell and he was never known to flinch. For war was no novelty to the old veteran of many wars, but to us he seemed slow and fumbling. The skipper (Capt. Austin C. Shofner, USMC) was young and energetic, a man who got things done, and done in a hurry. We like to think of "Shifty" as one of our bravest and certainly the most resourceful officer in the regiment. His Corregidor career, his escape from prison camp in Mindanao, and his exploits as a fighting commander in the Pacific Islands bolster up this statement. The "Old Swede" could not meet the required standard, and the "Old Man" (Lt. Col. Anderson) was spoken to. The "Old Swede" came up for officer hours [nonjudicial punishment] in the bombproof, and there ensued hard, scathing words and a sharp warning. He returned to his duties and there were no more complaints. Perhaps "Shifty" had a soft spot in his heart for the "Old Swede," for he tolerated him and kept him as his first sergeant of the battalion reserve, exasperating at times though he might be.

I watched him for signs of a relapse, but there were none. There was liquor to be had on the island, for a price, and even afterward in prison camp for a still higher price, but I think the "Old Swede" kept his resolve. I feel sure, that from the day Major King slapped that thirty-day restriction on him, with that black mark in his service record book, he never touched another drop of the Demon Rum.

There was a first sergeant in the same battalion who certainly did not come up to some men's standard of what a Marine Corps "first soldier" ought to look like. Men who did not know him shunned his company, and he hid his light under a bushel for he was modest and self-effacing. But he was capable, courageous, and competent, and other Marines began to realize his worth under fire. He also acquired a sudden popularity because he gave away his scanty food when it was not kosher.

The "Old Swede," like any wise Marine in war, was always on the prowl to keep his belly full, and some thought Joe Pearlstein's Orthodoxy attracted him. But I, who knew them both so well, prefer to think it was their loneliness that drew them together. Both strong men in their own diverse ways, they drew strength from each other. A biblical student might recall a resemblance to those steadfast friends, David and Jonathan, the little Joe and the big "Old Swede."

After the fall of Corregidor they went together to prison camp. In Cabanatuan, Joe, who had discovered his heroism under fire, just could not stand confinement. He began to lose weight and developed a shaking of his head. He grew morose, to the point where he shunned his fellow Marines and sat out in the open by himself. His body became covered with "Guam blisters," for there was little water in which to bathe. The blisters turned into repulsive ulcers.

"So went Satan from the presence of the Lord, and smote Job with sore boils from the sole of his feet unto his crown. And he took him a potsherd to scrape himself withal; and he sat down among the ashes." For vigorous and meaty description, one cannot hope to equal the Book of Books, divinely inspired.

Despite his listlessness, Joe had taken care of others. Even when his heart was breaking behind the barbed wire, he got some of his friends sulfathiazole. This I know to be true—he saved my life with it. Always there hovered around him the "Old Swede," taking care of him. Now he seemed free of the blighting influence of alcohol, and despite hunger, amoebic dysentery, and imprisonment he began to improve. He was well liked, and a naval officer prisoner made him his barracks first sergeant. Handling some 150 men, starved and resentful of discipline from any American officer, the "Old Swede" worked wonders. I began to think he would be able to make the grade at last.

In October of that year of 1942 the first of the details for Manchuria and Japan were made up. Some volunteered, some were sent regardless of their wishes, and some were just too far gone in heartbroken listlessness to even care whether they went or stayed. Joe with his ulcers, his shaking head, and his moroseness had to be sent out. Another naval officer had put him on the list, for Joe was in a different barracks from the "Old Swede." When the latter heard the news, he was Homeric in his wrath. His protests were futile, so he did the only thing left for him to do—he demanded to be included on the list. His friends tried to dissuade him, and it was pointed out to him that Joe would not last very much longer. He denied an ear to the voices of reason, and reluctantly his name was placed on the detail.

We who did not make that trip, the first of the so-called

prison ship voyages, were never to see either of them again.
We do not know exactly what happened, but we can guess,
only too horribly. Japan is a land of damp, bitter cold, where
winter sets in early. And these prisoners of war had no
woolen clothing, only their flimsy poor khakis that were
rapidly becoming rags.

I heard that both died in Moji. Who went first I do not
know. "Pneumonia" probably was the recorded cause of
death, but I think "starvation" was the real reason. And then
Joe had the broken heart of a man who could not stand confinement.

I remember the "Old Swede" as I last saw him, looking
brighter and years younger. Again he was the thirty-year-
old, the average age, mentally and physically, but not noted
in the records, of average Marines. As he marched in his
Götterdämmerung to that Valhalla, where all good Swedes
go, he was last seen alongside Joe, offering to help him with
his pack, and being refused.

> Thus seamed with many scars,
> Bursting its prison bars,
> Up to its native stars,
> My soul ascended.
> There from the flowing bowl,
> Deep drinks the warrior's soul,
> Skoal! To the Northland, Skoal!
> Thus the tale ended.[13]

We may indulge in the pleasing hope that the poet's
fancy might be applied to the "Old Swede," for he certainly
loved his drink.

---

13. Longfellow, "Skeleton in Armor," last verse.

12

THE STORY OF FIVE GALLONS OF RUM

It may not be amiss to briefly define rum, as condensed from an article in the encyclopedia:

A spirit distilled chiefly in the West Indies from the fermented skimmings of the sugar boilers and molasses, together with sufficient cane juice to impart the necessary flavor. Its peculiar flavor is due to butyric ether. Caramel is added for coloring. Much of the rum sold is merely plain spirit colored with burned sugar and flavored with rum flavoring. The Medford Rum, manufactured in Massachusetts, is largely exported to Africa.

It may not be further amiss to muse briefly upon the old pirate chantey from *Treasure Island*, which runs like this:

Fifteen men on a dead man's chest,
Yo, ho, ho, and a bottle of rum!
Drink and devil had done for the rest,
Yo, ho, ho, and a bottle of rum!

For most of the characters mentioned in this tale are dead, although not from the ravages of "drink and the devil."

A philosophic mind might reflect briefly upon the fact that the subject of rum could be made into a very singular history. I am not aware of the existence of a good, readable volume on rum. To many, rum may be considered a sort of elixir of the gods, for so many, alas, wear the red ribbon of that leering old satyr, Silenus, the deity of intemperance. The good ladies of the National Women's Christian Temperance Union might have reason to call it Beelzebub's Broth, as they wear the white ribbon of that chaste virgin, the goddess of temperance. (I wish I could remember her name, and I imagine an inquiry to the local WCTU could quickly supply it.)

For some ex-police court reporter turned war correspondent, whose present views on the future of European countries command profound respect in the public prints, there is the opportunity for profit in a very congenial subject. Clio, the muse of history, is not a difficult lass to woo.

Further browsing in the encyclopedia discloses the fact that "Butyric Ether, . . . when imbibed by man and the lower animals, first produces stimulating and intoxicating effects, but afterwards causes drowsiness, accompanied by complete insensibility." Some of the words in the article forcibly strike the eye, as "volatile," "great mobility," "high refractive power," "fragrant odor," and "fiery taste."

The town of Medford recalls to mind the lovely, limpid waters of the Mystic River, its close proximity to Boston, that Athens of America (and likewise the birthplace of John L. Sullivan), together with Tufts College, founded under the auspices of the Universalist Church. This communion holds the pleasing doctrine that all men, and also the devil and fallen angels, will be forgiven and enjoy eternal happiness. A cynical mind may discover a close connection between the phrases "largely exported to Africa" and "forgiven and enjoy eternal happiness," to further bestow a tolerant smile upon the very close connection between New England piety and the Demon Rum.

Captain John Smith, who founded the first settlement of English colonists in these United States at Jamestown in 1607, is credited with setting up the first still on American soil. He is supposed to have used the fermented juice of wild sugar cane, the "sweetenings" of the hill folk in the Big Smokies of the Appalachians today. Virginia has a statue of the doughty captain on the site of his colony, but there is no monument of stone or bronze to commemorate the event, so pregnant with the destinies of our land, of the setting up of that instrument of the devil, the still. What evil genius in the Old World first set up that device for the distillation of rum? Our muse, the fair Clio, is silent on the subject.

From the isles of the West Indies, washed by the clear blue of the sparkling Caribbean, whose waters are the home of hurricanes, let us turn to those fair lands of the Far East, the Philippines, where the blight of war has left its cruel scars and the typhoons rage in destructive fury. (Note the words "hurricanes" and "typhoons," for our subject is rum, as I reflect upon the strife and disorder that follows in its train.) Here the evil genius of man had implanted the seeds of the Demon Rum.

Until recent times rum was not made in these islands. Gin, largely distilled from the juice of the nipa palm, though some came from the product of the sugar mills, was the popular beverage. In the days before the war, it was possible for the "Old Sunshiners" to procure a five-gallon demijohn for as little as two dollars and twenty cents. The more popular-sized containers were of two types, the "grande" of two liters, and the "peck," of one. It is possible that the term "peck" was derived from the Spanish *pequeño*, a "little one."

The military and naval elements fancied the "San Miguel" brand, called "A-1, Number 1." On its gaudy label was delineated the holy archangel St. Michael, his flaming sword at the throat of the prostrate Satan. Here is the counterpart of New England piety and booze, half a world away. Gin was very properly prohibited to the enlisted personnel, but the ubiquitous Chinese bazaars would always oblige with a "peck" of San Miguel for some thirty cents. (The San Miguel Brewery and Distillery were both owned and operated—and still are—by the Roman Catholic Church!)

Collectively these native gins were referred to as "loco-motive," from an obscure brand whose label depicted a small Spanish steam engine. Great and thunderous were the fulmination of all commanding officers against locomotive gin. The first question asked of culprits at captain's mast (in-variably cases whose origins arose in liquor) was usually, "What kind of gin were you drinking?" And the wise reply was, "Gordon Gin, sir," for it signaled moral turpitude to the "Old Man" if one admitted any indulgence, however slight, in native gin.

For some years there had been an earnest movement toward the manufacture of a satisfactory type of native rum, for there was great demand for a beverage of the West In-dies brand. The Bacardi possibly led in popularity, with their "Blanco" and "Oro" kinds, the latter being the more expensive. (I recall these names with nostalgic longing, and I further remember the time that good firm ventured forth with an attempt to improve both the white and the gold la-bels. It was called Elixir of Bacardi, but to my taste it seemed to be merely gilding the lily.) And just before that year of 1941, when the Japanese unleashed their fury on these smiling isles, success crowned the movement. The se-cret so long sought, was discovered, and to a pleasing drink was added the more pleasing discovery that it cost but little more than locomotive gin! Gloom must have settled in the Bacardi portals in faraway Santiago de Cuba.

Among those native brands now placed before the pub-lic, the Elizaldo and Añejo shone forth in glory. The latter, lovingly pronounced in liquid Spanish as *ahn-yeh-ho*, is the subject of this tale, and when I come to it, its singular ad-ventures will be duly related.

In 1941 a belated attempt was made to increase the armed forces in the islands and, among other discoveries, the new reinforcements came upon the joys of good, cheap rum. At Fort Stotsenburg, in cool proximity to the hills of Pangasinan Province, away from the heat of the low-lying rice paddies, there sprang up a tent city. The field officers' street they themselves referred to as Scotch Alley, for they drew enough stipend to indulge, not too freely one hopes, of that elixir of the

> Land of brown heather and green wood,
> Land of the mountains and the flood.

But the company officers, whose pay was less and whose standards of decorum were not on the more exalted plane of that required of their superiors, ribaldly called their street Rum Row. These strangers justly scorned locomotive gin across the sea and those "old Sunshiners" whose stubborn resistance to the wheels of progress was noted in their fondness for native gin were contemptuously referred to as "old dobes" and "bamboo Americans." In fairness to the efforts of disciplinary standards striven for by the commanding general of the post, it must be pointed out that the names Scotch Alley and Rum Row were entirely unofficial.

In connection with this struggle between the forces of rum and those of native gin, in respect to tenacity and stubbornness of military character, it may be noted that the last strongholds of locomotive gin, where rum had scarcely made an entry, Corregidor and her fortified islets, tiny Forts Hughes, Drum, and Frank, were the very last to fall in the entire Luzon area.

From much digression, let me turn to my narrative of the five gallons of Añejo rum. The 4th Marine Regiment, serving in Shanghai, had been gradually reduced to the strength of seven hundred or so Marines. Hurriedly evacuated, we had arrived in the islands around the last days of November 1941. Here we found ashore the Marine detachment of the USS *Augusta*, the Cavite Navy Yard garrison, the 1st separate Marine Battalion, and the small force that guarded the Olongapo naval station. While these detachments were being consolidated into the 4th Marine Regiment to swell its strength to some sixteen hundred–odd, the enemy struck on the seventh day of December 1941. (On the wrong side of the 180th meridian, you are one day ahead in time.)

By now our 1st Battalion was largely in the Mariveles

area to help defend the navy's section base, the 2d Battalion lay in and around Olongapo to guard the approaches to Subic Bay, while regimental headquarters and service troops were quartered in the Olongapo naval station itself. Our tale begins in Olongapo.

We did not have long to wait for an enemy bombing. One clear morning, twenty-seven Japanese planes were counted on their way down to Manila and Cavite, passing us far off on the eastern flank. Puffs of smoke and the faraway booming of cannons behind the jagged peaks of the Zambales Mountains indicated that our forces were very actively receiving them. Soon our power house whistled its three deep, long blasts followed by a series of short ones—enemy bombers were headed our way!

Now we saw them, etched sharp and clear against a cobalt blue sky. There was a line of V's, three aircraft to a V, but on our left flank only two planes were in that V, for the antiaircraft bursts had crashed one of them down in flames. We cowered in our ditches and foxholes at this promise of lethal, terrible might.

Under the far edge of the line of enemy planes, where the town of Olongapo touched the reservation's edge at the quartermaster buildings, was a small Marine patrol commanded by QM Clerk Frank C. Ferguson, USMC. Next to them in the town was a large crowd of Filipinos gathered under a huge mango tree that shaded a cluster of nipa shacks, watching in curious ignorance the oncoming line of V's some five thousand feet above. They had been warned time and again not to expose themselves like this, and the Marine patrol yelled at them, but they refused to scatter.

Someone in the patrol was excited, for it was their first time under enemy bombers. There were flashes, and a .30-caliber automatic rifle barked its staccato sound. Whether the planes noticed such puny, pitiful efforts will never be known, but we received our first glimpse of the opening of a bomb bay, heard the *scree-ee-ee-whish* of falling bombs and the dull *crump, crump, crump* of the explosions, and shuddered in our shelters when the ground rocked with vibrations. The majestic line of planes passed overhead, and we saw them working over the army's Fort Wint on Grande Island, the bottleneck stopper of Subic Bay.

There was other work to do besides following the flight with our eyes. The few bombs dropped by one left flank plane had found their mark among a few Marines coming up the road toward the patrol, and some of them were wounded. Beneath and around the big mango tree was a scene of horror, with some twenty-five or so dead and a larger number badly hurt by those steel splinters. Doctor Wade and his force worked in among them on their errand of mercy, laboring far into the night. When morning came there was still much to do.

The Filipinos had learned their lesson, and there was a mass exodus from the dangerous vicinity of the naval station to the shelter offered in the hills.

Thus was the curtain raised on that Dead Men's Overture that preceded our Symphony of Death. We saw with tearful clarity what it meant to fight a 1941 war with 1918 weapons. And, at long last, we have come to our particular five gallons of rum. From now on it will remain with us until its sad end comes.

Later that same day one of our very senior officers, Lt. Col. Herman R. Anderson, commanding officer, 2d Battalion, 4th Marine Regiment, cruised over into the town with his orderly, Sgt. Wendell N. Garden, from Norfolk, Nebraska, who doubled in brass as the sergeant major's clerk, and prudently bought for himself five gallons of Añejo rum. It was well that he had this foresight, for John Chinaman, who controlled the retail business in that quarter, was hastily moving himself and all his goods away from a place of such peril.

The rum was securely boxed in a wooden container, labeled with its owner's name and rank, and marked "medical supplies." Such was meet and fitting, for it is well known that a daily dose of quinine as a malaria prophylactic is mightily increased in potency if chased down with a slug of rum. It was rumored that the farseeing officer had also purchased a few bottles before he left Shanghai. These potent fluids, some yet reposing in his baggage, would suffice to help ward off the deadly "malignant quartan" for some time. When these had become "dead Marines," their "duty performed and well done," the box might be opened, medicinal quantities taken only at seasonable intervals, and all would be well.

The orderly was solemnly charged with the safeguarding of the precious fluid. The sergeant major could be trusted, for he had recently gone on the wagon for the duration, so he said, before he left Shanghai, and the colonel noted this with pleasure. The remainder of the battalion staff might have come in time to know of the contents of this box labeled "medical supplies," but the colonel was highly respected and his property was safe. They were sure to be sharers when the cargo was broached, for the owner was a generous soul. In a smaller way, the rest of the staff, too, had been prudent.

A few days later the regiment received its second baptism of fire. Seven fine PBY flying boats of Patrol Wing 10 had been up in the air that morning to escape the Japanese planes. They were now nestled on the waters of the far side of the bay, some three thousand yards from the docks, to refuel. In less than fifteen minutes came the air raid alarm, and four little light attack bombers peeled off in their slow and unhurried dives with great precision. Their landing gear shielded by streamlined hoods gave them the appearance of striking falcons. Soon all seven of the PBYs were smoking wrecks and the bombers turned and headed our way.

We fought back valiantly with what little we had, our .30-caliber rifles, automatic rifles, and machine guns, while some sanguine souls emptied their .45-caliber pistols and Thompson submachine guns at them. On the dock, Chief Gunner's Mate William Grady Smith, hastily recalled from the reserve, and his force of a few Marines futilely fired a 2-inch naval gun, with Smith's own brand of homemade antiaircraft sights. And this was all we had.

We heard the droning whine of the enemy planes' power dives, the *rat-a-tat-tat* of their machine guns, and the slower *pow-pow-pow* of their 20mm nose cannons. There was the dull *crump-crump-crump* of the bombs along the seawall— there is no screaming *whish* when you are subjected to dive bombers—and the enemy was gone, to give Fort Wint their full attention. Our futile and furious small-arms fire died away scatteringly, there was one final *crack* from Smith's gun, and it was over.

The Marines took stock of themselves. No one was hurt; not even a building was hit. Suddenly a ripple of laughter commenced, rising to a loud crescendo.

Our water tank was spurting from a dozen places, the work of one of our green machine gunners, a private first class named Albert, from Company H. Further inquiry revealed that a young reserve corporal, Mike Winters, also from Company H, had managed to shoot his own combat pack full of machine gun bullet holes. There was much merriment over this, and to this day the mystery of how he could have done such a thing without injury to himself has never been solved. We could laugh then; we could still find things to chuckle over before we were to fall with Corregidor, but afterward there was seldom any occasion for merriment.

The rum emerged unscathed, for the sergeant major himself had sat on it during the fray. (The bottom of his foxhole oozed seawater.) The colonel did not inquire about his property for his mind was occupied with much more important matters. But the orderly, after a while, went over to the "Old Man" to report with a salute and solemnity, "The medical supplies are secure, sir!"

Then followed much scurrying around, much digging of trenches and foxholes, and much laying of underwater barbed wire on the beaches, for an attack was expected from the north. We saw the Filipino army stream by on the Manila Road toward the pass in the Zambales Mountains, with their guns, trucks, and commandeered buses filled with soldiers. We saw their pathetic waving of the "V" sign at us and we returned it gladly, for while we fully realized what we were facing, it would never have done to depress them.

We continued along with much of our old routine, for old

habits are strong and hard to break. There were three deck courts, for offenses committed in Shanghai before our departure, with "not guilty" pleas and attendant paperwork. Discipline had to be preserved, and both deck and summary courts-martial, even in the midst of war, remained to plague the sergeant major to the bitter end. The orderly typed the three deck courts out as he sat on the box labeled "medical supplies," and it was curious to reflect that these offenses had originated in liquor. To add to the paperwork, these Marines pleaded "not guilty," but it did them no good, as they were found to be guilty by Major Bradley, the deck court officer.

By day we guarded the naval station and by night we found security in the hills. On our way back and forth we saw the bomb damage in abandoned Olongapo. The church's gaping wounds were open to the sky while the adjoining cockpit was untouched. The rum went along with us, lashed on a machine gun cart with the orderly plodding alongside. At night he slept with it, for there were some thirsty men in the battalion whose morals of "mine and thine" were not entirely above reproach.

By echelons we departed for Mariveles on the heels of the Filipino Army. The command post was now located in the Riverside Cabaret, owned by a "bamboo American," a character named Gordon, since Doctor Wade had moved his sick bay far up the Manila Road. "Gordon's Farm" had long been an institution there. It could hardly be called a place one could write home about, as the recreation there was a subject of some concern to the doctors. Now the little "ballerinas" had flitted away, but the old gray "bamboo American" hovered around, dispensing drinks from his much-depleted stock, and for cash only. The orderly did his clerical duties, and well. The rum was still safe under his watchful care.

The mess sergeant, Leon B. Ellis, had scraped together a very nice Christmas dinner and served it out from the rear of his little truck. I like to think of him as one of the best I ever knew in his line. He tried to inveigle Gordon into a free drink, and when that was not forthcoming, offered to sign a chit. Gordon refused, with a show of anger, and locked his private door, sitting down in front and guarding his treasure. The mess sergeant looked wistfully at the box marked "medical supplies"—one would imagine that he knew the contents by this time—and broadly hinted that a drink would be appreciated on Christmas Day. The sergeant major denounced him roundly for thinking of such a thing with a war on, for there is no one more intolerant toward the Demon Rum than he who has recently forsworn its use. The orderly, Garden, sitting on the box, grinned broadly.

The air raid alarm sounded in the station, and men ran to foxholes and ditches along the road. Small white clouds were visible far off to the south, and there was even a cry of "paratroopers," but after an interval of suspense it was real-ized that they were only bursts from antiaircraft guns. Since no planes were seen coming our way, our interrupted dinner was resumed. It was noted that the orderly had not taken shelter, but remained with his box in the command post. He was but too well acquainted with the mess sergeant.

As the little truck began to chug away, old Gordon went up to it and asked for a bit of Christmas dinner, saying it had been a long time since he had enjoyed an American meal of turkey with all the fixings. The mess sergeant now had his inning, with profanity and insults. Gordon got no dinner from him, and he slunk back to his lair.

The old USS *Rochester*, ex–*New York* and *Saratoga*, a veteran of more than fifty years, long decommissioned and lying at the dock, had been loaded some days before with mines. The day after Christmas she was towed into the chan-nel under the direction of Major Schaeffer, to be sunk by his Marines. The naval station was burned, and the last echelon of our battalion left for Mariveles. In Bataan we leapfrogged the retreating Filipino army as it prepared for its stand against the Japanese. In the hills we bivouacked. It was here where we met our Cavite comrades and anxiously asked the fate of old friends, for the navy yard had been heavily bombed. The colonel never inquired about his "medical supplies," for he was very preoccupied with the duties of command and knew he could depend upon his orderly.

On the night of 27 December we moved to Corregidor Island to take over the beach defenses. In silence and without lights, we loaded our barges with our guns, ammunition, food, and seabags along with our records and typewriters, for the written accounts had to be maintained at all costs. We could see the pillar of flame-colored smoke rising from the burning Cavite shipyard. The colonel set an example by lugging his share of boxes in the loading chain and winking his confidential wink as he sat down in the bow of the barge alongside his orderly and sergeant major. Between their records chest and field desk was the box labeled "medical supplies," with his own name visible in the gleam of the rising moon. He made no comment.

We were greatly heartened by listening to the workmen, both American and Filipino, on the Fort Mills dock. "They will never dare bomb Corregidor, with all of the antiaircraft guns we have! General MacArthur has assured us that help is on the way! It won't be long now before we sight that five-hundred-mile-long convoy!" They raised their right hands in the "V" salute and we gave it right back to them. By streetcar in the eerie moonlight, we rode up to Middleside Barracks, with the strange rock canyons glowing huge, the long shadows gray-black, and here and there, as we passed an open space, the bare ground showing blue and yellow-green. And in the east, the pale yellow orb of the rising moon was reflected in the rippling bay.

The whole of the twenty-eighth was spent in getting bedded down, while companies were assigned to specific areas. Offices were set up and typewriters clicked with busy industry. We met the men of the 60th Coast Artillery, for they shared the barracks with us.

On the top deck, neat and shipshape, were the quarters of the colonel and his staff, in the same compartment with the battalion office. The "Old Man" remarked to the orderly that his Shanghai "medical supplies" were just about used up, and that on the morrow he would begin to use those he had so prudently secured in Olongapo before the last Chinese shopkeeper had departed for the hills. The orderly was thanked with charming politeness, and the sergeant major was also included. Both were relieved of their charge in this matter, and they looked at each other and winked. It is more than possible that the colonel, who smiled and winked back, for he was like that, noted this.

The army had not yet made up their collective minds about what to do with these sixteen hundred strange Marines, so we idled in the barracks now that our work was done.

The next morning, the twenty-ninth day of December, when we had just finished our breakfast and were ready for quarters inspection by the army, came the air raid alarm. We quietly went to the lower deck while the noncommissioned officers in charge of quarters of each company remained behind to clear out all of the stragglers. The *scree-ee-whish-sh-sh* and *crump* of bombs mingled with the *pow-pow-pow* of our .50-caliber machine guns, punctuated with the *boom-boom-boom* of the 3-inch rifles. (It was later said that only seven seconds elapsed between the alarm and the explosion of the first bomb.) There were cries of "First aid, Corpsman, wounded men!" from the lower deck, and the dull stench of picric acid permeated the yellow-colored smoke.

On came the enemy planes, wave after wave. Some were downed, and there was cheering. The Japanese resorted to high altitude bombing, and cheers were heard no more. It was said that our antiaircraft fuses were too short to reach more than twenty-four thousand feet. Later, the precious longer fuses were brought in by the navy in a submarine that ran the blockade, coming all the way from distant Pearl Harbor, and that was when we learned what had really happened to our battleships. We knew then that there would never be that promised five-hundred-mile-long convoy. But some of us wondered why those longer fuses had not been thought of sooner.

The nearby army canteen was hit and belched forth black smoke. Darting figures were seen to run in and out of the place. Later, orders were issued threatening condign punishment on the heads of those who might be caught with looted wristwatches, fountain pens, and other small articles plundered while the canteen burned. We like to think our Marines were innocent, for they had not been there long enough to find out who was next door. Still, one never knows.

There were heroic deeds, for wounded men were rushed to the Malinta Hospital over twisting, hilly roads while bombs and machine gun strafing fire rained down from the skies. Comrades were dug out of caved-in bomb shelters while ammunition dumps, open and uncovered, burning fiercely after being hit, made rescue hazardous with whining, red-hot steel splinters flying through the air in our vicinity.

In the lower deck compartments men cowered against the bulkheads and speculated on whether the walls of Middleside Barracks might not cave in under repeated bomb shocks. The orderly was seen seated in a chair, immersed in a *True Detective* type of magazine. He had always tried to cultivate a poker face in his gambling, and now the odds were none too good, for a Marine lay dead in the compartment adjoining us. He might have been a bit theatrical, but he was under the eye of the "Old Man" and the sergeant major, and he was not going to be outdone in calmness. Just a nineteen-year-old he was, with a smooth, clear skin that in China had caused our "room boys" to christen him Pai Mien, for "White Face." If he thought of the "medical supplies," he gave no sign of it. And between lulls in the waves of enemy bombers, the "Old Man" strode gallantly outside the barracks on the parade ground to give timely warning, and then strolled slowly in with his reassuring smile.

The three nightmare hours came to an end, and the welcomed "all clear" was sounded. The rolls were called to check on who might be dead or wounded. The sergeant major sped up to the top side, for he was very concerned about his battalion's records and knew that a bomb had burst up there. He stumbled over the prone figure of Cpl. LaVerne

Murphy, of Company E, dead at his post of duty, as a good Marine might be, for he had been in charge of quarters in his outfit with the duty of staying behind to clear out any stragglers. He called down to 1st Sgt. Wayne K. Miller and later that day "Dusty" wrote down in his neat handwriting on the master roll card, "Instantaneous death in line of duty, multiple head and chest wounds, bomb, direct result enemy action, in line of duty."

The sergeant major, now joined by the orderly, began to clear the debris from their records chest and field desk, and were much relieved to find both unharmed, though somewhat scarred. Their typewriter was smashed, but they knew they could loot another from the army if they had to. In the "Old Man's" berth compartment, the sunshine streamed in brightly through a jagged hole in the roof. The shreds of his baggage and that of his staff littered the place and were yellowed with plaster dust. We figured it must have been a five-hundred-pounder that blew up in there.

There were a few wooden splinters located beneath the piles of powdered plaster and broken concrete as they kicked here and there, and they identified them as being from the box once labeled "medical supplies," and marked with the name and rank of its owner. The sergeant major sniffed carefully, but he could detect no odor of the contents of the box, for the clinging picric acid still lingered on. The orderly was told to get down below and break the sad news to the colonel while the sergeant major dug around for his own clothing and pack.

Below, the colonel and his staff were receiving orders to get their Marines out of that death trap and into the beach defenses. The orderly waited quietly until high command was finished and the staff hurried away to give orders to the companies. The "Old Man" strolled out into the sunshine to glance up at the sky, for he still worried about his men until they could clear the barracks and get into trenches and fox-holes.

The orderly saluted, reported the destruction of the office, the safety of the records chest and file desk, the damage to the baggage, and lastly, the total obliteration of the "medical supplies."

"Very good, very good, and thank you! But, what the hell, it doesn't matter!" And then he grinned, shook the orderly's hand warmly, and slowly gave him his well-known familiar wink.

13

THE STORY OF THE OLD ARMY GAME

Late in the afternoon of the ninth day of April 1942—while the Bataan Force was being herded together to begin their Death March, while the ammunition dumps on the Bataan shore still burned fiercely, while the Corregidor defenders took extra measures to meet this new threat from the rear—the amazing Japanese ran their cannons up to Cabcaben and began to shell the island from the back door.

Over at the 1st Battalion of the 4th Marines, on Officers Beach, while all this activity was going on, some ten Marines huddled in a foxhole, oblivious to all around them, intent only in their gambling. A shell made a direct hit, and a rescue party under the direction of Maj. A. J. Mathieson rushed in to dig out eight dead bodies. The other two men could not be immediately accounted for, but a few days later there came forth out of that hole the awful, sweet smell of death, and as Marines dug deeper they found the remains of two of their comrades.

There were strict orders, reiterated over and over again, about such grouping together under fire, but gambling had such a hold on its devotees that they could not be well enforced. This tragic death of ten men from a single shell is the largest score we knew of among those who met their fate while pursuing the Lady Luck. We are aware of other cases besides, but not quite so tragic. So a disclosure of the Old Army Game may be enlightening.

Gambling, particularly among Marines and sailors, while it has a distressful prevalence, had never had the hold upon its addicts that one sees among the soldiers. These men take their gambling far more seriously, the games running for several days after payday, and the money wagered in a whole regiment generally winds up in the hands of a very few. Unless forced to do so by adverse circumstances, a Marine, and perhaps a sailor, too, will very seldom play in a house game; both Marines and sailors dislike the practice of cutting the game or bucking the tiger. The "dogface," however, is seldom happy unless someone is brutally taking a large rake-off for running the game, or he is permitted to buck odds of about four for him against five for the house, with a limit imposed.

When the 4th Marine Regiment was finally assembled at Fort Mills on Corregidor Island for beach defenses—after Shanghai, Olongapo, Cavite, Mariveles, and other places in the war zone of the Far East had taken stock of their dead and wounded, been assigned defensive sectors, and begun to fortify them—they looked around at their new companions among the soldiery, both white and brown. They discovered the island to be a gambling hall.

A type of dice layout called variously the "Philadelphia layout," the "sweat board," or more popularly the "crap table" seems to be a standard article of equipment in every unit of the U.S. Army the size of a company, battery, or troop. The percentage of the "line" and the "come" are all but little in favor of the house, being simply a come-on for the unwary, while those on the remainder of the board average about five to four in favor of the gamekeeper. It is to his best interest to bark his sucker bets, and quite well some of them do. Soldiers seriously doubt this game to be honest, but honest it usually is. It stands to reason that a dealer or payoff man, surrounded by twenty or more clients and kibitzers, some of them very tough citizens, would not be in the army if he had the ability to switch the fair dice for those with a college education. Such a character, combining both skill and chilled-steel nerve, would be found where pickings are more lucrative, at forty dollars or better for a four-hour shift plus a cut of the total take. These are the gentry that work as stickmen around Palm Beach or Saratoga's gilded palaces of chance.

Now and then such a man is discovered in the service, but his too-apparent skill drives away his clients and he languishes. The penalty for detection in using loaded dice in a house game is generally a free-for-all fight, loss of the bank, and, what is worse, loss of goodwill when the game is started the next payday. There simply are not any customers, unless there are new men in the organization.

There were several of these deadfalls set up on Corregidor that we saw in our wanderings, before the shellfire from the Bataan shore started to sharply restrict our travels to our own defensive sector. Just outside of either end of Malinta Tunnel, the headquarters of Gen. Douglas MacArthur, such games were openly carried on at breast-high tables covered with crudely lettered canvas. No chairs were ever furnished, for enemy bombers were liable to be around at any minute. Another hazard, besides that of losing your money, was the sporadic shellfire of the enemy's 105s dug in on the Cavite shore some seventeen thousand yards away. These cannons inflicted casualties, but as far as is known, no gambler was ever hit by a Cavite shell. James Ravine had one or more of these games, Sunset Battery was cursed by a like plague, and there were others here and there. The Cold Storage and Bake Shop wolf-traps had the name of being the largest on the Rock. Shellfire from the Bataan shore drove the Bake Shop gamblers in with the Cold Storage men, where shelter was better. The operators of institutions, for these games were of hoary antiquity, combined forces to trim their suckers during the last few days left to them before the Japanese would overwhelm them all.

Another game of dubious fame that might rival the Bake Shop and Cold Storage activities in its years of service to the military community was located in the Middleside station. Middleside was a large bunker complex on the middle of the island. The total destruction of this place by enemy bombing on the twenty-ninth of December 1941 caused but a temporary lull in its operations, for it soon located new quarters in the vegetable bins located in the rear of the barracks. Of this deadfall we will have occasion to touch upon later, as our story unfolds.

Of the sums wagered upon these galloping dominoes, it is hard to divest fiction from truth. But the fact is well attested that, when the Filipino Air Corps cadets, grounded because they had no planes, were assigned to Marine Corps units in James Ravine, one of them, a boy named Lopez, started to buck the tiger with a money roll of fourteen thousand pesos, won from his comrades on Bataan. The dealers in the ravine, all sure-thing men, had established rigid limits, which they would not raise. This proved their honesty, for there was a fortune going begging, and the sucker was crying to be separated from his money. As this client was demanding bigger action than they would give, the head of the clique, a first-pay-grade noncommissioned officer of the 91st Scouts, so rumor ran, had the cadet taken over to the Bake Shop game by a "roper-in" and duly delivered to the gamekeepers. One rumor credited this boy with receiving 25 percent of what might be obtained from the client. In three hectic days and nights the cadet lost his money, his watch, ring, and fountain pen. During this same period the father of the cadet, a colonel in the Filipino army Medical Corps, was killed in the bombing of "Little Baguio" in Bataan. The cadet was notified to come, but he did not stop his gambling.

The checker station game, now located in the vegetable bins behind Middleside barracks, was run by some army soldiers; the place was shelled and bombed daily, but the spud lockers seemed immune. Down at Bottomside, the lovely little church of San Jose Barrio had been bombed and ruined, and the army moved in a few men to be quartered there and a game sprang up at once. The come-on man stood out in the road and pulled in his customers as they passed by between the North Mine Dock and the Malinta Tunnel. The Bake Shop operators protested this infringement on their time-honored privileges, but to no avail. We heard that the chaplain of the 91st Scouts, a Captain Beau-mont, deplored this desecration of a shrine, but they kept on. The gamblers there seemed to have the protection of the devil himself, for no one ever heard of the church being hit again by either bomb or shell. By observing proper black-out rules, both the checker and church games operated all night long. In the few days before surrender, their winnings had so multiplied that the operators were forced to use small suitcases in which to stuff their banks.

At Middleside some Marines set up a competing game in the spud locker next door. They erected a table and a layout capable of taking care of twenty or more clients, with a dealer, payoff man, ladder man, and several shills to simu-late and stimulate play. The customers reversed the usual procedure, to repeatedly break the game. The Marines were still stubborn; gamblers from far-off James Ravine were induced to finance the game for a 50 percent cut, but the operators still lost money. The winners went next door to the army game, only to be promptly separated from their money. The principal toiler in this unfortunate syndicate was a corporal named Frank Forsythe, who had a chow dog he had brought along from Shanghai, a cold black beast of vicious tendencies. He called this creature "Lucky" and re-tained him around the gaming table, but Lucky brought no luck. And during all of these activities, men were being killed and wounded in and around Middleside Barracks some yards away.

Most of these games were brazenly run in the open, to at-tract their clients, until enemy shellfire forced the gambling men to take cover. Bombing alone could never have driven them away for very long. In James Ravine bombs hit in the vicinity, wounded men in defensive positions, demolished several gaming tables with their attendant devices, and scat-tered the gamblers. But only for a short time, for in about an hour the tables were repaired, the ground cleared and swept of debris, and the games were back in the battery.

The army attitude seemed to be that gaming could never be stopped, because a soldier with money might go to town on payday to buy drunkenness, disorderly conduct, and social disease. Permit gambling, and the money would center itself in a few hands. These gentry were always of the well-behaved type, who never got drunk or into trouble, and in some units they were cherished so much they were given the dayroom concession. There suckers were thus, willy-nilly, made into plaster saints, and all was serene. With a war on, and while men were beleaguered and besieged, this type of complacency continued, even though the men had no place to go to spend their money.

The navy and Marine attitude in time of peace was just the opposite. Our regulations were blunt and to the point, for "Gambling, being conducive of bad morals, is prohibited." Even an innocent kibitzer might be given a deck court if the game were seized, along with all the players. While they were never able to stop such practices, so deeply is gaming rooted in the human race, they at least made gamblers discreet, trying to drive their games to cover and concealment. Hence there was far less gambling among those who went down to the sea in ships than among those who served in the army on shore. But close association with the army on Corregidor, alas, contaminated their righteousness, and there was a letup in vigilance. At the same gaming tables one often saw sailors and Marines mingled with the Filipinos and soldiers.

An attempt was made during the siege to help reduce the size of the regular payments to the troops. We Marines were supposed to be limited to twenty dollars a month. But we had all sorts of reasons to tell the first sergeant why we needed more money; the Pay Department is notoriously kindhearted as long as they get a signature; the games continued. The professional gamblers seldom drew pay, for they didn't need to. Their clientele drew all the money they could, to the enrichment of those smarter than they. Many men were sensible enough to let their pay ride on the books, and some lucky winners were shrewd enough to deposit their winnings with the paymaster at 4 percent interest before they could be enticed back into the games. Their money would stay on deposit until their discharge. If they lived, they could collect; if they died, their heirs would inherit the money due.

The next type of game from the standpoint of popularity was stud poker. A dealer's choice game ran a close second, with the choice generally being stud. Cards being at a premium, the owners either ran the games themselves with a takeout of 10 percent or more, or else they rented the pasteboards to those who conducted such activities. These individuals built tables with attached seats, supplied a blanket covering, and moved their game right next to the crap table on the theory that the larger the crowd, the more of the unwary would be enticed in to see what was going on, with more profit for both games. Unlike the dice tables, the honesty of these card games is sadly open to question.

The dice used by the crap table folk were usually on the up-and-up, as I have said previously. The crooks were among the customers, who might try to introduce their own loaded "bones" into the game for their own benefit, in addition to the thousand and one petty thieveries they tried on the operators. One individual in James Ravine had his table dice cunningly engraved with certain Chinese characters. An old China hand, he could read them while none of his customers could. If he lost a pair of his dice, he always had another set of four pairs marked with different characters to take their place.

It is certain that no customer was ever able to put in his own pair loaded up for the long shots, or a set of tees that could never make a seven, for the come and line points. But in some poker games, various devices often marked the cards, and several players would gang up on a sucker.

The ethics of these card games were not those of a gentleman's club; a detected cheat merely paid up the current bet and was allowed to continue in the play. If one lasted long enough in the game, a pair of sharp eyes could detect the markings. But the 10 percent cut of the gamekeeper from every pot sharply reduced the chances of anyone else leaving his table a winner. The houseman in the end got all the money.

Blackjack, the game of twenty-one, pushed the poker tables very closely in popularity; there are some that would place this game even ahead of poker in the number of its devotees. The cut was much smaller for rented cards, being only a peso for each blackjack turned up. In the beginning, the army house games were run according to the rules set forth by Hoyle; the dealer was required to hit sixteen or under, stand on seventeen or over, paid double for blackjacks, took all standoffs, allowed a pair to be split unless they were aces, and prohibited bets on down for a double. This type of game is brutal for the clients, so the sailors and Marines, when they came to get in these games, demanded a change in the rules to pay off one and a half for blackjacks, with the dealer to take no pushes or standoffs. These men absolutely refused to contribute to the more abundant life led by the gamekeepers unless their demands were met, and the rules were changed to the apparent benefit of all.

The percentage in blackjack cannot be estimated with any certainty, but the game, even if honestly conducted, is sure to separate a player from his money as long as there is no traveling deal. The Hoyle rules possibly took in twice as much as the new system the sailors and Marines had demanded with such vigor. In the former method the custom had been for the dealer to make his own hits with faces up, "in the air" to use the vernacular. In the new deal now in vogue, the operators made all dealers hit down, and, to speak in their peculiar jargon again, "squeezed them off." This gave unscrupulous individuals a splendid opportunity for dirty work at the crossroads, and to some extent sharply reduces the material benefits so recently gained by the change in the rules.

It is necessary for the benefit of the uninitiated to explain that the very nature of this game makes it seem expressly designed for dishonesty. There are such simple tricks as turning the deck, marking the cards to deal seconds, and marking the cards to employ a "third baseman," to mention a few of the more common. To this hazard the game dealt by Filipinos added another. As was their custom, the Filipinos always dealt their cards from the bottom rather than from the top, like monte dealers. They were credited with devising finger rings that had tiny, protruding needle points with which they pricked the cards, to read them by feeling. If one got into a Filipino game, one seldom objected to this practice. It was simply a case of "When in Rome, do as the Romans do."

Another type of dice game, ranking after blackjack in its number of players, consisted of a table marked off with the points alone. The dealer furnished the dice, marked the point, made the change, and handled all bets, but covered none of them with the funds of the house. In the language of the game it was called a "head and head game." The gamekeeper took a peso on every other pass. If not too closely watched, he took more. As long as a reasonable amount of play could be obtained, these games averaged some three hundred pesos per day profit to their operators.

The Filipinos sometimes tried their native monte, played with a Spanish deck of thirty-six cards, with another set of pasteboard cards glued face up on a paper layout. They were never able to entice American clients of the white race into this form of diversion, so monte died a languishing death.

All of these games huddled together like so many food markets in big cities. If the craps layout did not appeal to your tastes, a few feet away you could buck the tiger at blackjack. Obliging gentry were all around to make change, at a percentage, rent out a deck of cards; sell sandwiches, cigarettes, and coffee at high prices; and even agree to stand your watch for a reasonable figure. These harpies were themselves in turn victims of their vice, for every centavo they could obtain was played over the board, to the profit of the dealers. The gamekeepers made sure their areas were kept clean and in good police, for they wished no trouble with their officers; in James Ravine, for instance, a decrepit old bandsman of the 91st Scouts, named Solomon, was paid a peso daily from each game for his services as a sweeper.

Apparently the venerable, white-thatched old man, bent over and limping with his old-age arthritis, was assigned no other duties. Perhaps the first-pay-grade noncommissioned officer of the 91st Scouts, whom rumor credited with being the master of the games, had something to do with this.

Chuck-a-luck, whose percentage is five to three, we never saw. Only on army transports, where the men cannot get away from it, does it flourish. This is the same game as the British soldiers' crown and anchor, only the numbers are one to six, while our cousins like their four aces, with crown and anchor.

Roulette was nonexistent among the enlisted men. Its percentage being only nine to eight, it does not appeal to the professional element. There was talk that a war correspondent had a wheel in the Malinta Tunnel for play among the officers with whom he chummed, but we cannot verify this fact. But we can state with reasonable assurance that among the ranks no barker ever made the night hideous with his cry of "Round and round the little ball goes, where she stops, nobody knows."

Soldiers are naturals as suckers, and nine to eight is not enough to justify a roulette wheel.

Draw poker, so popular in other circumstances, we never saw. The reason was quite simple, for in rake-off games, stud gives a bigger pot and is faster. When one is renting his cards for play at so much per hand, he looks with repugnance upon a game that takes some time for a showdown.

Bingo, bango, tombola, or keno, to give this type of game some of its names, we likewise never saw or even heard of being operated. There appeared to be possibilities for a small operator to pick up loose change among those men who had lost their pesos at the tables and had a peseta or so left. One thinks no one had the foresight to procure such a game in the children's toy department of the Manila stores before the siege came. This layout works well on the crowded transports at a dime a card, to enable the players to escape that sheer boredom of the voyage; it works better on shore in a port exchange or club beer garden, where the operator takes his 10 percent usual cut, and 10 percent more to buy brew for his clients, but there was no beer on Corregidor.

If there were other games such as hearts, red dog, honest john, bar the roll, banker and broker, or fan tan that one might see in civilian houses of chance, they did not come to our notice. Servicemen do not look upon them with the same favor as those other games I have described. And, of course, there was no policy or lotteries, since the war had closed down all such *jueteng* games, normally big business.

In the Philippines the national sport is cockfighting. This sport, so brutal and debasing in its effects upon those who participate in its degrading joys, had been curiously permitted a legal status on Corregidor for many years by the army authorities. In a land where not every barrio (small town) of size might have a church, but all had cockpits, this could be understood. Two regiments of Scouts served the cannon of Corrigidor, and there were numerous native civilian employees on the island. In addition, there were many soldiers among the white men who may be considered to have "gone native," who became addicts to the cruel sport of fighting chickens to the death. Hard by the little church in the barrio of San Jose stood the cockpit, and on Sundays the military police preserved order among the bettors.

The war abruptly shut down this scene of blood and carnage among the chickens. Those fowl that survived the initial bombing were carefully looked after by their owners, in hope of a return to better days. But the breakdown of the quartermaster food supplies, the issuing of half rations, and the hunger of the troops caused a letdown in morals. Some of these men had been chicken thieves before they came to be in the armed forces, it cannot be doubted, and these prized birds gradually disappeared to fill hungry bellies.

To sum up our survey of the Old Army Game activities, it may be repeated that shellfire never broke up these pastimes, but merely drove them to seek shelter under cover; aerial bombs never worried the hardy devotees, except that they might take cover when the air alarm went off, but as soon as the "all clear" sounded, the games were resumed.

What happened to the sums of money won is a matter of some speculation. When Corregidor was surrendered, much money was buried. In the majority of cases, it is thought, the owners did not survive imprisonment. Captain Fleming told me by letter that of some 22,500 white men who were taken in the islands, some 4,150 were known to have survived, and he had gotten his figures in Manila from army headquarters. And we know that the death rate among the Filipinos was far higher. Those paper pesos buried in the earth lacked proper containers, so it is believed that the deteriorating effects of the tropical rainy season during the next several years turned each of these small fortunes into a useless moldy mass.

The astute Japanese shook down quite a number of men, to rob them of all their money in addition to wristwatches, rings, jewelry, and fountain pens. Despite this, a great deal of these sums made their way to Cabanatuan Prison Camp, and, after a seasonable interval, gaming was openly resumed. Layouts of the professional type, carried all the way on the Death March from the Bataan lines or from Corregidor, appeared. In addition, certain of the brethren made new layouts using indelible pencil, red and blue crayons, ink, and even paint stolen from the Japanese, on shelter halves or scraps of canvas.

The Old Army Game was not confined to gambling alone. It may be described as "Never Give a Sucker an Even Break." And now the human leeches, the army's "20-percent men" who had been in obscurity and eclipse during combat, reappeared on the scene. Now they charged 100 percent, or more. The gambling element that had money pooled it in small groups; an officer would sign an ironclad note with two or more officers as cosigners, with the note to read, say, 500 pesos at legal interest. The borrower might get 250 pesos given to him, if he was lucky. One wonders if they are collectible today, either from the man who signed it, if he survived, or from his estate. An enlisted man could hardly borrow money from these gentry unless he was a personal friend; such men do not have many friends. After a time, when the moneylenders had lent their all, an underground was established. Money was procured to be lent at an extraordinary rate of interest.

The open flagrancy of the gamesters soon caused orders to be published against them. They were issued in the name of the Japanese authorities, but I suspect they were inspired by the senior officers, some of whom, having no money of their own with which to gamble, may have resented seeing it in others. Again, the navy and Marine element, now in the saddle, could have told their army brethren that "Gambling is conducive to bad morals," and the seed would have taken root. Also, the "haves" were spending a goodly sum of money on food while the "have-nots" were starving and dying. If anyone displayed too much money at a gambling table, his friends and acquaintances for a loan importuned him. Thus gaming for money died its natural death. It is more than possible that a sort of 10 percent takeout poker game, with chips in lieu of visible money, still continued, in cover and concealment.

After a while the Japanese began to pay the officers. Wiser than their men, they seemed to spend their funds in the commissary, for tobacco and food. Bridge for free was their pastime. Occasionally one of them might be enticed into a poker game with the men, only to be promptly fleeced, but such things were considered rare.

The arrival of Red Cross food, in December of 1942, marked a revival of gaming; mostly poker and blackjack, for the dice layouts were still barred. American cigarettes were the medium of exchange. A twelve-ounce can of "big-meat" was worth four packages of smokes, a chocolate bar, three, and a two-and-a-half-ounce coffee tin of the soluble variety was worth two. (If one were a navy man, he might have to pay three packs, for such men are known as coffee addicts.) Not all of these men were fools enough to gamble, by any means. Those four little twelve-pound packages given out to us that Christmas saved lives; beriberi began to disappear and the lame began to walk; eye ulcers grew smaller, while the blind saw. The death rate dropped from some twenty-eight men per day to less than two men per month!

Perhaps the horrible example of overeating on the part of a sailor may have contributed to the revival of the games, for at least some of the professional brethren offered it as an excuse. A seaman whose weight had been some three hundred pounds was now down to a bit just over one hundred. His ravenous appetite had been remarked upon in peacetime, for his shipmates told of his being "shanghaied" from his submarine for eating a case of oranges put out by the commissary steward for the boat's crew. Now down to wrinkled skin and feebly animated bones, he received his first twelve-pound package while his comrades, sick of rice, gave him some seven bowls full at the noon meal. By suppertime he had finished the whole box, along with some seven or so more bowls of free rice. After midnight he expired in the agonies of acute indigestion.

When the Red Cross food was gone, hardly a game was to be seen in those early months of 1943. A few hardy individuals, among the unrepentant, risked their Filipino "dobe" cigarettes at cards and dice, but such displays were rare. The "have-nots," the chief supporters of the gambling profession in the more abundant life, now had nothing, and the "haves" spent their money and food, not to be enticed into games of chance.

In late May the prisoners were informed that those who worked The Farm would soon be paid, fifteen centavos per day for noncommissioned officers and ten for privates. There was now much activity in the making of layouts and the construction of tables. There was a market in the sale or rental of cards, while ingenious men carved a reasonable facsimile of dice from the black wood of the *camagon* tree, with spots touched with white lead stolen at great risk from the Japanese.

The word got around that nothing would be barred, as long as some discretion would be used and a lookout kept for the Japanese sentries. So when the happy day arrived, games of poker, blackjack, and craps blossomed in full force. The general carnival spirit to contribute to the game-keepers infected even some of the "haves." One might think that persons starving slowly to death would have spent their pitiful mite—for they were paid in "Mickey Mouse" money—in the commissary for a coconut or for half a cup of peanuts. But many thronged to the gaming areas. As before on Corregidor, these games were grouped together, each advertising the other. Most of their play was by boosters in an attempt to attract the suckers, yet considerable sums were wagered. The Farm was very, very tough about this time, with the torture squads out in full force. A gambler would give a sick man on the "quarters" list up to ten pesos to take his place for half a day. And I know of one gambler, a fellow named Ted Levin, who before the war had run a nightclub in Manila, who hired men to take his place, daily, for over two years!

In Group Three, composed of dysentery ward graduates segregated from the others but required to work on The Farm, was a dice game barked by a former professional in civilian life, a strange fish caught up in the net of the draft. The superior crooning of his wares was the envy and despair of his competitors, for he gathered unto himself nearly all of the suckers addicted to dice. One of our Marine game-keepers hired an Englishman, one Thomas Crook, originally from Grimsby, Lincolnshire, a former Shanghai policeman with a broad Lincolnshire accent; the former limb of the law was taught carefully how to bark and operate the game. The crooning professional, who worked as the group barber, now had this new competition set up alongside him in his own shop, a shed with a nipa palm thatch. The loud cries of "Now 'e fawncies the hite" as ten centavos were placed on "big eight," or "Pie hoff the hunder seven, mite" as he paid off the winner of a two to six number in the space marked "under seven," were a distinct novelty and helped attract trade. The crooning barber was driven to exceed his former efforts, and there was laughter and merriment at his quips and sallies. Such was greatly needed, for far too many men had forgotten how to laugh.

But after a while the starvation increased, and the suckers did less gambling in order to buy more food. Again the games became nearly as dead as a dodo.

Then some of us were sent to Japan. Packed 1,035 in a single hold, as tight as peas in a pod on this prison ship, there was no gaming for there was no room in which to spread out. The Japanese had forbidden smoking in the hold, so precious tobacco was hoarded for the future, for no one knew what it might hold. During the four-day train ride in Japan, with one hundred men packed in a single narrow-gauge car, we saw no wagering, for likewise there was just no room.

For several months, until Christmas 1944, when a twelve-pound box of Red Cross food was issued, there was no gambling to be seen. These men were all too beaten, dispirited, and starved to think of their gaming. Besides, they had no money, and there were no cigarettes issued, other than a tiny few. The delicacies from their homeland revived the spirit of chance, and several "friendly" games, with no cutting, except a small rental for the cards, started for food, with cigarettes as the exchange medium. Efforts were made to break up this vicious practice by the Japanese and our own officers, but the gamblers were discreet and hard to detect in the act. There, right before us, we could see that "Gambling is conducive of bad morals," for thievery increased to an alarming degree. There were fights, disorder, and cruelties practiced by the prisoners on each other. But the games continued until word came of the Japanese surrender.

The contrast between these vicious food gamblers and a group of players on Corregidor may be instructive. Some Marines and hospital corpsmen of the 2d Battalion, 4th Marines, all well acquainted with each other and friends from their Shanghai days, started a credit type of poker game in James Ravine on Corregidor with the battalion orderly clerk, Sgt. Wendell N. Garden, keeping the books. To the surprise of the cynical, the game met all of its obligations the first payday, but did not survive another one. A corpsman, losing heavily, plunged deeper and deeper in debt. In an effort to recoup, he soon owed more than he could repay in ten years. Not being able to pay in full, he paid nothing, the other losers followed suit, and the game broke up with anguished howls on the part of the winners because they could not collect. On the whole, the incident caused much merriment, especially on the part of the "I told you so" element. There was no further bitterness and the game was soon forgotten.

Not so was the case in this bleak and dismal prisoner of war camp in northern Japan, with its fifteen feet of drifted snows, its scanty heat, its starvation food. An army technical sergeant of the air forces had lost his all, but it was not common knowledge. He got back into the game, and the banker trusted him to the extent of fifteen packs of cigarettes before his inability to pay was found out. Great was the wrath of the players. Corporal punishment of this emaciated creature was gravely considered, to be finally rejected, and it was decided that he would forfeit sixty bowls of rice, the current price being four bowls for a pack of smokes. His audacity in bucking a game in which he had nothing to lose and all to gain was roundly denounced, and his section leader, T.Sgt. Ralph H. Pope, from Berryville, Virginia, approved the sentence, for he thought that making a cheat pay up might deter others who had like ambitions. He was permitted the cruel clemency of losing only one bowl of rice per day, his noon meal.

This man's name I do not recall, but he had spent two years studying at MIT, and so was highly respected, until he was caught. The man was already suffering with advanced malnutrition. When thirty days of his sentence had passed, he had completely lost his voice, was barely able to stagger around, and Doctor Dan placed him in the hospital. Here the doctor saw to it that he received a little more food than the others, and his voice partially returned. In the month or less between surrender and our final release, with American food dropped to us from planes and reinforced by American drugs, he recovered most of the use of his limbs, but not his voice. I wonder today just how he is.

The philosophy of one of the old-time gamblers, 1st Sgt. Emanuel Hamburger, AT Co., 31st Infantry, proved enlightening. "In 1917 and 1918, when I was a dumb john, I was a sucker for the seconds dealers and the dice table men. I used to hand over all of my pay each month. It took me three years to learn the tricks, and by then all of the rich suckers were out of the army. There was nothing in it but a lot of twenty-one-dollar-a-month guys, and company collections took up most of their dough before I could get them into a game. All these years of peace I prayed for a big war so that I could stay in the States in a training camp, trimming suckers and thinking of how I could make five thousand dollars a month. And here I am, in a prisoner of war camp, my hands so shaky with starvation that I cannot even deal off the bottom anymore without getting caught. Think of all those dumb johns in the States just begging to be separated from their dough, with me here, in jail!" (His remark about getting caught dealing from the bottom was sadly true, for he had been detected in the act a few days before our talk, and he was somewhat in the dumps over it.)

The worthy man was released, to go to Guam by plane. Here we heard about his activities, how he had some old shell splinters cut out and was on crutches, and how he had located a sign painter and had a dice layout made on a brand new white hospital blanket. He found an engraver to make his secret marks upon his dice, for he feared some of his clients-to-be might inject their own loaded bones in his field dice game, with attendant disaster. He gathered unto himself a dealer, several boosters, and even made provisions for his ropers-in. He drew substantially upon his back pay, and chose for his location the colored mess attendant's heads.

Some hours after pay call, when all was running serene, a client asked to change a twenty-dollar bill; the old gamekeeper reached into his shirt for his roll when a chill voice was heard, "Drop all that money on the table!" There stood the chief master at arms of the hospital, Chief Pharmacist's

Mate Phillips, and his henchmen blocking all of the exits. In the resultant turmoil someone seized the roll of bills while another made off with the "Bob Evans" white hat that held all the silver coins. The layout and dice were seized, and the gamekeeper and his principal assistant went up for captain's mast (nonjudicial punishment). They were released with a warning, and they gambled no more on Guam.

It was noted that the old man was soon busied with a new layout; he was procuring new dice and applying for more of his back pay. He requested ship transport to the States rather than to go by plane, for only thirty men or less could go by air while the transport holds would contain a thousand or more suckers. But they sent him by air, which almost broke his heart. Another gamekeeper, who became my friend while in the hospital in Cabanatuan, gave me some additional insight on the subject of gambling. A tiny drafted man of Sicilian ancestry from Brooklyn, one Private Pelligrini, whose friends claimed was in civilian life a "petty racketeer," confided that "there's no sucker as nice as a soldier sucker, see? Here I am hustling for a living these twenty-six years before I find out what nice suckers these soldiers are. I should have had the sense to come into the dogface army when I was eighteen, instead of fooling around Brooklyn and going to Elmira [prison] for a stretch. When I get out of this stir, I'm going to dobe over right here for all of these nice soldier suckers."

He was perfectly sincere in his attitude, for when a Marine (myself), who had an acquaintance with that chapter of college algebra called "Permutations and Combinations," began to inform some fellow prisoners that six, seven, and eight were not three-way points, but that the odd "big six" or "big eight" versus "seven" was five for the gunner against six for the house, the distressed little fellow called me aside, begging me to desist from such dangerous enlightenment. "Never educate a sucker, pal. What they don't know don't hoit 'em. It's the old army game, you know, where you never give a sucker an even break. There's a sucker born every minute, and I sure love to hear one squeal."

There may have been some truth in this frank, revealing attitude on the part of my friend, for his companions in his battalion of aviation engineers stated he had won some eighteen hundred dollars on the voyage out, from soldiers who sought to relieve the boredom of a transport ship. His complete ignorance in military affairs was shown by his conduct before a special court-martial, for he had gotten into some difficulty on the transport while a member of the guard. The president of the court was explaining to him his rights as a witness, if he, the accused, chose to take the stand. Facing the court, he shrugged his shoulders, turned his palms upward in the age-old gesture of futility, and said, "What's the use? Even if I had Clarence Darrow for a mouthpiece, I couldn't win!"

Few of the gamblers gave us such an insight into their philosophy as this engaging little man from Brooklyn. But a certain army sergeant, whose long years in the prison camp had stripped away his ordinary caution, gave another sidelight. "It's like this with me. I'm awful careful never to rub a guy the wrong way. I look on everyone as suckers for my game. I try to carry out my duties as a sergeant, of course, but in such a way as not to make enemies of my suckers. I want the same gangs at my layout every payday. I never want to trim a big sucker. He might squawk, and there would be trouble. The sucker I love is the man with only five dollars left after he settles up with the company collection sheet and the 20-percent man. That ain't enough for a decent liberty, so he comes to my table. He knows I've got the percentage on him, and I've always admitted it. But he sees me with several hundred dollars, and he's got five. He couldn't get in a decent poker game with that kind of dough. But he is welcome in my game. If he can double his money, he makes a good liberty. If he goes broke, he ain't hurt. He's got a place to eat and sleep for the rest of the month, jawbone for his smoke, movies, and supplies. That's why, when I pull sergeant of the guard, I don't have a lot of guys run up before the 'Old Man.' I keep order and discipline, a good

fire watch, safeguard prisoners and property, and my suckers all like me."

I recall that, years ago, in our Marine Corps manual,
there was once a sentence that was the work of genius. It
was simply, "Tact is the keynote of discipline." Our army
sergeant had never read these words, but he had somewhat
of the right idea. The army does not seem to try too hard to
keep its noncommissioned officers from gambling with the
privates. It may be that wise officers like this type, as exem-
plified in our sergeant.

"It's the old army game! Never give a sucker an even
break!"

14

THE STORY OF SOOCHOW

This is the tale of a little dog and his odyssey. He was whelped in Shanghai, served there as a Marine mascot, went through five months of continuous campaign, suffered nearly three years as a prisoner of war of the Japanese, and made it back alive!

Soochow served some six years in Shanghai as the official mascot of the 1st Battalion, 4th Marine Regiment. In late November 1941 his unit took him with them to the Philippine Islands, where he went through the Bataan and Corregidor battles. As a prisoner of war of the Japanese, he saw life from behind barbed wire on the aforesaid Corregidor, then in Bilibid Prison, Cabanatuan Number Three, and Cabanatuan Number One, all of these places of evil memory in these islands. The army Ranger battalion rescued him in February 1945.

In Manila, after release, he was duly processed along with his released comrades, deloused with DDT, showered with Red Cross gifts and dainties, and given, I hope, a large, tough, fried steak à la US Marine Corps, of which he is very fond.

Then he was returned to the continental limits of the United States, a strange land for him, for duty in the Marine Corps base at San Diego, California. Unlike his fellow prisoners, he was given no convalescent or rehabilitation leave or reenlistment furlough for, like the good Marine he is, he was ready for duty at all times. Under the heading in his Service Record Book of "Specialist Details," his entry is merely "Mascot," hence he needed no time off.

He is still in the big San Diego base, on duty with the recruit depot, and he should prove to be an inspiration to the new Marines. His old regiment is somewhere out in China, but Soochow is well content where he is. Marines do not as a general rule pay very much attention to the names of the units in which they are currently serving— they are simply in the "Marine Corps," and that is all they care about. By now they must have outfitted little Soochow in a splendid blue coat, red-piped, with perhaps the chevrons of a noncommissioned officer, gold on a red background, old issue–type as befits an old-timer. They ought to have his ribbons pinned on, for Soochow was there when his comrades got the Yangtze Service Medal; the China Service Medal; the Philippine Defense Medal with two stars; the Asiatic Pacific Medal, likewise with two stars; the Presidential Navy Unit Citation with two stars; the Presidential Army Unit Citation with two oak-leaf clusters; an American Defense Medal with one star for being on foreign shore at Pearl Harbor time; the Victory medal; and he might have gotten the American Theater ribbon for a year in the States, if he got back before early March 1945. For personal medals he can wear the Purple Heart, with possibly two stars [in lieu of second and third awards], for the little fellow on some three occasions was lacerated by flying steel and rocks, and of course he has the Good Conduct Medal, with the numeral "2" for his more than twelve years of service. I might hesitate in this last award at the numeral "2," for in the days before the war when I knew Soochow, his conduct was not the best. But he has the impressive list of some ten medals, and maybe eleven, which is quite a number for any Marine to wear, and most unique for a little dog.

I guess they make much of him nowadays; generals and colonels may honor themselves by being photographed with him, and certainly the public relations branch can always write up a colorful story about Soochow. This last is useful, for Marine Corps publicity is needed when a penny-pinching Congress forgets the lessons of this war and begins to shave down our commandant's requests for money. In addition, if the recruit depot Marines make proper use of Soochow as a morale builder among the young lads of their boot camp, he can indeed be quite a valuable citizen.

To cap it all, the Marines might even have a gunnery sergeant detailed as his orderly, or rather, I should say, keeper. In those pleasant days at the San Diego base, between the Nicaraguan wars and this last Pacific expedition, the official mascot there, one Jiggs II, just an ordinary, pedigreed, pampered English bulldog, had a noncommissioned officer of that rank (G.Sgt. Don Beeson, later captain, and now dead. The depot's baseball field bears his name) to attend to all his wants. For the muster roll records, so scrupulously gone over in the Department of the Pacific and the Washington headquarters, this dog was carried as "AsstNCOinC (assistant noncommissioned officer in charge), Athletic Store-room, Base," but any informed Marine who was there during any part of those years will tell you that all this fellow ever did was to act as orderly for this mutt. So, I hope that our little friend has an orderly of proper rank assigned to him—even the lofty rank of sergeant major would not be too good—for Soochow saved the lives of many of his Marine comrades.

The highest military award in ancient Rome was the oak leaf crown, not for killing, but for "saving the life of a citizen." Julius Caesar won this award in his youth; his busts in later life show him with it. It helped conceal his baldness, of which he was very sensitive, but he was mighty proud of this wreath just the same. The keen senses of Soochow detected, time and again, the sound of "motors in the west," and his furious barking often preceded the air raid alarm so his comrades could rush to their shelters and reasonable safety. His duty done, Soochow would likewise rush, and often get there ahead of the Marines, being a little speedier in the face of danger. On at least three occasions he was not quite fast enough in the face of shellfire and got cut quite a bit, but fortunately he received no broken bones or severe wounds. The numerous scars on his back bear mute witness to his right to wear the Purple Heart. If the few survivors of that 1st Battalion get together and start the paperwork on Soochow, he might even get another personal award, like a Silver Star, for his gallantry in action. I repeat, this little dog saved a lot of Marine lives.

We few who came back alive, if we ever see him, will make a fuss over him, for our own reputation in the Corps. We will be inwardly thankful that the little dog's memory is short, however, for we all ought to be heartily ashamed of our neglect of him. This indictment should embrace nearly the whole of the regiment who served along with him as prisoners of war. For there came a time in Soochow's life when the little fellow truly needed a friend, and no Marines would lift a finger to help him. In his hour of anguish, this Gethsemane for a little dog, he was befriended by a civilian, Mr. Ray Foss, a man who had never known Soochow until they came to their common misfortune together. Thereby hangs a tale, none too creditable to we who survived, and we should be thankful that Soochow, in his present bliss with his adored Leathernecks, has a short memory. This I am sure of, for he has forgotten all of his knowledge of Chinese.

For the story of the early life of Soochow, I must rely on hearsay. He is said to have been brought into the 1st Battalion by a hospital corpsman as a tiny puppy sometime in 1937, but his owner soon abandoned him for the delights of White Russian girls and the cabarets. By then his winning, comical appeal had so captivated the Marines of the battalion that he had no trouble in hanging on as the official mascot, for he had that quality so dearly loved by the Marines, a fighting heart.

It may be of interest to the uninformed to note a peculiarity of Marine mascots acquired on foreign soil. With the exception of cats, most animals in a very short time developed a most decided antipathy for their former owners, the natives. There was little Jocko, a tiny capuchin monkey, who chased natives away from the old fort in Managua, in Nicaraguan days. Old Riley, a disreputable, drunken female of the rhesus species, is better known. For some years she was chained at the entrance of the carpenter shop in Shanghai by members of the maintenance gang in the compound on Haiphong Road. "Slick" Fullerton, the gunnery sergeant in charge, was as astute as his nickname, for if any Chinese workman tried to leave without a Marine there to hold this lady monkey in, she would attack him with her fangs. She simply hated all Chinese. I recall many dogs that were the subject of "officer hours" for unwarranted attacks upon peaceful natives, with minor international consequences. The "room boys" may feed the animal, but it knows its superiority and will show it with growls and bared teeth. Sometimes it even bites deeply, particularly if the native stands his ground.

Soochow was no exception to this peculiarity of Marine mascots. As he approached adult doghood he was positively ferocious, and the "Old Man" began to get concerned over him, for his pugnacity endeared him to the file, if not to the rank.

While he was pondering this problem, for the morale of his Marines was a matter of concern to the battalion commander, Lieutenant Colonel Collier, the "room boys" took direct action. They did not dare to make away with the little dog, for their known fear and antipathy toward Soochow would make them immediately suspect. His prolonged absence would have resulted in a wholesale dismissal, and "room boys" were easily procurable in an overcrowded land. The Gordian knot was cut by a "snatch job," and by taking him, securely bound and muzzled, to a local blacksmith to have his teeth filed flat. For Soochow, not being able to talk, it was some time before the outrage was discovered.

At first there was great indignation, but after reflection, cooler counsels prevailed. The ancient Greeks had a word for it, called the "act of oblivion" in such a case. The indignant Marines were untutored in the annals of classical antiquity, but they did the same thing by deciding to forget the incident. Mayhem, that crime defined in common law as "mutilation of the person so as to make him less capable of defending himself," had been performed upon Soochow, but his ferocity remained unabated. The "room boys" could now laugh off his futile attacks, but the rickshaw men and street hawkers who infested the compound gate did not know of his handicap, and they still feared him. So did other dogs, for Soochow was a jealous dog and immensely proud of his position as sole battalion mascot. The "room boys" piously denied having had any part in the foul deed, but the colonel must have been secretly pleased by their action. The civilization of China is older than ours, and it has been remarked, "China always absorbs her conquerors."

In appearance Soochow was ludicrous, hence some of his appeal. In his veins may have flowed the blood of a terrier, a pointer, and a bulldog along with the basic Chinese "wonk." His face bore a comic resemblance to the sad, austere look of a mastiff, his ears curled down, and his tail curved gaily back over his rump. His weight was about twenty-five pounds when his admirers were seeing his absurdly short legs, indicating a trace of dachshund. The saying of the Roman emperor Tiberius (A.D. 14–37), as quoted by Suetonius, "A man is his own best ancestor," could be applied to this little dog, for he certainly had a fighting heart.

His conduct record, however, left much to be desired. On more than one occasion Lieutenant Colonel Collier awarded Soochow up to five days' solitary confinement on bread and water for his frays and disorders. These punishments were duly entered into his Service Record Book.

Despite Soochow's jealous rage at the entrance of another canine into his domain, he was suspected at times of harboring criminals, fugitives from justice. The 2d Battalion had three dogs of nondescript ancestry for mascots. Their supreme joy was to participate actively in parades, with all of Shanghai present in top-hatted dignity. After little Brownie had made his historic attempt to use the shiny boots of the regimental adjutant, Capt. Robert B. Moore, at Kiaochow Field, as a canine comfort station, the commander of the 2d Battalion, Lt. Col. Donald Curtis, was chided for his neglect to secure the dogs and perhaps spoken to sharply, for the presence of the dogs at parade had before been deplored.

So to the duties of portly, majestic "Big Jack" Taylor, the 2d Battalion's lordly police sergeant, was added that of capturing and tying up these miscreants. After two such frustrating experiences, the dogs went over the evening before parade to hide out. Normally Soochow would have driven them away with bared fangs, but this time he admitted them to his sacred domain. The next morning "Big Jack" hunted high and low for his canine charges, but they were not anywhere to be found. Promptly at the first notes of "Adjutant's Call" they appeared and took their usual festive part in the military solemnities. It is presumed that the battalion commander was again chided, this time with severity. Being an astute man, the colonel soon discovered what had happened. From then on, Brownie and company were always placed in durance vile the night before parades, and all was serene. Soochow went unpunished. He had the old timer's dislike for parades. Anyway, there were enough cats in his bailiwick to keep him away.

His name, Soochow, was always a source of laughter. The Soochow Creek divided the International Settlement of Shanghai into two parts. It starts near the city of Soochow, some sixty miles from Shanghai, and unites the waters of the Grand Canal with those of the Whangpoo River. Its slate-gray bosom carries a cross section of Chinese river traffic with flagrant disregard for our Western sanitary ideas. Hence its color and pungent odor! Prior to 1932 and the first of the "Shanghai incidents," the Marines paid little attention to it except to cross its bridges, seeking relief from the boredom of military life in the fleshpots of the Hongkew. Later it became the boundary between the encroaching Japanese and the Shanghai Volunteer Corps, the Italians, and the Marines. Guard posts bristling with lethal weapons controlled its bridges. The Gordon Road ordure loading station was a place to be avoided if possible. Defense maneuvers were frequent along its banks, and it was the scene of many minor "incidents." So we all knew it, only too well.

In a spirit of distressful levity, the Privates' Club had a medal struck with a mustard-yellow-and-brown ribbon (you may guess the why of such colors) and some nonsense engraved on the medallion about "Soochow Creek Defense," with a figure of a Chinese coolie pushing a night-soil cart. The medal cost a dollar, and they were awarded with great ceremony at company beer parties to Marines who had been found guilty of some outstanding act of stupidity.

The story was current in most posts in the States of dumb Marines who had served in Shanghai going into the first sergeant's office, saying, "Put me in for the Soochow Creek Defense Medal, Top!" Some with a sense of humor gravely collected a dollar, sent it out to the Shanghai club, and in due time the medal and certificate arrived and were informally awarded with laughter and merriment. Other first sergeants, lacking such saving grace, indignantly threw the applicant out of their offices. Then the joke was revealed. Of course, Soochow wore such a medal attached to his collar.

If you look at a map of the Marine sector of the Settlement, oriented north as is proper, from the western boundary to about two miles east, the creek makes the area to its south look exactly like a dog's head. And of course that sector was called Dog's Head.

So giving such a name to a little dog of such comical appearance was considered meet and fitting. Like the second lieutenants and field musics [bandsmen] of those days, who were considered the most useless men in the Corps, so was Soochow. He toiled not, neither did he spin, nor was any man his master. His was a very happy life.

It is further related that he visited the clubs and cabarets daily, as do gunnery sergeants and certain other folk who do not have to stand guard duty. He learned early the trick of

jumping into one's rickshaw, for he abhorred walking, and
after a time the coolies would ride him alone in solemn dignity. Arriving at his destination, his imperious bark would
summon one of his Marine friends from the club to pay his
fare. On his return, the gate corporal always paid for him.
The Peking Marines of the twenties used to tell the same
story of their mascot, John Bunny. Unfortunately, it can be
related with sad truth that Soochow's admirers often gave
him beer and strong drink, which made him all too familiar
with the morning hangover.

Soochow's idyllic existence was suddenly shattered by
the coming of war. The regiment was hastily embarked on
the *President Madison* and the *President Harrison*. A fund
was raised, a crate made, and Soochow went aboard. A certain private who shall be called "Tex" and Soochow had developed a mutual liking. They had in common none too
good conduct records. Tex saw his little friend safely ashore
in the Philippines and looked out for him.

The story of Bataan and Corregidor may be read elsewhere, but suffice to say that Soochow survived, fed by Tex
and other Marines. It has already been related how the keen
ears of the little dog detected the sound of enemy planes before any of us heard the air raid siren. He did this many,
many times. Whether or not his abilities extended to the detection of shellfire in advance is an open question. Serving
in another battalion, I seldom saw Soochow during those
days, and one knows that Marines will gild the lily when the
subject is one they admire.

On the sixth of May 1942, Corregidor fell. Now the adventure of Soochow became singular indeed. By some
miraculous process, Tex and other Marines got Soochow
through the barbed-wire prison that was now on Corregidor,
Japanese ships, the Old Bilibid Prison, and the trains of the
Manila Railroad, and he arrived at Cabanatuan Prison Camp
Number Three. Even more strangely, they taught him not to
attack the Japanese soldiers, the enemies of his adored
Marines. Several dogs, mascots of the soldiers, were imprudent enough to "insult the honor of the Japanese army" and

were killed by bayonet or torture. (This was, in fact, the wording of the charge read to us, with threats of death sentences for its violation. Of course, the Japanese never defined just what "the honor of the Japanese army" was.) Soochow learned to obey the order after a fashion, but his bristling hair and low growl was always a matter of concern when the guards were around.

Now real hunger began for this little dog. Tex and his friends fed him from their meager rations of rice, but one by one the "friends" dropped off, and soon Tex alone fed him. Both of them lost weight. Tex had dysentery and the beriberi shuffle; the gay curl of Soochow's tail was now seen in a disconsolate droop. By this time Soochow was well known to all the prisoners and submitted to the caresses of the hands of soldiers, sailors, and those civilians who had stuck with the armed forces. All of these men wore rags, and all had the same despondent look; all were friends to Soochow, but their friendship stopped short of feeding him regularly. Now and then one might toss the little dog a bit of well-gnawed bone or a spoonful of rice, but had it not been for Tex, Soochow would not have lasted long.

When Camp Number Three was closed in October 1942, Tex carried Soochow along with him to Camp Number One. Here he made new friends and soon became a familiar figure. The arrival of Red Cross food helped save the lives of these men. They could now afford to feed Soochow, and he regained much of his former weight. But soon this small amount of extra food was gone, Tex was shipped out to another work camp, and Soochow grew gaunt and thin. His gay tail that had begun to joyfully curl up over him again resumed its dismal droop.

Under pressure of their gnawing hunger, men began to eat strange and weird foods. Cobras, killed on The Farm, hidden beneath shirts—for the Japanese loved them, too— were smuggled past the gate and emerged in stew pots as a tasty delicacy. Beloved mascots died in order that their owners and others, not as scrupulous of the rights of "mine and thine," might for a little while satisfy the cravings of eternal hunger. Scrawny tomcats added the flavor of their lean, stringy bodies to a rice stew, while kittens, soft and tender, sold for a very high price. Dog traps made their grisly appearance. Their owners were warned of what would happen to them if Soochow disappeared, for even if the Marines could not feed him, they would protect the little dog.

It was at the nadir of his fortune that Soochow finally found a friend in his strange odyssey. Not merely a friend who caressed him, but a friend who fed him while they both were starving. And this friend would go out to play ball with the little dog, to his infinite delight.

"Big Ray" Foss was a civilian, a longtime resident of the islands best described by that adjective of the army folk as an "old dobe." (Nautical types and Marines would say "bamboo American.") He was full of tall tales of pesos, of big jobs, "nipa" gin, and native women, and some figured he may have thought too well of himself. He was in his early sixties, a man with a face carved from granite, a shock of iron-gray hair, and six feet or more of big, bony frame. The outbreak of war had found him a civilian workman in the Cavite Navy Yard.

The second day of January 1942 marked the capture of both Manila and Cavite. Most of the civilians had by that time turned in to the comparative ease of Santo Tomás concentration camp, where they were later to know what real hunger was. But "Big Ray" and certain of his fellows were made of sterner stuff, for from the beginning they had cast their lot with the armed forces. Many did heroic work, many more did valuable service, and some few cowered under the *scree* and *crump* of bombs in rock tunnels. Just like servicemen, not all were heroes. Someday their story will be written, these forgotten men of Corregidor.

"Big Ray" had none too much to eat himself, yet he adopted Soochow and took real care of him. The little dog had gotten some form of paralysis and now dragged his hind legs along the ground. I think it was beriberi neuritis, so common among the prisoners. This brought Soochow to "Big Ray's" attention, and somehow he procured a few cans of precious corned beef for the dog. The black market kings charged twelve pesos a can at the time, and I still wonder how "Big Ray" got the money. Soochow slowly recovered, and after a while he would go out and scamper after the wooden ball that "Big Ray" had carved out for him from a piece of scrap *tanghili* wood.

There was much talk among the Marines about the disgrace put upon them by a civilian taking care of their mascot dog, but like much of such talk, it came to nothing. Occasionally a Marine might give Soochow a bone or a spoonful of rice, but it was "Big Ray" who kept the dog alive. Soochow still made his daily inspections of the camp, his short hairs bristling when he passed close to the Japanese guards, much to the concern of "Big Ray." He tried the expedient method of tying the little fellow up, but it did no good. After Soochow was given a long talking-to about this danger and released, he would only repeat the offense. Why the Japanese never killed him was a great mystery.

Soon "Big Ray" could barely feed his little friend, so sharply had the rice rations been reduced. He himself was now a gaunt bag of bones, starved and very sick. The droop in Soochow's once gay tail was now permanent, and he became too listless to make his daily rounds of the camp. Many hungry men eyed that dog with a dangerous gleam in their eyes. Soochow must have been fully aware of his peril, for he stuck close to "Big Ray." The grim protector loudly proclaimed what he would do to anyone who dared eat his Soochow. His big, hard fist was feared, and Soochow lived. I like to think that no Marine would have eaten him. A soldier, a sailor, or a civilian, perhaps, but Soochow had saved Marine lives, and those Leathernecks did not forget that much.

The old man used to talk wistfully of keeping his beloved "Soo," as he called him, in Manila with him after they were released, but he thought the Marines would want to take their mascot back with them. I used to think it strange to hear him say this, for even if Soochow was the property of the survivors of the 4th Marine Regiment, "Big Ray" certainly had some rights of salvage in the matter.

In the fall of 1944, I went on the long journey to Japan. With the hardships of bitter cold weather, short rations, and climbing the mountain to the mine, I gave Soochow little thought. If I ever reflected on him, I figured him long dead of starvation. News from various sources came of the capture of the Philippines by the Americans, and perhaps I idly mused over the fate of "Big Ray" and Soochow, but I am not too sure.

I do not know whether "Big Ray" lived to be released by the Ranger battalion. We who had gotten to know him liked him for his many good qualities, one of which was his unselfish devotion to a little dog when the going was really tough.

After I was released from Japan, I came upon a copy of our *Leatherneck* magazine that had a picture of Soochow and a long article, but there was not a word about "Big Ray" in it. One guesses that no one spoke of him to the public relations branch, for it would not have been the most desirable type of publicity.

Soochow is now back with his beloved Marines. He who so often dodged bombs and shells ought to be able to keep out of the way of speeding cars. Besides, over at the Drills and Instruction Office of the recruit depot, where he now resides, there are not many, and they go by slowly. His principal worry seems to be acute indigestion after eating too many fried steaks, and if they give him a good gunnery sergeant for his orderly, he should survive to a ripe old age.

His present bliss is untroubled by rival mascots, and if a strange dog shows up in his domain, he is the old, ferocious Soochow again.

Should I see him, I will tell all of his mighty feats. For my own reputation I shall be silent about "Big Ray." But, as the little dog submits resignedly to my caresses, I will wonder just how much he remembers of the big, grim "old dobe" and his hand-carved *tanghili* ball that he so delighted in chasing.

Soochow died in December 1949 of old age, being about twelve and a half years old. He was buried with full military honors at the Marine Corps Recruit Depot, San Diego, California. A fitting granite monument on the recruit training regiment side of the depot marks Soochow's final resting place.

15

THE STORY OF PRIVATE GIZMO

During the First World War the term "shell shock" was applied to those men who broke down in screaming terror, many of them without getting close enough to the front to hear the sounds of drumfire. In this Second World War they call it, on our sick reports, "war neurosis, hysteria, acute." It helped in the wrecking of one man who had been a good Marine, and he ultimately committed suicide. This is not a pleasant story to recount.

I shall call him "Gizmo," that Marine Corps slang term for something indefinite. In China, where he had served previously, it would have been "Jay guh nay guh," if you will pardon my flagrant disregard for the phonetics of that mystery, the "Wade System of Romanization of the Chinese Characters." To the Chinese it means, "This or that," spelled *che ke na ke* in the system of the good professor Wade. Civilians like the word "gadget." The modern Marine does not know Chinese as well as his more immoral predecessor did, for, alas, inflation has made it prohibitive to use that so-convenient method of studying a foreign language, the "sleeping dictionary." "Gizmo" is short, convenient, and your hearers know exactly what you mean.

This entire preamble boils down to this: our "Gizmo" was a distinct discredit to the Marine Corps; therefore it is best to draw a decent veil over his true identity.

In the latter part of 1940 the wanderlust came upon him,

or it might have been a transient form of patriotism, for the bugles were sounding, the drums were beating, and the Marine Corps recruiting posters were brightly colored and alluring. So he came into our midst to be duly indoctrinated in boot camp into things a young Marine should know. The post sergeant major had to make up a China detail. The department gave him the names of the first three pay grades; sergeant down through private; all he had to do was take from his personnel cards those with the longest time to serve on their enlistments, and notify their units. The company commanders then had a chance to battle to retain their "key" Marines, but the sergeant major was usually victorious in such skirmishes. Our young "Gizmo" was fresh from boot camp; no one knew him or cared very much about him. The sergeant major took just one glance at the personnel card and inscribed his name on the detail. "Deus ex machina," just like that!

In the spring of 1941, he came to join the 2d Battalion of the 4th Marine Regiment in Shanghai. It can be assumed that he had the usual trip across the Pacific; that he had been seasick the first day or two; that he had fallen for the old gag, "Mail closes for the mail buoy at twenty hundred tonight," and hopefully carried his letter to the ship's post office in mid-Pacific; that he got liberty in Honolulu, Guam, and Manila, with no better behavior than that of his fellow Marines in those wide open ports; and that he stood a lot of guard duty on what he considered useless posts on his transports.

As his ship carried him by Corregidor, in the Boca Grande Channel that enters into Manila Bay, he may have been solemnly told that tiny little Fort Drum was a "concrete battleship, an experiment of the 1918 war; see her cage mast, fourteen-inch gun turrets, and stack." In the mists of early morning, the little island certainly could have passed for such. Gizmo probably gave it but little thought. To grim-looking Corregidor on his port side he possibly gave less of his attention. Yet, just a year later, almost to the day, he was to die there, by his own hand, in terror and in fear.

In the Haiphong Road billet of the 2d Battalion, Gizmo did well. His first sergeant (Richard Duncan) even developed a fondness for him, for this young man was not an athlete and he stayed out of the hospital and off the misconduct list, for if not a moral lad, he at least was sanitary. He was seldom, if ever, up before the skipper of his company, Capt. Paul Russell, until 25 September 1941, who was replaced by 1st Lt. B. L. McMakin, and when a Marine was wanted to walk post, he was always available. This last feature is what endears privates to their "top sergeants."

The battalion sergeant major never knew Gizmo in those days, for he was never up for "office hours," the term called by our British cousins for their "crime parade." If the sergeant major did not know a private, it was to the latter's credit. It meant that this humble private had properly learned the first lesson of all Marines—"It is not what you do, but it is what you get caught doing that counts." He who has progressed this far along on the road of knowledge is no longer to be considered a recruit.

I suppose he gave the girls in the Majestic and Carton Cabarets a part of his attention, that he was an inveterate habitué of the 4th Marines Club, that he explored certain dark and devious sides of native Chinese life, and that his average amount of common sense taught him to distinguish the gold from the dross. Just a normal young Marine he was, and no one paid much attention to him or had cause to worry about him.

In one trait he was a bit different from his young comrades. Somehow, somewhere, in the days of his pious youth in the Middle West he had conceived a tremendous respect for constituted authority. His devotion to his top soldier and particularly to G.Sgt. Felix Szalkewicz was not unusual, for they were men of force with high professional attainments, but his worship of commissioned officers was a thing to cause wonder. The better type of Marine officer, if he had observed Gizmo carefully, might have channeled this adulation properly.

When war came and Gizmo came into contact with the enemy, such a trait might indicate a potential Medal of Honor winner. But there were too many things on the mind of "Big Ben" McMakin, the H Company CO, in those China days—guard, defense, standby, machine gun patrols, and the ever-increasing "incidents" around the Ichang Road bridge, where the sentries of the Japanese naval landing party glowered menacingly at the handful of Marines who barred their way to taking over the Settlement.

One cannot blame "Big Ben" for not preventing this excessive hero worship, for, after all, Gizmo was only a private in a company of 140 Marines. The skipper was a very busy man.

Most of us hated the parades, for the novelty had long ago departed. The conditioning marches, hiking at top speed with full packs, we hated even more. But Gizmo reveled in them, for his admired battalion commander, Lieutenant Colonel Henderson, would be there, and at the preliminary "troop and inspection" the battalion executive officer, Maj. Lewis B. "Chesty" Puller, might even call him by name, for that Marine officer knew every man in the battalion.

Gizmo, being a trusting soul, soon began to believe there was nothing the American nation, through its representatives in the Marine Corps, could not do. The Japanese would never dare start a war with the Marine Corps. Their army might be a bunch of mad dogs, but their navy knew the United States Marine Corps and had common sense. The Japanese navy would be the balance wheel for peace in the Far East.

When our regiment evacuated Shanghai in late November 1941, Gizmo's faith in the invincibility of his Corps was touching. He remarked, "It's just a tactical withdrawal to the islands. We are sending a big force out there, you know, and they do not want us here in China, out on a limb. As soon as they have enough Marines in the Philippines to make Tojo think a bit, the Fourth Marines will be sent back to China. From what they tell me about the Japanese out here, they have nothing but a third-rate army. The poor Chinese even have them stopped at the Yellow Bend and the Ichang Gorge. It would be a slaughter to hit them with a full division of Marines."

War came on the seventh day of December 1941. The regiment was scattered in the Olongapo-Mariveles area, digging defenses, ducking enemy bombs, burying their dead, and beginning to realize that there might not be any relief until it was too late. Gizmo kept his spirits up, and his cheerfulness was quite a contrast to the more realistic attitude of one of his fellow Marines. "They ought to lock some of you guys up, talking like that. They told us we lost two old battleships, the *Arizona* and the *Nevada*, and a worthless old target ship, the *Utah*. You people are talking like they sank a whole fleet, bah! In a short time that five-hundred-mile convoy will be here, with the Marine Corps on board. Then watch these little Japanese run!"

Even when he found out that ninety-odd enemy transports had filled up the sixty-mile-wide Lingayen Gulf to debark an army and its equipment; that eight American submarines had left Cavite to attack them around Christmas Day and had returned without ever firing a torpedo; that the Filipino army was withdrawing in plain sight of him to make their last stand on Bataan, he never worried. He dodged his bombs with the same feigned coolness of his officers and learned to take care of himself in the field, and he was a good Marine.

His company was the last one in his battalion to go to Corregidor that night of the twenty-seventh of December, for the army's coast artillery had more than enough to do in firing their guns against what they saw coming. The Marine regiment could be most useful in beach defense.

Two days later he might have been a bit disillusioned, under the heavy bombing Corregidor had taken. There were a lot of people killed, a lot more were wounded, and Bottomside was made into a shambles.

Gizmo had his cover in Middleside, just hard by the army brig. The place held several prisoners, for when war came, these men had flatly refused to fight for their country. The army had locked them up while they pondered what they were going to do about such goings-on.

The sergeant of the guard on the morning of the bombing was quite a character. As an old regular, those prisoners were poison to him, a disgrace to the Coast Artillery Corps. As the bombs screamed and burst against the crescendo of *pow* and *boom* of antiaircraft guns, there were cries of "first aid" at Middleside, and here we first heard the battle cry of the Marine Corps, "Corpsman! Corpsman!"

The sergeant of the guard took great pains to inform his detested charges of all the gory details, adding the fictitious observation that, "The barracks are on fire at the other end, and the wind is blowing this way!" The smoke from the burning post exchange, a wooden structure, lent realism to his tale, and the fumes of picric acid from the bombs further heightened it. As the air raids continued, the prisoners screamed in fear, shaking the bars of the cellblock in a piteous attempt to obtain release. The sergeant sadly informed them that he had no orders to let them out. From time to time the prisoners were apprised, all too faithfully, of their danger. The Marines laughed heartily at the efforts of the sergeant to be entertaining and spurred that good man on to further heights. Gizmo thought the situation was as funny as the others did. This sadistic performance lasted some three and a half hours while the bombing went on.

A day or so later found all of the battalion in defensive sectors, for the army had moved them from that death trap of Middleside Barracks onto the beaches. Gizmo was posted in James Ravine.

Here he came to know and to respect the white officers and the brown soldiers of the 91st Scout Artillery. Frequent bombings, replied to energetically by the 60th Antiaircraft Regiment, taught him to think that the army was quite a good thing, almost up to the standards of his own Corps. Like all Marines, in the beginning he was very earnest and

careful to hide his fear and worry about getting killed. It is
almost a religion with Marines to keep our comrades from
knowing how scared we are. In the First World War the fatalistic attitude was expressed as follows: "If the shell or
bullet has your number on it, there is nothing you can do to
avert it. So long as your number does not come up, you have
no fear of going west." The new philosophy was: "It might
happen to all of you other men, but never to me." Like reli-
gions, philosophies change with the times. The splendid indifference to danger shown by army officers of the 60th and
90th Regiments, as well as that put on by his own Marine
officers, gave vast confidence to Gizmo. In his ignorance, he
fancied the Bataan and Corregidor lines as impregnable.
Never for an instant did he doubt what he read on the battalion bulletin board. When the dramatic radio message as-
cribed to Mr. Frank Knox, secretary of the navy, appeared,
saying, "Hold on for seventy-two hours, for help is on the
way," his simple Marine's faith of believing implicitly in
what his superiors told him remained unshaken. Others
laughed bitterly and derided the "Help is on the way" statement, but Gizmo's faith in that five-hundred-mile-long
convoy and the coming of the 1st Marine Division was
touching.

The news of the fall of Singapore, depressing as it was to
others, bothered him but a little. He was heard to say, "What
can you expect of a nation of slaves and a few white men?
The Malayans see no reason to fight merely for a change of
masters. These Filipinos are fighting for freedom, not for a
change of chains." He had been listening to the Manila
Japanese radio, broadcast in English, to break down our
morale, and had picked up some of their phrases, no doubt.
Still, they had failed to depress him.

He was greatly impressed by the biography of Gen.
Douglas MacArthur as it was read out to him and as he
heard it over our own radio station, "The Voice of Freedom." He had never seen the supreme commander, but he
worshiped him with a devotion born of implicit confidence.

Even in the evening, as the Cabcaben airfield across the North Channel from the James Ravine received its regular daily bombing, Gizmo had no doubts. Even when the enemy set up their guns on the Cavite shore, and our Rock began to find out a little of what enemy shellfire was like, he still seemed to have no worries. He stood his defense watch like the others, did not run from bombs and shells, and came to the notice of Gunnery Sergeant Szalkewicz, who suggested he be promoted to corporal, with profit to Gizmo himself and to his platoon.

One day, early in the morning, we got the rumor that General MacArthur had left for the south. The current talk ran, "Just as far as Cebu to check up on things. Maybe he'll go a bit further and look-see at Mindanao and then come back." There were other more biting remarks about our Allies, that, "Our general is not like those cowardly limey generals who bailed out just before Singapore fell. He'll be back, we know it!"

But the rumor persisted and was confirmed the next day by an order couched in a well-known, exalted style. Some phrases stick in my memory after all these years: "The front has now become stabilized"; "I am ordered to Australia, to lead back the relief force for the Philippines"; and that classic line, "I shall return!"

For most of us, such verbal reassurance was useless. We had more or less known all along that there just was not any help coming. Like death, we had refused to think much about it. We had all taken out our insurance, written our letters of false cheer home, set our affairs in such order as we could, and tried not to worry.

I'm not sure, but I believe this was about the same time that Gizmo began to show the beginnings of "war neurosis, hysteria, acute." In the beginning there was very little of it visible among us, for we tried extremely hard to hide our fear from our fellow Marines. But after two months and more of almost daily bombing and shelling, like a contagious disease, it was beginning to rear its ugly head. Gizmo was seen to go around in a sort of daze, his mouth half open, his lower jaw quivering, and his hands held alongside his waist, trembling and shaking.

The shelling from Cavite hit a three-inch ammunition dump in the ravine, just above us, and that caused hundreds of rounds of ammunition to be fired off. Bursts and the whining of red-hot steel splinters hurtling through the air to maim and kill made us take cover in that exposed area. Gizmo's post was in a trench on the beach, perfectly safe from that inferno up in the ravine, yet he slipped away to cower in the gloom and darkness of the nearby Dirt Tunnel. The gunnery sergeant missed him, searched the tunnel, and yanked him out. He figured it was just a case of temporary jitters, as he had seen it happen to lots of good men during the First World War. There was earnest talk with the sergeant and the corporal in charge of the beach position, and all three of them conferred with Gizmo himself. Their combined efforts might have borne fruit had not the young man been able to see so clearly the flashes of the 155mm guns of the Filipino army up by Cabcaben, just across the North Channel from the trenches. Closer and closer those flashes backed up to Corregidor each day, for the Bataan lines were slowly withdrawing under the Japanese assault. One could not argue convincingly with that sight across the channel. The gunnery sergeant had to admit failure.

The matter was one that obviously required some pondering. The army used to read off to us some of its courts-martial cases "for the encouragement of the others"; I vaguely recall the words, "To be dishonorably discharged from the service, with forfeiture of all pay and allowances due or about to become due, and to be confined at hard labor for a period of ten years." I think it was in the case of a sentry who had deserted his post. First Sergeant Richard "Bozo" Duncan was informed of how matters stood by the platoon leader, First Lieutenant Tistadt, for it was felt he might have influence with Gizmo. He set out to look up the erring one, but he didn't find him at first for there were bombs falling in the ravine. After the debris and the wounded had been cleared away, "Bozo" found Gizmo in the James Ravine bombproof, a deserter from his post, shaming his regiment before a startled group of 91st Filipino Scouts, for these men had never before seen a Marine give way to such an uncontrolled paroxysm of stark, naked fear. Big "Bozo" seized his man with no gentle hand and led him away. The "top soldier" had been a Quantico football and baseball player of some fame a few years back, and he feared no man, only his wife.

In the seclusion of the Dirt Tunnel he spoke earnestly with Gizmo, and it is to be feared that he may have used physical violence in his efforts to put some sense into what, in his opinion, ought to have been a good Marine.

A day or so later the Bataan front fell (9 April 1942). Across the channel the ammunition dumps, set on fire by the defenders to prevent the Japanese from getting them, turned night into dreadful day. All that day and all of the next, fugitives streamed across the channel by boat, by raft, on broken timbers, and some even by swimming. The same day that saw the collapse of Bataan marked the advent of the enemy's artillery fire in our back door. It was never to cease as long as we held out.

At Gizmo's position, open and exposed to the enemy a little over forty-one hundred yards away, all of the camouflage was knocked down by the exploding shells. The indefatigable Marines and Scouts of the beach gun positions managed to keep a covering of a sort continually in position, but without any help from Gizmo. He was generally cowering and shaking in the bombproof nearest at hand.

The first sergeant was finally forced to admit to his company commander, Capt. Benjamin L. McMakin, that he had failed in his duty to bring Gizmo back to ordinary standards and had to ask "Big Ben" for help. The captain was fully aware of the trouble and in his wisdom he had held aloof, for he had hoped that "Bozo" and the gunnery sergeant could take care of the matter properly. Now it was thrown up to him officially, and he was required to act in the duties of his commission.

The army had a more modern and humane way of taking

care of such men. They put them in front of the doctor, who looked them over with care and marked some for the hospital with the diagnosis of "war neurosis, hysteria, acute." Some others of whom we are aware were retained at Middleside with no duties, but they were required to come down to James Ravine for their meals, over a mile of tumbled ground and under much bombing and shellfire. It was felt that the urge of hunger would overcome that of fear. I may add that this remedy failed, and the "patients" were placed in the hospital.

The mind of "Big Ben" ran to simplicity and old-fashioned ideas. (He never was to live to see release and learn the new term, "combat fatigue." Had he done so, his snort of contempt can be imagined for the foolish doctors who devised such frills and fancies for fighting men.) He was fully cognizant of the danger of the contagion of fear, for cowardice might spread like wildfire at the wrong time. At the present moment it seemed decidedly that the Japanese were going to honor "Big Ben's" beach position with a landing party.

He went through the formality of a talk with Gizmo, yet he felt it was hopeless from the beginning. Gizmo had lost all of the simple, childlike faith in the officers that he had once had and now, if one talked to him, he began to get incoherent and helpless. There were by that time no berths left in the hospital, for it was flooded with the wounded and even the malaria patients could not be admitted.

"Dose them with quinine and keep them in the lines," seemed to be the order of the day. So far, no Marines had appeared on the casualty lists of the hospital with this "war neurosis, hysteria, acute," and "Big Ben," a proud man, surely did not want this dubious honor to fall to his company. One heard rumors that Gizmo was slapped with stinging blows, for "Big Ben" was forthright in his simplicity. Gizmo was returned to his beach trench to be especially watched, and the skipper hoped for a change for the better.

Soon began the terrible bombardment by the enemy's 240mm guns. Incoming shells from 105s and 150s were certainly bad enough, but these huge shells with delayed action fuses dug into the ground, shivered it like an earthquake, and then blew up with terrific force. You could not patch up your emplacements any too well after the 240s paid you a visit. So after the first of these violent bombardments and Gizmo's escape from his keepers, the "Old Man," Lt. Col. H. R. Anderson, had forced upon him the unpleasant duty of "office hours."

Gizmo was not alone in his disgrace. One sergeant who had a dangerous post on the Topside tennis court was allowed a reasonable length of time to eat dinner. When it was proved that he had exceeded it, the "Old Man" decided to make a corporal of him, for this sergeant had been on Marine Corps expeditions before in his time. If he showed up well in his new rank, the "Old Man" would give him back his third stripe. Several of the new men, none of them Marines attached to us after their escape from Bataan, including white soldiers and Filipinos, were charged with "war neurosis"; the "Old Man" was outraged, and properly so. The offenders were scathingly denounced and their officers were ordered to put a guard over them in their positions. Two Marines were then brought in for the same offense, and the battalion commander appeared to be both shocked and hurt. In his stern warning he appealed to the honor of the Marine Corps, for these were his old Shanghai men.

There was no brig safe enough from enemy shellfire in which to lock up these men. Under the Articles for the Government of the Navy, they were liable to be court-martialed and shot for their crimes. The "Old Man" did not have the heart to do this, as a general court-martial was a thing of shame and disgrace, and to be avoided if possible. He had hopes that a personal appeal to their better natures would be effective.

Last of all in the dismal parade, the sergeant major marched in Gizmo.

"Big Ben" stood at attention beside the trembling Marine, while now and then the ground rocked from the shock of a 240mm round exploding just outside the sandbagged revetment at the mouth of the bombproof. The battalion commander minced no words in his judgment, saying, "Captain, you've tried everything in the world to keep this man on duty at his assigned post. I hereby solemnly order you to detail a tough noncommissioned officer over him with a club to beat him unmercifully if he runs away under fire. If this does not cure him, we will have him court-martialed before a general court, and, if found guilty, he may be properly shot."

These were decidedly words of a most nonregulation nature coming from a commanding officer, but these were strenuous times. I still remember the set, grim look on the "Old Man's" face, made more so by the shadows of the flickering candles, for the incoming shellfire had severed the lighting cables. I knew his sentence to be hard, but just, under such circumstances. And while the ground rocked again and again from those horrid bursts outside our shelter, there came a dull stench of picric acid into the stifling air, for the shellfire had also broken the ventilators upon the hill above us.

There came a lull, and "Big Ben" took Gizmo away and turned him over to the gunnery sergeant. A very tough corporal was given his instructions and departed in search of a suitable club. While he was on this mission, the big cannons opened up again on the beach defenses. Gizmo ran for the safety of the Dirt Tunnel in his hysterical fear. The corporal, coming back with his "tommy gun" slung over his left shoulder and a formidable bludgeon in his right hand, was directed to Gizmo's place of refuge. With grim purpose written on his features, he located his quarry.

Just what happened next will never be set down with exactitude; you know how eyewitnesses differ in their testimony, and the Dirt Tunnel was lit by only a single candle. The consensus seemed to be that Gizmo, when he heard his name called and saw his nemesis loom up in the shadows before him, put his rifle muzzle to his breast, paused for a dreadful, fear-stricken second, and then pulled the trigger.

The hole blown out of his back was as big as the palm of a man's hand, for a Springfield bullet usually "keyholes" through flesh and bone. There was an agonized spasm, a heave of his chest, and Gizmo lay dead. No longer would he fear the Japanese bombardment or, more fearsome still, the expected enemy landing on the shores of James Ravine. Now that knowledge had ceased, he knew all the answers.

The sergeant major and the orderly clerk cursed bitterly when they heard the news, for they would have to write up the precept, the proceedings, and the findings of the court of inquiry together with certain other writings, for there is much paperwork in connection with a suicide case. Courts and boards demand perfect work, free from erasures, smudges, and strikeovers. There was no light except that of candles in the bombproof, but they wearily shrugged their shoulders and began typing.

The findings had such phrases as "death from gunshot wound, self-inflicted, while mentally deranged," and kindly Doctor Wade saw to it that there was the very important "Death in the line of duty" inserted, so that the dead Marine's parents would come into his insurance and perhaps six months of dependents' pay.

The "Old Man," quiet and subdued, read over the papers and signed his approval. It was the last such document he was ever to sign as a reviewing authority. A little less than three years later he was to go to his judgment before the Highest Court of All while his prison ship was sinking. He was a Marine who never shrank from his duty.

"I wonder what makes a man crack up that way?" asked the sergeant major of the orderly. "Gizmo was a damned good Marine up until six weeks or so ago."

The orderly busied himself in the files and finally placed an open one before his superior noncommissioned officer. The latter read, while the former's finger stabbed out phrases as "The front has now become stabilized," "Bring back the relief force to the Philippines," and "I shall return!"

The eyes of the sergeant major narrowed. "Sergeant," he

said, in his most rasping, official tone, "any more such insinuations and I'll run you up in front of the colonel for stirring up sedition to the detriment of morale in the face of the enemy, the United States now being in a state of war! What you need is a good biff in the jaw! Put that damned file away and get busy on today's strength and casualty reports!"

16

THE STORY OF FIRST
SERGEANT SANTALESES

His first name I have forgotten, if I ever knew it. I am none too sure that his last name is spelled correctly, but it is close enough. He served as first sergeant of the Headquarters Battery of the 91st Regiment of Coast Artillery, Philippine Scouts. This last entry should thoroughly identify him.

I got to know quite a number of Filipinos in the early days of World War II, as long as Corregidor held out. I often marveled at the ability of the Philippine army, starved and half wrecked with malaria, to hold the Bataan lines in the face of the overwhelming strength of the advancing Japanese for as long as they did. If this force had a fair percentage of "first soldiers" of Santaleses's type, there was my explanation.

His regiment manned the minefields and the mobile 155mm guns. Their crest was a griffin, a mythological beast, with some sort of Latin inscription that few of us understood. Being Marines, we had only slight interest in such matters. Santaleses himself, with quiet pride, answered my query in his precise, correct English, and told me just what a griffin was.

"Sir, it is a fabulous animal with the body and legs of a lion and the head and wings of an eagle, signifying the union of strength and agility. We employ it as an emblem of vigilance, since the animal is supposed to be the guardian of hidden mines and the key to untold treasures. Sir, our regiment mans the hidden mines by laying them, maintaining the electrical connections, and operating them from the mine casement. Also, sir, our Corregidor in Spanish means the governor or controller of the entrance to Manila Bay, our key to these untold treasures. We are very proud that the American officers gave us such a crest for our regimental insignia. All of our men can tell you just what I have said, for it is taught to them as recruits. I thank you for your interest in our Scouts, sir."

In the beginning our feelings about our Filipino allies had been uncertain. In the Cavite Navy Yard we had known only workers, servants, and civilians of a nondescript class. Our contacts at the Olongapo naval station had been much the same. Too many of the natives had been purveyors to our vices and foibles, for one finds these folk the world over, wherever men are in uniform with payday money burning holes in their pockets. Our seaport towns should not be judged solely by those carrion crows that infest the waterfronts, only too eager to separate a Marine from his money. Too often the uniform is a password to the underworld. When we came to know the Scouts we changed our opinion.

An irate old colonel of field artillery (he earlier had commanded a regiment in Bataan), when he was senior officer prisoner in a hospital ward in Cabanatuan, once gave way to his anger. The listless efforts we Americans made toward keeping the barracks clean and our flagrant ignoring of the doctor's orders, transmitted through him, caused his ire. "I have said it before, and I repeat it now," the fiery old soldier told us, "had I my choice of commanding Scouts or Americans, I would take the Scouts every time. When an order is given to the Scouts, it is carried out to the best of their ability. But among the Americans there is a large percentage of men who immediately try to see how they can circumvent what they are told to do."

By this time we knew and respected the Scouts. The colonel's words stirred some to anger and low, muttered curses. I knew him to be dead right. And I reflected on Santaleses, an outstanding Scout. Was he not a first sergeant?

We came to know the man and his battery around the end of December and the early days of January, in the years of 1941 and 1942. In the following four months we came to know them intimately. We Marines take our hats off to them.

The 2d Battalion of our 4th Marine Regiment had its command post, the Headquarters Company, Company F, and Company H located in James Ravine, manning the beach defenses of the North Channel, with the rest of its units located at Middleside and the South Shore. We had been under severe bombing and knew what it meant to have comrades wounded and killed. We had marched down to James Ravine under severe nervous tension to relieve the 91st sentries in the dark. The rest of us were assigned to billet areas and turned in to sleep, mostly on stony ground.

The next morning we took stock of our cover, the defenses we were required to build, and our new comrades, the Headquarters Battery and Mine Detachment of this strange 91st Regiment. Under their seemingly careless, quiet attitude was concealed an amazing efficiency, though we could not see it then. We asked one another, "Don't these fellows realize there's a war on?" to be answered by, "My God, what else can you expect from a bunch of dumb gooks?" Marines use this term to describe natives in the countries where they go to "protect American lives and property," the "situation well in hand" stuff, as the newspapers like to describe it. It is worthy of note that in a short time the term "gook" was seldom heard. It was replaced by "Filipino" and finally by the simple word "Scout."

The Japanese air raids came with deadly frequency. There was much damage to our defenses, and every now and then a Marine was killed, and more of them were wounded. The Scouts mingled with us. We shared their shelters, we partook of their freely given rations, and we began to be aware of First Sergeant Santaleses.

He was a little man by our physical standards; among Filipinos he would be considered medium-sized. He was broad-shouldered, lean, and wiry. His walk was the strut of the born soldier, proud of his uniform and corps. Looking at him, I thought of the adventurous Chinese traders with their frail junks, beating out the typhoons of the China Sea; I mused on the conquistadors of Spain, and Manila galleons; and the dons who had mated with native Malay and Chinese stock, with their ultimate product being this first sergeant of the Scouts. His face, that mirror of the soul, was firm, without a trace of that arrogance so commonly attributed to "topkickers" in cartoons and comic strips. His manner was respectful to his officers, and equally so to all of us Marines and those sailors who later came to join us from their beached ships, but never deferential or cringing. He was the first sergeant of his battery and very proud of that fact. Altogether, I decided he was a most satisfactory sort of man to have on one's side in a tight spot, and a very tight spot we were in, I can assure you.

The white men had done considerable looting of burned-out buildings. I recall the first time we were bombed at Middleside, when in the midst of death and attempting to conceal our terror, for we fancied the barracks walls were going to cave in on us, the nearby post exchange building was set afire by five-hundred-pound bombs. Men were seen darting in and out of the black cloud of smoke. Afterward, orders came from the army threatening with punishment those men found in possession of stolen wristwatches and other such small articles. Those miscreants who had drunk up the beer stores in a burning inferno were not chided, for that would have been a mere waste of paperwork.

Then I recall with delight the barge of some two thousand ton capacity that broke loose from its moorings in Manila Bay. Under the seaward current it drifted south from Manila and gently came to rest in the shallows under the cliffs at Battery Point on our Rock. Our 3d Battalion discovered it to be loaded to the gunwales with case goods. There were prunes, raisins, apricots, apples, and figs— all first-quality dried fruit. There was also sugar, canned milk, chocolate slabs, and tinned butter. All of us were then on half rations, for Lieutenant General Wainwright was prudently hoarding the immense supplies in the Malinta Tunnel. There was the Bataan army to feed, besides us. We had settled down for a siege with some hope of relief, for had not Secretary Knox's radio message said, "Hold out for seventy-two hours; help is on the way!"

The 3d Battalion was hungry and could not be blamed too much for helping themselves. They remembered their comrades of the other two battalions and passed the glad word. Our mess sergeant, Leon B. Ellis, procured a truck and filled several hiding places to capacity. He then thought of his friends in the Scouts and offered his truck to the battery mess sergeant. Santaleses was informed and asked his colonel, for being a good soldier, he knew that looting of such stores was strictly forbidden.

The colonel gave approval; a detail was furnished; several trips were made, and a good supply was covered with a convenient tarpaulin. Our mess sergeant never told his colonel until he had finished looting and placed a case of raisins in the "Old Man's" command post. Good soldier Santaleses asked his commander first, before his men took a single thing.

The gorged Marines then cut the army in on the deal, and the 60th Coast Artillery was busy for several days. After a week of this happy life, the army quartermaster, from the depths and gloom of the Malinta Tunnel, discovered the skullduggery. The military police rushed forth to safeguard the cargo—there was nearly a third of it left, surprisingly—while the quartermaster's merry men labored to swell the stores in Malinta. And there issued forth from the headquarters of the high command stern mandates about looting.

For a while we stuffed ourselves with rare viands and drank lovely chocolate flavored with milk and sugar and even buttered. But, an end must come to all good things. Our stores ran out and the kindly Scouts shared theirs with us, for they did not have our gluttony. I remember that barge with much pleasure.

Before the Scouts left their pleasant Topside quarters they had amassed a good library. The place had been heavily bombed by now, but there were lots of books left, and reading matter would be appreciated. First Sergeant Santaleses got permission to enter the place with his men—all bombed and burned buildings were *verboten*—and we had books in plenty.

The married Filipino Scouts and native employees, together with some of the "dobe" white soldiers married to the natives, lived in two barrios, the smaller at Middleside and the larger, called San Jose, located at Bottomside. This latter enjoyed a cockpit, for the army is tolerant in such matters, especially where cockfighting is the national sport. Heavy bombing had destroyed much of the church, and the adjacent cockpit had suffered but to a lesser extent. The Sunday morning spectacle was now a thing of the past. But the ancient battery mechanic of the Scouts had a few cocks and a setting hen that the battery watched with anxious eyes, for some of the Marines had been looking at the birds with evil intent. Repeated bombings killed off the cocks, one by one, but that mother hen was able to hatch her little brood in James Ravine. Santaleses told some of us that he deplored cockfighting, but that his men were wild over it and he perforce had to tolerate it. Someday he hoped his people would substitute baseball, perhaps, in place of this brutal pastime. He remarked that Americans in northern Luzon had induced the wild tribes to cease their quaint custom of taking heads from the next valley by having them expend their exuberance in baseball games and track meets against each other. When he retired he had vague plans of joining a movement and devoting some portion of time to gently weaning his people away from the degrading sport of cockfighting.

A shell killed the mother hen, but her little ones survived the surrender. I fear the victorious Japanese discovered the chicks and put them in their stew pots.

We Marines took shameful advantage of the Scouts. We moved in on their rations and took much of their bunk space in the bombproof. We preempted their radio and abused their gentle natures in diverse ways. But, our little brown brothers had the last laugh on us all in the end. One was an inveterate gambler with a high degree of skill, and his years of association with American soldiers had made him an expert at dice, poker, and blackjack. Alas, one is reluctantly forced to admit that of his many virtues, honesty in games of chance is not his most outstanding one. Bombs and shells might hit in the ravine, but the gaming went on, day and night. Naked lights after dark were strictly forbidden, but the illumination afforded by the bright moon was sufficient to read the cards. Daily the Marines and sailors with an occasional soldier left the gaming center sadder, but no wiser, men.

These games appeared to be conducted under the auspices of the regimental supply sergeant of the Scouts, and he was reported to be taking a cut of an undisclosed amount of money. The professionals who owned the tables hired a decrepit old private of the regimental band, one Solomon, and gave a peso per table to the white-haired ancient to clean and police the area, besides repairing bomb and shellfire damage. Santaleses, when chided by some of the virtuous element among the Marines about the propriety of his battery being a gambling hall, frankly laughed at them. His fixed opinion was that it was futile to try to stop a pernicious vice long established by custom, and besides, where else could the men spend their money? When a man was wanted in a hurry, the first sergeant knew where to find him. Woe betides the Scout who slipped over to the Cold Storage or Bakery games if Santaleses found out about it. While he never said so, it was most obvious that he preferred keeping the battery's money at home. Santaleses, I might add, was never seen participating in any game.

The Scouts set up a shoe shop under a corporal named Andales. This fellow was one of the better known gamblers, always on the lookout for a loose dollar if it could be honestly made. He found out that Marines would pay a peso for a shoe repair job, and soon after, Santaleses found out the same thing. What was probably said to the good Andales was not disclosed, but the practice ceased. All shoes were fixed free, and with charming courtesy.

Over in Fort Frank, a tiny islet in the bay and some eight hundred yards from the Cavite shore, a continual fight with the enemy was being carried on. Besides the usual artillery duels, they sprayed one another with machine gun fire. The baffled Japanese tried night landings to silence such audacity, but the battalion of the 91st, with their white brethren of the 59th Heavy Artillery, repulsed them bloodily. The angered Japanese then moved in a big 240mm battery and really worked the place over. The little steel and concrete fort, so strongly built, resisted all efforts until one Sunday morning when disaster struck. The men were all lined up in their main tunnel for some kind of inspection—the army is most particular about these things, even in the midst of war—when a "two-forty" shell hit the top deck, did a ricochet, discovered an air vent, went down the opening, and burst with deadly force. The Scouts told us the death toll was 140 men. Replacements were in order, and fast.

A number of officers' servants had elected to stay with their masters instead of leaving the Rock for Manila before the siege started. Some of these men performed their humble chores in James Ravine, and some were prominent among the gamblers. First Sergeant Santaleses and others spoke to them, and a number of them agreed to enlist in the 91st for duty at Fort Frank.

I remember the scene very well. In the rear of the James Ravine bombproof, by the flickering light of candles stuck in bottles, before the colonel and the adjutant, a group of young boys nearing twenty years of age stood at eager attention during the impressive ceremony of the military oath. The color sergeants stood by the national and regimental banners of silk, and all available officers were at attention. First Sergeant Santaleses stood alongside Sergeant Major Umbrero, both noncommissioned officers resplendent in starched khaki, pistol belts, and leggings with glittering brass eyelets, and shoes polished like mirrors.

Outside was heard the dull sound of exploding shells,

bursts from the battery of "One-o-fives" on the Cavite shore mixed with the more frequent explosions of one of our burning ammunition dumps. We Marines who had duties in the tunnel looked with bored indifference at such military foolishness. Had we been capable of understanding, we too would have stood at rigid attention, for we were witnessing the secret soul of a regiment. The formation was at last over, the first sergeant barked his "About face, march!" and the lads strode proudly from the bombproof, for they were now Scouts. The personnel adjutant took them over to Fort Frank, for he had the pay duty and could kill two birds with one stone.

It was noted that First Sergeant Santaleses accompanied him. The noblesse oblige of the first sergeant rank was shown in its clear purity, for it was a perilous voyage by boat and in the darkness, being beset by bombing and shellfire. One imagines that there were other such scenes taking place elsewhere on the island, for there were 140 replacements needed for the dead alone, and James Ravine could furnish only a part of that number.

A reserve line some eight hundred yards long was established up the ravine and manned by twenty-seven Filipino mess attendants, reservists called back after sixteen years of naval service, and some fifty of the Scouts—bandsmen, clerks, carpenters, cobblers, messengers, motorcycle riders, tailors, and such other gentry that one may find in a regimental headquarters battery. A sergeant major of Marines was in command with Sergeant Larsen of the Pay Department, a property corporal named Morvan, and First Sergeant Pearlstein, all from the battalion Headquarters Company of the 2d Battalion of the 4th Marines. The sergeant major spoke long and earnestly to the army colonel, asking for Santaleses, for he knew his man. He got him.

The position was dangerous. A barrage might indicate a coming landing. When the curtain of fire descended, these men had to go out and man their foxholes. They had one good break—a Marine lieutenant and his men had already started the holes in that rocky soil.

Those Marines took Santaleses and the leader they had chosen from the mess attendants to go over their plans for defending the position. There is nothing like a good, personal reconnaissance—what they call in China a "look-see"—if you have time to do it. The foxholes were a little too shallow, so it was decided to send the men up in small groups, each man to dig his own little hole a bit deeper. There were twenty-one ammunition dumps along that Upper Belt Line Road, all open and all highly dangerous if a bomb or shell should set them off.

The Marines were gratified to learn that First Sergeant Santaleses knew quite a bit about this type of work, of fields of fire, of command posts, and of mutual support. They had imagined him as only an artilleryman. Questioning revealed Santaleses to have learned his soldering trade originally in the Philippine Scouts infantry, before a wife and numerous progeny had required him to transfer to the coast artillery and the quarters at San Jose barrio. He spoke of eleven little prospective Scouts and army nurses whose fate in Japanese-held Manila was unknown to him.

The paymaster Marine was told to prepare a detailed sketch, for he was known to have some slight skill in such matters. The next day Santaleses submitted a map complete with ammunition dumps, culverts, road junctions, trees, foxholes, and all the things that delight the heart of a to-pographer. His foxhole printed the name of each Scout, and the mapmaker said if the sergeant major would give him the names and assignments of the others, he would insert them in their proper places. He did this and was thanked, for that Upper Belt Line Road was under intermittent shellfire and had been for some time.

Colonel Anderson was informed and given a copy of the sketch, with full credit being given to the first sergeant. Santaleses glowed with pride when his own colonel and the Marines' "Old Man" took time out to thank him personally.

Bataan fell, and this put the enemy at our back door. Singapore was built to defend against a sea attack, and when the back door on land was taken, they were finished. So it was with us, only we lasted a month, less three days, where they lasted hardly a day or so. Now 290 cannon—105s, 150s, and 240mm guns bolstered with enemy plane bombings—began pounding us day and night. It was death for the crew of any fixed gun emplacement to try and fight back, for a single outgoing round brought back a reply of hundreds. The 91st Scouts manned roving tractor-drawn 155s and rendered a good account of them.

Some radio commentator in the States, whose broadcast was heard faintly over the shortwave radio, likened life on Corregidor and the fortified islands to "living on a bull's eye on the target range." His phrase was very apt, much truer than he probably had realized.

When barrages were slammed down on the ravine, the word was passed to "man the reserve lines." The pay man and the property corporal got the mess attendants out of the galley tunnel and were not entirely pleased with the dilatory way these men left their shelter for their foxholes. But the sergeant major and the first sergeant of Marines found no fault with Santaleses and his Scouts. They were usually there ahead of their men.

The morning of the emperor's birthday, 29 April 1942, was a thing of terror and a foretaste of the hell to come. For some thirty minutes, "two-forty" shells had been hitting the island every five seconds, in addition to artillery of other types and much bombing. The Scouts manned a 75mm cannon just above the reserve position. The casement was hit by a two-forty shell and the crew was buried. Despite the intensity of the fire, rescue parties ran out in the open, climbed the cliff, and began to dig out the survivors. Of twelve, five were pulled out alive, but all were wounded. Marine Gunnery Sergeant Davis directed the rescue, but he always gave the credit to Santaleses. First Sergeant Joe Pearlstein was very active in this affair and he, too, spoke highly of the Filipino first sergeant. It took a lot of guts to venture up to that place that terrible morning.

On the night of the fifth of May the long-expected landing came, but at an unexpected point. James Ravine was the

closest place, a scant forty-one hundred yards across the
North Channel from Bataan. Instead, the wily Japanese
struck at the waist of the island, where the pollywog's head
that stops at Malinta Hill becomes the long tail leading out
to Monkey Point. Here the 1st Battalion, 4th Marines had
only a few tunnels, and those of small capacity. The soil, of
virgin rock, made foxholes nearly impossible to dig. There
was a scarcity of dynamite. For several days there had been
a heavy bombardment in that area, but the other end of Malinta, next to the North Mine Dock, had been even more
heavily bombarded. Likewise, James Ravine had been given
close attention by the Japanese artillery.

The 1st Battalion, with the Reserve Battalion of sailors
and a few Marines, met the enemy bravely and well. A few
Scouts of the 92d Artillery and some other Filipinos stood
their ground with the Marines. There was an epic fight, but
the odds were just too great. All of the big cannon, except
for very few, were damaged beyond repair, and the lone
searchlight left that stabbed out at the landing barges was
quickly shot out.

Over at James Ravine, a heavy barrage was laid down as
a feint. Reserve lines were ordered manned. The Marine pay
sergeant and the property corporal ran through exploding
shells up to the galley tunnel, and by their valiant efforts the
mess attendants manned their flank, for the mess tunnel was
just below the position. Santaleses and the Scouts had a
longer route to get to their right flank and they had two
strong culverts, some deep ditches, and good cover for part
of the way. One would have expected them to move slowly,
stopping under such cover as this route afforded while the
shells burst and sent red-hot, screaming fragments of steel
hurtling through the air.

The sergeant major and his first sergeant were now at
Middleside. A phone call routed them out and they raced
down the hill. As they reached the position the barrage
stopped. They heard a resolute voice call out, "Who goes
there?" and they saw Corporal Viola, the quartermaster's

clerk of the Scouts. As he stood by his foxhole in the road, his fixed bayonet glittered in the moonlight and his extra bandolier was swung across his chest. Receiving an affirmative to their question, "Is Santaleses here?" they raced on. The first sergeant of Marines dropped off at his place in the center of the line, while the sergeant major ran farther on to see about the mess attendants. When he found them all in their places, he reported over his field phone, "Position manned and in readiness, sir!" Since Santaleses was there, he felt it unnecessary to check on the Scouts. He knew they would be in position.

First Sergeant Santaleses reported he had no men killed or wounded. It was a miracle. When he was asked, "Why didn't you stop for cover under the culverts or use those ditches on your way up here?" his reply was simple and direct: "Our battery commander said nothing about stopping to take cover; he told us to man the line." This answer was worthy of the highest traditions of the Scouts.

He never got the chance to close with the enemy, for the island was surrendered that morning. Now and then I saw him during the next eighteen days on Corregidor, and he helped Doctor Wade as a stretcher-bearer for the sick and the dead. I lost sight of him in the Old Bilibid Prison when they sent the Scouts to Camp O'Donnell while we went off to Cabanatuan.

I heard they released the Scouts after a while, for too many of them were dying in Camp O'Donnell. Strange to relate, the Americans stood imprisonment better than the native Filipinos. Doctor Weinstein, who was there, said the death rate was 440 men a day at Camp O'Donnell!

On our way to Japan in the fall of 1944, while in the Old Bilibid Prison for processing, I asked Dr. Wade whether he had ever heard from Santaleses. "Yes," he said, "I think so. I feel sure I saw him on the street one day, while I was under guard coming back from the port area. Since then I have been receiving a little food and some native medicines. How they are slipped over the high prison wall, I do not know. I feel sure it is Santaleses's doing. Think of it! He has quite a large family, yet he manages to remember us at the risk of his own life. You know the Filipinos here are starving."

I have never heard of him since. I feel sure he mixed himself into the Battle of Manila, for he was a fighting man. Of course, I hope and pray—for some Marines do pray, occasionally—that he and his tribe of little prospective Scouts and army nurses are alive and well. With some four years of back pay coming to him, and his family allowances, a prudent man like him could live in affluence in the islands.

I like to think of him for his simple, direct answer, "We were ordered to man the position, sir. The battery commander said nothing about stopping to take cover." I also like to think about that griffin, that "fabulous animal with the body and legs of a lion and the head and wings of an eagle, signifying the union of strength and agility." Within the lion's body is his heart, and First Sergeant Santaleses, Headquarters Battery, 91st Regiment of Coast Artillery, Philippine Scouts, certainly had the heart of the king of beasts.

17

FISH STORIES

No collection of Marine Corps yarns should be without its fish stories, so for the Isaak Walton trade some are being included.

During the siege of Corregidor in the spring of 1942, the Japanese were the unwitting cause of adding to the scant rations of our beleaguered garrison. They can by no means be considered among the world's best bombers. The little island was a hard place to hit, at best, and, in addition, the antiaircraft guns of the 60th Coast Artillery unnerved the Japanese pilots to the extent of causing the bombers to deflect from their courses. Many bombs were dropped in attempts to hit the Rock, but exploded harmlessly in the waters offshore. Consequently, large numbers of fish were stunned and floated to the surface.

Filipinos are generally good swimmers and absolutely fearless in the water when they are hungry. So after each bombing, the water was black with the heads of the swimmers, and they bagged large quantities of fish. Frequently the white soldiers, sailors, and Marines would join in the foraging.

Among the many varieties of fish thus added to our scant rations, I recall with pleasure barracuda, sardines, *laplapa* (a kind of bottom-fish, but tasty and tender), and a fellow we called a banana fish, a yellow-tinted one with a scalloped dorsal fin, weighing nearly a pound.

After we became prisoners we were occasionally fed salt fish. The smell of these fish, partially decayed, was enough to lift off your hat, but we knew our desperate need for the phosphorus and protein they carried, so we ate them gladly, if not always with relish. In addition, the camp commissary sold a form of fish sausage, generally swarming with worms. If the sausage was cooked well enough, it tasted fine. We thought the fish to be the *dalag*, a tiny specimen that frequent the rice paddies. During the dry season he burrows down deep for moisture and sort of hibernates, if that term can be applied to the finny tribe, and emerges from his oozy mud when the rains fill the rice paddy walls. We heard it was the most important food fish in the Philippines.

Some of the prisoners who were sent out on detail to Bataan reported seeing a strange tree-climbing fish. It was a little chap with large, sad eyes like a spaniel that gazed mournfully at you as he perched in the mangrove roots only a few feet above the water. These fish were very agile and difficult to catch. In my previous wanderings around the shores of Subic Bay, I had seen these fish and knew the tale about them to be true, despite the scoffers who loudly derided the story of a climbing fish. The fish lie in the roots at high tide. When the water recedes, the scum and debris on the mangrove roots retain much moisture. This fish seems to keep his nose close to this dampness and to get his water from this source. When the roots have dried out, he slides back into the cool depths.

In Japan the prisoners were fed, but very rarely, a bit of squid. This animal looks like a tiny octopus and is caught in schools floating near the surface. The taste of squid is not unpleasant, but long hours of boiling cannot reduce its inherent toughness. The only inedible part is its beak, a hard, bony substance something like the paring from one's big toenail. We ate the little bit we received with avidity, for we needed the precious protein.

Shark's head was occasionally fed to us while the Japanese feasted on the bodies. Boiled with soy or mesoy, a fermented paste of salt and the soybean, it was very good. We learned with surprise that a shark has no bones, only gristle, which is easily chewed. The Japanese stored the shark heads under the snow; hence there was a deplorable amount of stealing. The current price for a stolen head was four Japanese-issued cigarettes, the "hard rolls."

Whale blubber was sometimes on the menu. It has no real taste, even with mesoy paste added to it, but we were glad to get it, for we thought it helped in easing the effects of pellagra. Our skins were now dry, cracked, and splitting at our elbows and knees, while many men suffered from sores in their mouths. Whale blubber was seldom given to us, and when we got it, it worked out to about an ounce per starving man.

Now and then on our way back to the copper mine, as we ducked the sharp stones thrown at us by wolfpacks of small boys, we saw civilians carry huge porpoise heads that must have weighed twenty pounds or more. Some claimed they were dolphins, but we still resolutely stick to porpoise. Among us, this fish, or rather, mammal, is seldom eaten, by reason of the sailor's superstition that the porpoise will push a drowning man to shore and thereby save his life. We would gladly have devoured all of these sea pigs we could have gotten, but our hosts never shared them with us. All we could do was gaze at them wistfully as the sentries hurried us back through the melting snow on the road.

Semidried, partly salted fish were, once in a while, given to us, about two ounces per man. These fish swarmed with worms, so the doctors made sure the galley boiled them for a very long time. We had endless arguments as to whether they were herring or codfish. The Japanese guards had them strung on poorly guarded rice-straw lines in our compound. Worms or no worms, we stole them repeatedly, for starving men have no fear of sickness as long as their craving for food can be satisfied, even for a few pitiful hours.

Our own officers sometimes detected a fish thief and penalized him by the forfeiture of a week's tobacco ration. Our colonel, A. J. Walker, used to threaten the culprits with the brig, a very tough place indeed, but he never went as far as to have a fellow prisoner confined for filching fish.

Of the techniques of the thieves, the best seemed to be to take a water can and a pair of Red Cross scissors out to the wash rack and make a pretense of washing up. You looked carefully for the guards, the galley force, and your own fellow prisoners, for theft from your own stores was considered outrageous conduct. A swiftly raised hand, a snip of the scissors, and the severed rice-straw line dropped its burden—a fish plopped inside your water can. The penalty for stealing just one fish or a dozen was the same if the guards caught you. So fish thieves always went whole hog. Then there was the hazard of the guardhouse to pass, with its *Kiotski* salute, or ignominious bow if both hands were full. Now and then a water can was searched and the culprit beaten up. Sometimes the Japanese gave him five days in their brig, that place of horror and hell.

If we were lucky enough to escape these hazards, we then slipped into the latrine and gorged on the raw fish. We had to eat them all at once, for if we saved some, the smell around our bunk would give us away. Violent diarrhea was the invariable penalty for eating raw fish, and one usually contracted worms for the effort. When we went to the sick bay to ask Doctor Dan or Doctor John for medicine, they would chide us gently, giving us something for the diarrhea and also for the worms that were certain to follow. We were sternly warned not to eat raw fish, but these wise and kindly physicians never reported a man for stealing this food.

In time, the strangling Allied blockade came to shut off all fish from the dying empire. In the coils of this anaconda of "oil and steel," the "blood and guts" of Japan gushed out. By then we had only a few bitter months to go before release would come.

The fish story to end all of these fish stories has to do with a released prisoner who, after the war and while on sick leave in his hometown under his "vine and fig tree," was invited to a dinner party. Filet of flounder was the main course, and our hero (myself, at the home of Mr. William Boswell, Colonial Heights, Virginia) ate heartily.

This man had, while as a prisoner of war, suffered from dysentery, wet and dry beriberi, malaria, pellagra, scurvy, improperly treated wounds, and heaven knows what else. He had survived because he had an iron will to live. His stomach must also have been made of iron. He was now in pretty good shape and worried about his "Shanghai chest" coming back. From a low of about 85 pounds in Cabanatuan Prison Camp Number Three, he had slowly climbed back to 185 pounds.

Two days after the dinner party, his host called him and anxiously inquired as to how he felt. The fellow said he was fine, and wanted to know why anyone was concerned about him. The host told him that he was at that moment just recovering from an acute attack of ptomaine poisoning, and that he was in bed and under a doctor's care. He added that the other dozen or so dinner guests had been similarly stricken, but were also recovering. The flounder was blamed. Our hero expressed his surprise and offered his sympathy, but as for himself, he had felt no discomfort at all.

The story got around, and the town was convulsed with mirth. The men who survived nearly four years as "guests of the emperor" must be incredibly tough!

18

A BLACK MARKET KING

I knew his name and his outfit. The former I would rather not disclose, so I shall call him only "Gonzales"; and the latter I am sure was the 200th Coast Artillery, Antiaircraft, the National Guard of the State of New Mexico. He was of Indian blood, that was certain. In New Mexico, the Gonzales tribe is as thick as Smiths are in other states.

The 200th Coast Artillery was well spoken of among its Indian soldiers, or perhaps "Spanish-Americans" is a better term, and they had the reputation of being fearless. The regiment was among those overwhelmed on Bataan, around the ninth day of April 1942. The survivors were now locked up in various Japanese prison camps. I had come upon Gonzales in Cabanatuan Number One.

The working section of the camp was separated from the hospital area by a barbed-wire fence watched over by an interior guard of prisoners armed with clubs. On the outside of the camp were the Japanese, with rifles and naked bayonets. A person who had attained the status of a member of this prisoner guard company was indeed fortunate, for he did not have to work on The Farm. Mostly it was a refuge for broken-down old soldiers, well advanced in years, who scorned to try to deceive the doctors and make the "quarters list." There was, however, an occasional youngster in the envied group, and among them was Gonzales.

Those noncommissioned officers of the 200th who were

of [Native] American ancestry used to brag mightily about their Indian soldiers and always had a good word to say about their Navajos. They insisted that no Spanish-American troop ever ran from a gun crew while enemy bombers were overhead. It seems possible that a 200th officer, of the type who looked out for his men in misfortune, had secured for Gonzales this coveted assignment. It might not seem a coveted job to some men, but then, they had never heard of The Farm. No extra food went with the position, of course, but you did not have to turn out for "heads down and tails up" labor with the hazard of torture that went with The Farm.

On the north side of our encampment, where the barbed wire of the hospital partition met the fence, was a Japanese guardhouse. It was a simple, nipa-thatched shack with a partition in the back for sleeping and a covered porch in the front where there always sat several of the alert Japanese. It seemed that instead of a "two hours on and four hours off" as with us, these guards did a "one on and two off." With this unique system they had no time between watches in which to sleep. There they sat while off watch, alert and missing very little, while the rest of them walked post.

Their sergeant of the guard and the much-feared officer of the day made their rounds on a well-beaten path by bicycle. Woe be unto him found derelict in his duty! Corporal punishment of a brutal nature was summarily awarded on the spot, and in plain view of all prisoners. There were stories current of sleeping sentries beheaded by samurai swords, but one knows how such tales get exaggerated in their telling. Every few minutes during the night, as the sentries met one another at the end of their beats and before they about-faced to go back to the other end, they made the night hideous with their screams of *"I jo arma sen!"* We learned that it meant, "All is well!"

The Japanese had looted from the prisoners all that they could before their officers put a belated stop to it. Even now, quite a few of the prisoners had certain trinkets much coveted by the guards, such as wristwatches, fountain pens, automatic pencils, rings, and cigarette lighters. The prisoners were more than half starved, and money would buy food in the commissary. The Japanese had money, and besides, there were one-hundred-pound sacks of rice in the storerooms for issue to the prisoners' mess. Gonzales became acquainted with these guards and sold them his own pitiful possessions. Then he extended his field by acting as an agent to sell other prisoners' valuables, for a commission.

His first sergeant, a former Marine and now an air corps staff sergeant, and other men in his guard company warned Gonzales that he was risking death in going within the dead-line of that barbed-wire fence. His comrades did not know the entire story, for the boy was going farther than that. He was climbing under the barbed wire, with the connivance of the sentry and the guards, to exhibit his wares under the electric light of the little guardhouse. After his deals were consummated, he would slip back into the camp. Even if the "top soldier" had known this and relieved Gonzales of his sinecure, it would have been futile. Gonzales had found a way to get extra food; he was hungry, and under the spur of that eternal gnawing craving for food, he had lost his normal instinct of self-preservation and forgot the prisoner's fundamental rule, "Never trust a Japanese!"

Around ten o'clock one night he was in the guardhouse making a deal. The Japanese officer of the day approached silently on his bicycle. The sentry was barely able to tip off the corporal on post. When the officer of the day arrived, he found his men busily tying up Gonzales and eagerly beating him in the process. The prisoner was charged with an attempt to escape, and his futile attempts at defense were answered with more blows. Gonzales probably spoke no more than a dozen words of Japanese. The officer of the day left the lad to the care of his men in the guardhouse, with probably a warm commendation for their alertness. All night long the hospital patients heard the sounds of blows and groans as the captors beat Gonzales.

The grapevine spread the news throughout the camp, even at this late hour. There may have been sleepy grumblings, and remarks such as, "Well, he asked for it, he had it coming to him. These buzzards that sell rice at two pesos a canteen cup don't get it from the commissary. The damned Japs steal it from our own stores to trade it to those black market kings."

We returned to our troubled, tortured sleep to dream fitfully about food and more food.

The Japanese commandant at this time was a whitehaired major, weak and bent over with age. His name I do not recall, if I ever knew it. He never appeared to make any attempt to control the cruelty of his men, and he seemed to be under the thumb of his captain, his second-incommand. This man we called "Beat like carabao," for he often said that this was the only way to get work out of the prisoners.

About ten o'clock the next morning a small group of us were toiling with a ditch and latrine detail inside our camp. We, too, were objects of envy and hatred, for we received the burned rice that came off each galley pot for helping to fix their ditches. A fine young army captain, John Finzer Presell, Jr.,[14] was in charge of us, and we blessed his name, for he had arranged for this precious burned rice to be given to us. We heard he had been the cadet regimental commander at West Point before he was commissioned in the

---

14. John Finzer Presell, Jr., Class of 1940, US Military Academy. Born in and appointed from Maine, he graduated third in his class. He served in the 14th Combat Engineers and was taken prisoner on Bataan. He survived the Death March. He died on 12 January 1945, in the bombing by his own American planes of the *Enola Maru*, from wounds received in that tragic action. He was then thirty years old. He had been decorated with the Silver Star and the Distinguished Service Medal, and I imagine that this DSM was awarded posthumously after his released comrades had taken the trouble to tell the War Department what a splendid soldier he had been. He automatically received the Purple Heart for the wounds that caused his death. I knew him for only a short time, but I cannot praise this young officer too highly. To my mind, he represented the very best traditions of the United States Military Academy; in his manly figure was personified the motto of the academy: "Duty, Honor, and Country." He was posthumously promoted to major on the day of his death.

combat engineers. This was a great honor. He did five times as much work as any of us and accepted no rice for himself.

Our captain called our attention to a dismal procession coming our way along the main Cabanatuan Road. We looked up and saw four armed Japanese in front, a stumbling, ragged figure with his hands bound behind him, and four more guards in the rear. The morning sunlight glittered on their rifles and brightly polished bayonets. Off to the side marched the one we thought to be a sergeant, for we saw he carried a pistol. The firing squad and their victim passed in front of us only some hundred yards away. The sharp eyes of the captain told us the prisoner's hands were bound with barbed wire, and it was probably tightly drawn. The Japanese are a very economical people and make use of whatever is at hand.

They turned the corner and marched off into the adjoining field, a corner of The Farm. We looked and saw a farm overseer take away four prisoners carrying picks and shovels—the grave-digging detail. We stopped our work to see the final act of this tragedy. We commented on the fact that there had been no formal court-martial, and one Marine was heard to remark, "The Japs are practical people, like the Chinese. In their courts they figure that if a man intends to commit perjury, no oath will stop him. They do not waste the time of the court with an oath. They can still sock him plenty if they prove perjury. So, what's the use of trying Gonzales? The Japs figure he attempted to escape. The guards' lie convicted him before the officer of the day." For all we knew, General Homma down in Manila had been told by phone and had duly approved.

By the open grave stood the condemned man, the firing squad lined up in front of him with the sergeant standing off on the flank.

We watchers felt but little pity. A man who dealt with the Japanese had it coming to him. Our officers were continually telling us that black market rice could come from only one possible place—our own stores.

There was a sudden flash of movement that caught the eyes through the morning haze in the field studded with gray-green trees. "He's trying to run away! Look, his bound arms made him fall down! There, they've got him!" We saw the bayonets gleam as they rose and fell, stabbing the prone figure. We saw the flashes of the shots and heard their scattered reports. There was no need for a mercy shot, and it was omitted. The farm overseer brought back his detail of prisoners to cover up the huddled thing that had been so contemptuously kicked into the grave. We resumed our labors, for if we loafed too much on those inside jobs, the captain would relieve us, and back we might go to The Farm. We thought it might be nearly time for that welcome cry of "Burned rice!" from the galley.

The captain of combat engineers remarked that the day was the Fourth of July, 1943. We looked up, startled. We had even forgotten to keep track of time.

19

"ALL OF MY SUCKERS
ARE IN JAIL, TOO."

His name is Brown. I heard that he survived his imprisonment and was living in his native state of Mississippi and biding his time until he could get back to the Philippine Islands. He used to own the well-known Corregidor Bar in the Walled City of Manila, and he wanted to get back there to reopen it.

The town of Manila is now full of soldiers, and their pay has been increased. With his prestige and personality, Old Brown would draw in a lot of trade. But the Walled City is no more, and he would have to open up in the New Town, if there is any more New Town since the Battle of Manila. I hope he gets back there and names his new place the Corregidor Bar. Someday, on my way back to China, I shall stop in Manila and look him up, to our mutual intoxication, as should old friends who have been through much danger together.

I can assume with reasonable safety that he was one of that type of saloonkeeper who had come out to the islands in the "days of the empire" as a soldier in the ranks. A lucky hit in the company crap game, or it may have been stud poker or blackjack, enabled him to buck the select few who foregathered to determine who would have all the winnings in the regiment. Brown presumably came out on top and probably deposited his money with the quartermaster. There it would earn 4 percent interest, and neither he nor his friends could get hold of it until the day of his discharge. On that day he received his finals, in the islands, and entered into business in Manila.

Brown, who always had a large heart for the needs of his friends, became a boniface with a restaurant and bar. There were several fortunes in Manila founded on such humble beginnings, and in those early days Brown may have been quite ambitious.

His nickname was "Buster," which gives a clue to his age, for that hoary ancestor of the current plague of comic strips made its appearance as "Buster Brown" in the early days of the century.

By the time the war began, he was a big, tough-looking old man, with a hard look in his cold blue eyes, a square, jutting jaw, and a shock of snow-white hair. His grim appearance was somewhat tempered by a twinkle in his hard eyes, as though he shared a guilty secret with you. He had run through the ownership of several saloons, for he was addicted to gambling at times. Furthermore, he all too frequently violated the first commandment of all saloon-keepers, which is simply, "Never take a drink in your own place."

He had never been put to the additional expense of hiring a bouncer, for he always was able to take care of his own rows. In those happy days, when a submarine crew put in at Cavite after a trip down from Tsingtao up China way, and officers and men assembled together in merry wassail, it generally took the shore patrol and more to reinforce a bouncer when the situation got out of hand. Old Brown, despite his formidable appearance, had a mellow, genial disposition and was well liked by all the customers who patronized his Corregidor Bar. His injudicious extension of credit to members of Uncle Sam's armed forces and to others lately of the said armed forces, now called "Sunshiners," had prevented Brown's ever attaining much of this world's goods, for he was hardly more than a jump ahead of the sheriff and his creditors. But he always managed to keep his head above water and the bar and restaurant open. Friendships and hilarious times made up for what he may have lacked in filthy lucre.

When I became acquainted with him, the incongruity of his nickname was laughable. "Buster" as applied to such a character was comical. In his later years his chief delight was in the innocent diversion of a game of cribbage played with a customer, with the stakes a glass of cold San Miguel beer.

When war came to the smiling islands, one who did not know "Buster" Brown might well think he would have turned himself in to the Santo Tomás camp for internment along with the women and children and oldsters, and many who were not oldsters at all. But old "Buster" went exactly where his friends had known he would go. He made his way in back of the Bataan lines to serve in a semimilitary capacity and to help build an airport under continual enemy bombing. The Bataan collapse drove him to seek the safety of Corregidor, it was said, where he drove a team of mules by night, delivering rations while bombers were overhead and shellfire made life precarious for those men not fortunate enough to be safe in bombproof shelters.

Brown stopped shaving at the start of the war, and soon had a good start on a beard.

Now and then a mule would get killed by shellfire, to the great delight of the men in the vicinity, for then they could feast upon the carcass. Old "Santa Claus," as he now became known, was quite a legendary character. The quartermaster would generally dig up another team for him after these happy accidents, and he would resume his humble wanderings around the Rock, giving out the scanty rations to the outposts.

In the course of human events, as determined by the conquerors, "Buster" Brown finally came to anchor in Cabanatuan Military Prison Camp Number One. There he became acquainted with the Marines who had not met old "Santa Claus" of the Rock, and they liked him at first sight.

On account of his venerable age, for he was possibly in his middle sixties, the Japanese did not require him to work

The Farm. To add further to his look of senility, that old fox continued to grow the beard, which he started while on Corregidor. Now this snow-white hirsute adornment covered his entire face and even part of his chest. It effected a most remarkable change in his appearance, for the hard, shrewd look turned into one of benign kindness and made him look the perfect, genial old gentleman of the Christmas season.

His wit and humor made him decidedly popular, and his little table, built outside of his nipa barracks, became a sort of shrine for the hopeful, for this old man always had the latest rumors. As no one knew with any certainty anything of what was going on in the vast outside world, certain individuals set themselves up as military critics. A West Point colonel or an Annapolis commander, trained in the analysis and evaluation of military intelligence, now took a backseat to the new military critics: the chaplains and doctors, or the former privates first class of the air force who had been library orderlies and hence were men of profound strategical knowledge.

Besides, and what was also of prime importance, old "Buster" had a deck of cards and a cribbage board. When not playing himself, he would lend them out, free of charge. This was quite out of the ordinary.

We suspect he was somewhat involved in the underground, in a better way than some of its outstanding personalities. His friend and competitor, "Cal" Coolidge, of the famed Luzon Bar, was known on several occasions to procure medicines for the sick, and more than once was involved in the purchase of a whole gunnysack of native tobacco from the commissary for free distribution to the sick. In these affairs Brown seemed rather prominent, but his connection was somewhat vague. He never talked about it.

After we were released, I happened to see a group picture of some living skeletons taken just after they were sprung from Cabanatuan, surrounded by their rescuers, the Army Rangers. I spotted old "Buster" with his big beard and that twinkle in his shrewd eyes, and it made me feel very good.

The thing that sticks out in my memories of this old man

is a trivial one, but I like to reflect upon it. One day he was asked the usual question, so commonplace and trite, of "Buster, don't you hate like hell to be locked up here?"

The answer he gave was truthful and sincere, as with a twinkle in his eye the old man said, "Naw, not a damned bit. Before this war it was a hell of a tough job to keep scratching out a living, with all of you suckers on the loose. How could I make enough to keep even a nipa roof over my head, when all of you, all of my suckers, are in jail, too?"

20

SULFA DRUGS AND MORPHINE

I cannot vouch for the truth of this entire story, for I was never at Nichols Field. I knew the two soldiers well. One of them, to a certainty, has been dead since 1943, and the fate of the other I simply do not know. He was a pitiful, shrunken skeleton of a man a year later, under the watchful care of Doctor Wade, in the Old Bilibid Prison, and I heard that his chances of living then were small.

I learned part of the story from some of the survivors of Nichols Field Prisoner of War Work Camp while I was locked up in the Old Bilibid Prison with them, being processed for my trip to Japan. It was generally told in strict confidence, with vagueness as to names and details, for such knowledge, if true, was highly dangerous. "Old Doc" Decker, the chief pharmacist's mate from our 2d Battalion, gave us the missing parts of the story in the strictest of secrecy.

I shall call these two boys Damon and Pythias, after the mythological twins. I had come to know them in our Corregidor days in the old Middleside Barracks, where they used to sleep at night after a day's manning of battle stations with 3-inch antiaircraft guns. They were a refreshingly bright, alert pair of youngsters, respectful to Marines, and they had learned to call a gunnery sergeant by his full rank, not by the nondescript army title of plain "sergeant." They often sat at the feet of our first sergeant, Earl O. Carlson, the

"Old Swede," to listen to words of wisdom and his yarns of China, Nicaragua, France, and Alaska.

The boys were inseparable and shared between them whatever they might come across in the way of extra food. Their interests seemed the same. Once Damon told me he and Pythias had been schoolmates and had enlisted in the Regular Army together for service in the Philippines early in that year of 1941. I liked the way they gave us so freely of their tailor-made khaki when our clothes began to run short, and I liked better the time they showed us a cache of new M-1 rifles, the Garands, to replace our Springfields, for the army refused to equip us with such weapons from their own stores.

Then the lads left us to stay permanently near Battery Geary, and I saw them no more while the war business was current. I heard that Phythias was wounded the day the big 240s blew up the battery's magazine and threw a twelve-inch mortar barrel all the way from the gun pit to ruin our Middleside tennis court. (There was no tennis being played at that time, for we were otherwise well occupied.)

I saw Damon in Corregidor, when I was behind the barbed wire of the 92nd Garage area, and made eager inquiries of Pythias, for I genuinely liked the lad. He informed me that his friend was doing quite well in the hospital in Malinta Tunnel, that he himself had been volunteering for working details to get up there, but that he had been unable to see him. However, he had gotten messages to him and had received replies. Pythias had been cut across the back by a shell splinter that had chipped his spine a bit, but now he was limping around all right and would soon be out. Damon hoped to hang around the Rock long enough to be reunited with him.

I came across the boys again in Cabanatuan, when the final Corregidor detail came in. They had worked for some six months on the island, clearing debris and shipping everything valuable off to Japan, for the Japanese are economical people who seemed to be making an earnest effort to make the way pay for the war. They told us of old friends, and of how Chief Pharmacist's Mate Decker, of our 2d Battalion, had given Pythias his personal attention so that the ugly wound had healed almost whole, except that the boy could not bend over very well.

They were quite disappointed in Cabanatuan, for we were fed none too well, and our death rate was some twenty-eight men per day. By now, they both had contracted amoebic dysentery and a little "wet" beriberi. They worked on the wood detail together, two men and one axe, and under the circumstances seemed cheerful enough. Then came news of a detail to go out of the camp, and I heard they had volunteered. They thought, like so many others, that the grass was greener in other pastures, and that no place could be worse than Cabanatuan. They came around to tell me good-bye, to give old G.Sgt. Felix Szalkewicz a mattress made from rice sacks, a rare treasure at that time, and to carry some money from us to Doc Decker, whom we liked and admired. The grapevine had told us that "Old Doc" was in the Bilibid Prison with his beloved Doctor Wade, and the outgoing detail would first go there. We felt sure the boys could be entrusted with the precious pesos for Decker, and if they missed him, we would be glad for them to have a bit of cash. (Later we found our faith justified—Old Doc got his money all right.)

Nearly two years passed, and I had forgotten all about the boys, in my misery and hunger. Now came my turn for an outgoing detail, in Japan, with my first stop in the Bilibid Prison. There I saw my old friends, Doctor Wade and Doctor Decker. I reminisced with the latter about how he had been in the James Ravine rescue, when they dug out the entombed Filipino battery and Decker earned his Silver Star. He thanked me for the money and mentioned that Damon was near death right there in Bilibid. "No, he didn't get another man to break his arm down at Nicholas Field to get away," Old Doc said. "It was just the usual thing—starvation, dysentery, beriberi, and aggravated tuberculosis. They've got him in isolation, with a collapsed lung, and I don't think Doctor Wade can pull him through. The Japs won't let anyone see him. Pythias is dead, and between you and me,

Damon is dying more of a broken heart than anything else."
After these preliminaries he told me the rest of the story.

"One of the Japanese in charge of labor parties at
Nichols Field was called 'The Wolf' by the prisoners. He
was well named, and some of the prisoners who were
brought back from there, half dead, tell horrible tales of his
brutality. Or, rather, I should use the past tense, for we think
'The Wolf' is dead.

"Remember that stiff back of Pythias? He could do a
day's work as well as any other prisoner, when it came to
heavy lifting, the way those Japs wanted it done. One day
'The Wolf' had Pythias breaking dried mud, the stuff
that's as hard as rock, with a little short-handled Jap pick,
to load in the light railway cars for the airport. The poor
kid wasn't bending over far enough for 'The Wolf,' so
the damned Jap grabbed the pick and slugged him across
the face with it. You know that the sight of blood brings
out the entire sadistic urge in these people, and 'The Wolf'
just went crazy in his frenzied rage. He struck the boy over
and over again, across his back where he had been
wounded before, and the men had to drag him in from
work in a semicoma. He died just three days later from the
effects of that beating.

"Damon laid his plans for revenge. He is supposed to
have gotten together with several other dysentery men, all
chronically ill. The doctor had been treating them with Red
Cross medicines. They saved the sulfa-guanidine powder
the doctor gave to them. Then they all claimed to have violent cramps that kept them from sleeping, and the doctor believed their story. For several days running, each one of
them received enough of those one-eighth-grain morphine
sulfate tablets to bump off any healthy Jap, for they were out
to get 'The Wolf.' The doctor, in issuing these tablets, doped
off, for he told the men to place the pill under their tongue
to dissolve the morphine just before taps instead of coming
around and personally seeing that they did it.

"They gave all of their pills to Damon, who then ground up
the pills and mixed them with some of the sulfa-guanidine. I

guess they must have had three ounces or more of this powder, of which they mixed up about one ounce. They made up
three or four doses, with the morphone load made separately,
all tied up in tissue paper from sick bay.

"Damon now began to cultivate the friendship of 'The
Wolf.' This was ordinarily difficult, but his technique was a
new one. He began to turn out an honest day's work at the
airport, and it soon came to pass that 'The Wolf' noticed it.
The Jap stopped by and complimented Damon and even
gave him one of his cigarettes. In time they began to talk to
one another in broken Japanese and halting English, with a
good deal of sign language, for 'The Wolf' made Damon his
prisoner-'honcho' (boss).

"The other prisoners, not in the know, were very much
mystified by Damon's attempts to make friends with the
hated enemy. He was the object of open censure and criticism. He kept his mouth shut and simply refused to answer
his comrades when they bawled him out.

"One day 'The Wolf' suggested a black market deal to
Damon. A khaki shirt changed hands for three pesos, for the
Japs make their soldiers pay for clothing when it wears out.
Before long the Jap complained of the symptoms of amoe-
bic dysentery, for which the Japanese doctor had no more
American medicine, and the prisoners' supplies were all
gone.

"The doctor may have had a little sulfa-guanidine left,
hidden for his most desperate cases, but 'The Wolf' figured
it was all finished. Damon suggested a deal for some medicine. The Jap snapped at the bait and paid him a peso for
one of the doses of sulfa-guanidine tied up in the official
hospital tissue paper. This was not enough, so they traded
for the other doses.

"Then Damon supplied him with the last dose, the one
with the morphine sulfate mixed in it.

"None of these guys ever saw 'The Wolf' again. The Japs
suspected nothing, or if they did, they never made any inquiry. Some prisoners, not in the know, asked a Jap one day
in sign language where the overseer had gone. The sentry

cuddled his right forearm over his forehead, and replied *'Honcho, nai.'* We took that for the sign of death, and the words meant, 'Sergeant, he no more.' It could have meant that he was transferred, but I doubt this. We think that Damon had avenged his best friend."

21

CORNSTARCH PILLS

The first shock of meeting Japanese soldiers after our capture was unpleasant. The majority of us were smart enough to conceal our money somewhere on our persons, but many, in their innocence, carried their wallets in the breast pockets of their shirts and wore their wristwatches in plain view.

Marine captain Austin C. "Shifty" Shofner had assembled us at Middleside barracks that morning of the seventh of May 1942 in a column of fours, to be marched down the hill to the Malinta Tunnel on the little island of Corregidor, which we had tried so hard to defend. As our column of some four hundred men swung down the road, the conquerors passed us in small groups of threes and fours. They darted into the ranks and pulled out men to remove their wristwatches, wallets, and any visible trinkets, and in some cases looted prisoners of their precious eyeglasses. The word was quickly passed along the line of marching men as to what was happening up front. Valuables were hurriedly concealed, and there was a slowdown in the thefts.

As we neared Malinta, off on our right, we received the first real shock of our degradation. The Japanese had set up a large table for their morning meal, and the tablecloth was a large American flag, of the post type, some nineteen feet long and ten feet wide.

At Malinta we heard of no looting for the next two days.

The Japanese regulars seemed to be a civilized type of human being, soldiers like us, and in a very short time a brisk barter sprang up. But it was also noted that in every case the Americans came out on the short end of the trades.

In the terribly overcrowded camp of the 92nd Garage, where we spent some eighteen days in that month of May, we became wary. Our officers told us that the Japanese sentries were forbidden to loot, but there was little we could do when a man with a naked bayonet came up and said, "Give money, give money!" and ran his hands over you to see what you had. The more astute had concealed their valuables and the Japanese got but little.

On the landing barges leaving Corregidor, for the transports in the bay were to take us to Manila, the sailors of the Imperial Navy really reaped a harvest. They also worked the prisoners over by pairs as they lined up to climb the ship's "Jacob's ladders." They searched their clothes and even their baggage. They were after money and watches, and they found plenty. But even then, there were a lot of men who got through without being robbed.

In the Old Bilibid Prison, where I lay for a few days, the only hazard seemed to be from our fellow prisoners. It had come to light that clothing is not a free issue in the Japanese army. The Bataan campaigns had been rather hard on their uniforms, made of cheap Japanese cotton cloth, and the Japs could use our shirts and trousers. We slept in our clothes, with our baggage in a bundle for a pillow, to insure a fair chance of having our belongings at daybreak. We heard that three pesos was the current price with our guards for a shirt or a pair of trousers. Evidently the Jap officers had clamped down on the acquisitive tendencies of their underlings, for I heard of no more looting.

In the beginning at Cabanatuan, I knew of an occasional theft, but it was rare. Prisoners who worked on the outside details under guard openly waved money at Filipino peddlers selling food, and their captors paid no attention to them. I began to think the Japanese regular soldier was not so bad after all. A bit on the cruel side, to be sure, but on the whole honest. Of course every army has its quota of crooks, I knew, and I reflected that we might have been much worse if conditions had been reversed. In general, as far as the regular Japanese soldier was concerned, our money and valuables had less chance of being stolen by him than by our fellow Americans.

In October 1942, Cabanatuan Camp Number Three was closed down and we were moved down the road toward the city of Cabanatuan, to Camp Number Two, a distance of some eight kilometers. Here we found a highly organized black market, with even native gin for sale. The principal agents were those prisoners fortunate enough to drive trucks outside the camp, under guard, of course. These individuals reaped a harvest. By now the Filipinos had begun to feel the pinch of want, to know just what the "New Freedom, the Greater East Asia Co-Prosperity Sphere" meant, and they became in desperate need of medicines.

A tiny sulfathiazole pill sold for five pesos in the town by now, and our doctors were forced to take effective measures to safeguard their precious, pitifully small supplies. We could see a truck driver, entrust him with our shirt, and that night we might get a peso or so, if we were lucky. The drivers lived in affluence, and while their comrades starved and died, there were no living skeletons to be seen among these gentry.

The shortage of gasoline and alcohol for fuel caused the truck drivers to lose their envied positions one by one, and carabao trains replaced trucks, with prisoner drivers. These individuals were now the men "to see" in our business dealings, and like the Green Bay tree, a large flowering tree found in the Philippines, they flourished exceedingly well. Watches, cigarette lighters, fountain pens, and gold rings were standard articles of barter, but above all, the Filipinos wanted sulfa drugs.

And then began an amazing thing, a shameful thing, and a thing that was unbelievable.

The ingenuity of these prisoners in their handicraft was most remarkable. Possessing but few tools, and those few liable to be confiscated if discovered, they managed to make even more tools from material the Japanese had spurned as worthless scrap. We began to hear that molds for the manufacture of sulfathiazole pills had made their appearance, and that they were being made from Japanese cornstarch and coconut oil issued to the messes, and that these pills were so cleverly made that they defied detection.

It is presumed that in the beginning of this amazing racket, a small amount of sulfa drug was added to the coconut oil and cornstarch that constituted the base of these fraudulent panaceas. Many of the prisoners still had sulfa drugs, cunningly concealed, and even quinine. This latter drug was probably adulterated with cornstarch and oil at first, but the characteristic bitter taste of this malaria-specific medicine required a large amount of the drug to be used. For this reason, the manufacturer of fake quinine pills did not flourish for long.

To fleece the Filipinos, after all they had done and were doing for us, risking death and torture to smuggle food to us and give us news, was a sad reflection on the American character. By now the amount of sulfa drugs was so sharply reduced that the carabao drivers were being given pills of cornstarch and oil alone. This caused the wrecking of a very profitable business. The disillusioned Filipinos simply refused to buy any drug from an American prisoner of war.

There had never been any of these fake drug sales from one prisoner to another. If the drug did not work, there would have been violent recriminations. The Filipinos dared not say a word of protest, but the prisoners were different. It would have been very dangerous to sell fake pills to them. So the lucrative drug market seemed to be going the way of all flesh, and the manufacturers began to tighten up their belts, for starvation was now among them.

By this time the Japanese army seemed to have run out of drugs for their own men. They well knew that the prisoners had concealed sulfa drugs and quinine, and even had

Atabrine, another malaria-specific medicine. Orders were frequently issued to turn in all such medicines, but these were blandly ignored. Many of the Japanese had social diseases, contracted in the Philippines or in the isles of the Southern Seas. Their doctors were very stern with these unfortunates, hence they concealed their ailments and tried to cure themselves. By now almost all of the Japanese regulars had gone elsewhere, replaced by semisavage, ignorant, cruel little Taiwanese conscripts. These individuals were marched to Cabanatuan each Sunday for their liberty and led to Filipino brothels for the gratification of their lusts. As any social worker can tell you, a red light district, even if regulated by medical authorities, is no guarantee against acquiring a package not bargained for, and the ladies of the "oldest profession" were able, in an unwitting manner, to avenge slightly their invaded country's wrongs.

So the Taiwanese were forced to buy fake sulfa drugs from such prisoners as would sell them in this strange black market that had sprung up between conquerors and conquered.

The price of these pills sold to the Taiwanese started at a peso each and soared to nearly five pesos. For a while the drug manufacturers again lived in ease and affluence. With their ill-gotten gains they could hire sick prisoners on the "quarters list" to take their place on The Farm. The Taiwanese were not permitted within the barbed-wire enclosure as a general rule, and all was serene. In time the Japanese discovered the deception, the pill market died a natural death, and the manufacturers shuddered and trembled. They knew a warm welcome from the torture squads on The Farm awaited them should they be so imprudent as to show up there in a working party.

It is more than possible that those agents had corrupted the powers-that-be among the prisoner officers who made up these details, so now they must be taken care of in their moment of distress. Plank owners were shaken loose from inside jobs to work The Farm, and the black market drug kings went their several ways in comparative safety.

This distressing revelation of the use to which American ingenuity and inventiveness was put shows a sad sidelight to our own national character. The brazen audacity of some men in dealing with the enemy was a shameful thing, and never to be forgotten.

22

FALSE TEETH AND COCONUTS

Sergeant Major James J. Jordan, United States Marine Corps, may be described without exaggeration as possibly the best-known Marine in the whole of our Corps prior to the outbreak of World War II. In those halcyon days, when our Corps' strength was around eighteen thousand men, most of the old-timers knew one another, if not personally, at least by reputation. And old "Jimmy," as I have said, was known by all.

Jimmy, if my memory serves me correctly, entered the Marine Corps in 1915, and his first duty was Peking. It was said that he was one of the original members of the old mounted detachment or, as our navy files say, "He put the Mounted in commission." He was a burly little Irishman from New York City, with the entire native wit and shrewdness of a son of Erin. In military appearance he was a model for all Marines with his tailor-made uniforms, his leather gear shined to mirrorlike brightness, and his cock-of-the-walk strut.

I first knew him in 1928, when he was the first sergeant of the old 39th Artillery Company in those nostalgic days of long ago. How many years he had been around Peking and North China I cannot say, but it is possible he may have made one or two trips back to the States for a refresher course in his native land. I heard he was briefly topkick of the USS *Pennsylvania*'s Marines. As there was prohibition of alcoholic liquors in those days, in our "land of the free," it is more than possible that just one visit was enough for him, and he scurried back to China as soon as he could.

I heard that he did gunboat duty on the South China coast again for a while, a strange sort of exile, before I came to know him in Peking.

After Peking came Shanghai, then South China once more on a gunboat, and he finally came to anchor in the old Cavite Navy Yard, just eight miles across the huge sheet of water that is Manila Bay from the city of the same name.

Here in this *dolce far niente* land he came to stay, and acquired for himself a wife and a son. A lady named Angelina, whose last name I never knew, a lovely "ballerina" of the Dreamland Cabaret, attracted Jimmy's roving eye, for he was a connoisseur of the fairer sex. He settled down in domestic bliss and prepared to spend the remainder of his Marine Corps service there, with occasional tours of duty at the Olongapo naval station. In due course of time, as a thirty-year Marine pensioner, he might get himself a position as a navy yard workman, where his duties would be a sinecure, for a white man in those days in the yard merely supervised the labor of the natives.

The Marine Corps never looked with favor on its Marines becoming "asiatic," and it was difficult for a man to stay in the Orient for too long. The headquarters liked to get a man back in the States for at least two years, and then would let him go out again only with reluctance. So it came to pass that Jimmy had the axe fall upon him, and I came across him in "Frisco." He seemed a bit awed by the traffic, and I know the hurry and bustle of the crowds annoyed him. He commented upon the strange spectacle of white men unloading ships around the docks, of white men driving streetcars and taxis, and of white men tending bar. As we gathered in a gin mill, he had some difficulty restraining himself in the matter of clapping his hands and calling "Boy!" when his glass was empty.

Some six months later I heard he was back in the islands. It appeared he had gone all the way back to Washington for duty, seen some of his old friends among the high command at Headquarters Marine Corps, and importuned them for a special assignment to help evacuate the Orient, for war clouds were threatening and the Japanese were on the march to Cam Ranh Bay in Indochina and in a striking position to take Malaya, and a good sergeant major such as Jimmy was now needed in the Cavite yard, for the garrison was being increased.

I had a few brews with old Jimmy when I visited Cavite on my way out to Shanghai in the late fall of 1940. He had just returned from his enforced stateside exile and "had the situation well in hand." Like old Marines we talked about everything but what we feared was to come, and parted in high spirits.

The 4th Marine Regiment was hurriedly sent down to the islands from Shanghai before the jaws of the trap closed and arrived there a week before what we feared was coming to hit us. Scurrying between beach defenses at Olongapo, clearing out the naval station and burning it, moving to Mariveles, and ducking enemy bombs all the while, I thought but little of my old friend. I knew that the Cavite shipyard had been nearly destroyed by a high-level bombing attack and that many Marines had been killed, and that slaughter and devastation had been brought upon the old Spanish town. So on the morning of the twenty-eighth of December 1941, upon our arrival at the Middleside Barracks at Corregidor Island, it was good to see old Jimmy again, the sergeant major of our new 3d Battalion, from the Cavite garrison.

His appearance called for comment. His sharp Roman nose with its high bridge and his jutting battleship jaw were nearly touching one another. "Why, Jimmy, you look just like old Punch of the Punch and Judy Show" was my greeting, for old friends among the Marines are somewhat lacking in the ordinary delicacies. The old boy grinned ruefully and let me know that his new false teeth had been lost. A heavy five-hundred-pounder had blown him off his feet, and the blast had expelled his new "China clippers" into a gasoline dump.

Old Jimmy had barely been able to escape the flames, and it had been a very close shave with death.

The loss of his "store bought" teeth did not seem to worry the old sergeant major a bit, for his gums were tough enough to eat the Marine Corps food issued to him in the mess lines. I used to see Jimmy every now and then during the siege of Corregidor Island, over in the 3d Battalion command post or on the occasions he took a trip down James Ravine way. But after Bataan fell, the enemy shellfire was so hot and heavy that these visits had to cease.

I became a shipmate of old Jimmy's again in the Cabanatuan prison camps, in both Number Three and Number One. His freedom from all diseases was a thing to marvel at. He never had dysentery, malaria, beriberi, scurvy, pellagra, or a single other ailment as far as visible symptoms went, and he was never heard to complain. He grew gaunt and thin from starvation, as did nearly everyone else, but his morale and stamina remained outstanding. He worked on the labor details every day, kept cheerful, and was an inspiration to the younger men.

Jimmy's bosom buddy was a chief gunner's mate from the Cavite yard, one Alvin Grady Smith. Like Jordan, Smith had lingered too long in the Orient and had been captured at Corregidor after being wounded in a forlorn-hope bayonet charge. His desperate heroism was well known to all of us, and, like Jimmy's, his cheerfulness under adverse conditions helped us all.

Smith came down with beriberi neuritis of the "screaming feet" type that kept him awake and in agony all night long. Jimmy hovered around him, taking care of his buddy and, in the way of all Marines, laid Smith's troubles to the indiscretions of his youth. Smith replied in language profane and uncouth to the sergeant major's insinuations, and this banter kept the former's mind from his painful agony to a great extent. On those rare occasions when the Japanese issued coconuts to us, Jordan gave his to Smith, for, having no teeth, he was unable to eat them. The gunner's mate accepted them gladly, for they made a welcome addition to the scanty rice.

Poor Smith's feet became so bad that he could barely walk. The hospital became alarmed over these cases of beriberi and admitted some two hundred of the worst cases. And then came the blessed Red Cross food and medicines.

That Christmas of 1942 was a happy one, with four twelve-pound Red Cross packages for each man after those long months of starvation. Even the Japanese became infected with the holiday spirit and gave each man during the ten-day period about ten small coconuts.

Smith, who was quite a wit, always had a large audience gathered around listening to his sea stories and his remarkable adventures. As his daily coconut was issued, he publicly wrapped it up and addressed it to "Sergeant Major James J. Jordan, United States Marine Corps," with his compliments. A trustworthy runner then delivered it to old Jimmy. As everyone knew, the old man had no teeth, and these delivered coconuts caused great laughter.

Soon after the first of that year of 1943, when the Red Cross food had all been eaten and the pinch of hunger had again begun to be felt, Smith's feet were healed enough for him to be sent back to the working side of our camp. He immediately hunted up Jordan and hinted how much he would appreciate a few coconuts. He knew Jimmy had been unable to eat them, and he thought his old buddy would have saved them for him.

The laugh was on Chief Gunner's Mate Smith, for he learned that Jimmy had saved those nuts until the excess food had been eaten and when coconuts again had a high market value. They had been traded for tobacco and extra rice that Sergeant Major Jordan could eat with his toothless gums.

Smith took the loss good-naturedly, for he had learned his lesson from old "Punch and Judy." A wise Marine is always more than a match for a wise sailor.

23

"I CALL HER 'HEY, YOU!' "

In the beginning of the long years of our imprisonment, we relished the cool of the evening after a long day's toil on The Farm. Unless we were unfortunate enough to be assigned to a water detail (for there was no irrigation system in the broad, flat acres around us), our evening time was more or less our own.

Some men liked to watch the panorama of the glorious Philippine sunset, ever changing, always different. Others exhausted and sick, beaten and so dispirited, lay inert on their bamboo slates beneath the nipa-thatched roofs and slept with troubled dreams of food, food, and more food. The gambling element tried their chances with Lady Luck, with stakes of "dobe" cigarettes or rolls of native tobacco. Others worked at handicraft, manufacturing pipes from the native *camagon* tree or the lovely Philippine hard redwood, mistakenly called mahogany.

There was a certain peace and quiet behind the barbed wire, for the Japanese guards stayed outside of it as a general rule. Unless the prisoners got too noisy, they bothered us but little. And so the storyteller came into his own, as in the bazaars of Mohammedan lands. But there was no collection taken up from his hearers, for there was nothing for them to give.

The better educated and more mentally alert among the prisoners organized lectures on every subject under the sun, from coal mining in Cebu to gold digging in Baguio, from the geography of the South China coast to the topography of the Mongolian plains.

First Lieutenant John Paul Flynn of the Army's 31st Infantry told us of the campaigns of his youth, of American invasions of Murmansk and Archangel in the frozen White Sea of northern Russia and, half a world away, of American troops in Vladivostok and Khabarovsk. He told us of the Railway Engineer Corps in France, and guard duty on the Soochow Creek and North Station in the days of the 1932 and 1937 Shanghai "incidents," for this "old dobe" had been around in his day.

Captain Archer reminisced of revolutions and filibustering in the banana republics, and we came to learn of Gen. Lee Christmas in Honduras, for the doughty captain had been with him in his wayward youth. Capt. George Kaufman, late of the pack train of the 26th Cavalry, Philippine Scouts, gave us scholarly discussions on the breeding of horses, for he so loved the thoroughbreds.

Lt. Col. Everett E. Warner, recently brought in from his abortive guerrilla activities, gave us tales of the Cagayan Valley in the north, of how the Japanese burned and killed on the mere suspicion that someone was harboring guerrillas, of his capture, and most remarkable of all, of the kindly treatment he received from his captors.

The unique Fassoth twins, Martin and Bill, Hawaiian-born sugar planters of German descent, spoke of their refugee camp in the Zambales Mountains, of hiding the escapees of the Bataan debacle for over a year in the midst of the Japanese occupation forces until they came to grief and the hell of the concentration camp for military prisoners.

There were lectures on beekeeping, on military history, on the philosophies of the ancient Greeks, and on the story of Australia. Truly, it was a poor man's college, and many a prisoner acquired a veneer of culture merely by keeping his ears open.

Among those scholarly lecturers, travelers to the world's far places, builders of roads and bridges in backward lands, were raconteurs of a more humble kind. Their tales were ribald, with much profane and picturesque adornment, and were of people we had known, of places we had been, and of punishments awarded by outraged commanding officers, as soldiers like to talk the world over. Among such individuals, Sgt. Maj. James J. Jordan of the 3d Battalion, 4th Regiment of Marines had his little knot of devotees.

Jimmy may have stretched the truth somewhat, but the yarns of this shrewd old sea-soldier were so ingeniously woven that it was impossible to catch him in a lie. His tales embraced the days of old Peking, Tientsin and Chingwangtao, of Shanghai and Hong Kong, and of the intervening points of the China coast. He told of the Philippine Islands, of the vagaries of Marines in many lands, of the "shack masters" and the "squaw men." And his tales always made us laugh. This last thing was good, for in those bleak, bitter, hopeless days there was very little cause for mirth.

Of all Jimmy's yarns, I liked the one about old Joe Cerny the best. I had known Joe well, and was in Cavite when the tale Jimmy related had happened, and I knew it to be true.

Poor Joe has long been dead. He was too much addicted to drink, and after a session with a heart attack, was warned by the doctor in San Rogue that any further indulgence in the cup that cheers would very likely kill him. Joe took this advice to heart, at first, but the flesh was weak, and he began to slip. His friend and crony, an old Austrian woman, one "Ma" Slater, ran a bar called the Manhattan located behind the Cavite Marine barracks. Joe spent most of his spare time in the congenial company of Ma and her gin, so when Ma died, it was no surprise to find that, having no relatives, she had left Joe as her executor and heir. Cerny had just retired from the Marine Corps after twenty years of service, and this windfall of a profitable saloon was most welcome. He took over the place, locked it up, and began to inventory the liquor stock.

The next day the Manhattan was closed. The cash customers went over to the nearby Nutshell and to the Owl, while the "jawbone" men thirsted. After three days the Filipino boys who worked in the place called the Constabulary broke the lock and found Joe dead inside, with a look of perfect beatitude upon his face. That there was almost no stock left goes without saying.

About a year before this event, Jimmy told us that Joe had come to get legally married, a strange thing among the Cavite Marines, whose alliances were usually without the benefit of clergy.

At this time the happy bridegroom was a gunnery sergeant in his late fifties, for old Joe had been a soldier of Kaiser Franz Joseph in his native Austria long before he came to us in the Marines. Joe was big, sloppy, and fat, with ill-fitting clothing and a cap several sizes too small. Just how he ever attained the coveted rank of gunnery sergeant was always a mystery to us, and how he managed to retain it without being reduced was equally baffling, for Joe was just a genial, well-liked old incompetent. The colonels that commanded Cavite had all taken pity on him and had allowed him to remain there in the islands as long as he liked. His duty was that of outside overseer of the naval prison, a job that might have adorned the rank of any private first class since it involved only the handling of the leisurely labors of some seven or eight inmates. While some of the more energetic Marines, newly arrived from the States, deplored a man such as Joe in the rank of gunnery sergeant, all liked this good old man, for he was never known to say a hard word about anyone.

Cerny seemed to have a habit of marrying ladies of color. It was said that he married in Haiti, San Domingo, Nicaragua, and Hawaii, and that his wives ranged in color from saffron yellow to the black of a B-flat key on a piano. Some had died and some were divorced. It is suspected that he had contracted some alliances of a temporary nature as well, without the trouble of securing a marriage license. There had been some official correspondence about his marital affairs. He had been assured he was now a single man and that he was free to marry again.

The lady of his choice was a very young Filipino girl,

some fifteen years old, or perhaps younger. Housekeeping
was set up on the Calle Telegrafico, just around the corner
from the barracks. The love nest was handy to the navy yard
gate, and all wished the newlyweds well.

It occurred to Joe after a few months of married bliss that
it would be wise to fill out a beneficiary slip designating his
new dependent wife as the recipient of six months' pay if he
should die while on active service. He appeared in Jimmy
Jordan's office with his request, and the first sergeant started
to fill out the form.

"What's your wife's name, Joe?" asked the "top."

"Vhy, Mrs. Choseph Cerny," replied the "gunny."

"I meant her maiden name, the name she had before you
went and committed matrimony on her," Jimmy explained
to Joe.

"I go get it, you chust vait!" And in a short time Cerny
had returned with the name printed on a piece of paper. Presumably Mrs. Cerny or a neighbor had written it down, for
of Joe's many talents, writing was not his most outstanding
one. Jimmy, whose wise old eyes had seen many strange
things among Marines, thought nothing of it at all, so he
completed the form and took Joe to see the colonel, Lt. Col.
Maurice B. Shearer, to swear him in.

In the pleasant climate of the Philippine Islands there
was no door between the commanding officer's office and
that of his first sergeant. An archway sufficed, with a swing-
ing screen hung at shoulder height. Joe was sworn in with
all the formalities, and then the colonel leaned back to ask
some questions, for he had heard the whole conversation.

"How is it that you do not know your wife's name, gunnery sergeant?" asked the "Old Man."

"Vhy, Mrs. Choseph Cerny iss enough, sir," replied the
honest Marine.

The colonel was persistent, and he asked, "When you
speak to your wife, Cerny, what do you call her?"

"I call her, 'Hey, you!' " answered Joe straightaway.

24

"DONALD DUCK"

The Marines like to tell stories about some of their better officers while bragging to bored army and navy files. These men were forced to listen to the many glories of our Corps, for they, being locked up in the prison camps, could not easily get away from such tales.

By this time the prisoners had just about talked each other out. They had long been suffering from boredom and hunger, and food was by now almost the sole topic of conversation. Even in those dark days, and in the darker days to come, in Cabanatuan, aboard a prison ship, and in a Japanese copper mine, I occasionally heard this tale.

The first name of this Marine Corps officer was Donald (Col. Donald Curtis, USMC) and a hard, competent, aggressive man was he. In size you might describe him as big-little, and he had been both a basketball player and coach. Basketball is a hard game, and those who play it must likewise be hard, too.

They promoted Curtis from a leaf colonel to a bird colonel at the outbreak of war, but as there were no more regiments available for him to command, the new full colonel had to serve in his old capacity as the regimental executive officer. He was very well liked, after he and his men had gotten to know one another, and the files swore by him, for with this officer, his Marines came first. (There were a few who swore at him, but then you cannot satisfy everyone.) The men who had been his sergeants major at various times probably knew him best, and their verdicts seemed to be, "Tough, ice water in his veins for blood, fussy about details, and he always requires the quarters you live in to be spotlessly clean. Takes him three hours to inspect his barracks, but by the gods, it's worth it when you are living in filthy Shanghai. When you come to work for him, in the beginning you do just what he says and in the way he tells you to do. After a while, when you and he know one another, he lets you put out the orders he would give were he there, and you tell him, when he gets back, just what you did. And, you had better guess right, too. On the whole, I'd rather be his sergeant major than work for most colonels!" Coming from such Marines, this is high professional praise indeed. We Marines appreciated our "Donald Duck."

His nickname had nothing to do with his character. Some wag whose literary knowledge was gained largely from the comic strips had applied it to the colonel some years before, and the name had stuck, particularly among the irreverent, as such names always will. To most of the older noncommissioned officers, he was simply "the Old Man" or "the Colonel." I rather liked being commanded by him.

This anecdote has probably been told in various forms by military men of the officers they liked and respected since the dawn of the written, recorded history of the military art. We Marines are prone to seize upon such legends, to the greater honor and glory of our Corps. We recall in our recruit depot in San Diego, California, hearing a drill instructor tell a group of wide-eyed youngsters about a Greek Marine at Salamis, who seized the gunwale of a Persian trireme in his attempt to haul it onto the beach. A Phoenician boatswain lopped off his hand. The Marine clutched it with his other hand, and had it promptly severed. With both hands gone, he seized the rigging with his teeth. A swiftly descending sword decapitated him, but his indomitable fighting spirit animated his fellow Marines to ultimate victory. The tale may have come from old Herodotus, the "father of history," sometimes referred to as the "father of lies." A classical scholar may indulge in a superior smile and set forth the cold logic that the hero was a hoplite, an infantryman of the Athenian army, but I still like to think of him as a Marine. It is a very good tale to tell the young recruits when we nurture them so carefully in boot camp, for it helps to make them so intensely proud of their Marine Corps that their one ambition is to get into combat and close with the enemy.

Old 1st Lt. "Dobe" Flynn of the 31st Infantry, a sometime scholar in military lore, when he heard us talk of "Donald Duck," dryly remarked on the similarity of the careers of our colonel and that of U. S. Grant at the Petersburg siege. But despite gentle rebuke, we still like to regale our listeners with this tale. And, it is possible that in time it may come to be an established part of the recruit depot's curriculum.

There was scattered enemy artillery fire on the island of Corregidor in that month of March in 1942. We had been under constant bombing, and now the pesky Japanese had set up several batteries of 105mm guns on the Cavite shore some seventeen hundred yards away. While not particularly galling, this fire killed men every now and then. Orders were issued against crowding together, but like many such directives, they were all too frequently disobeyed.

To the twin hazards of bombs and 105 shells was added another. The industrious Japanese set up a big battery of 240s, a cannon whose shell weight was five hundred pounds and in inches its diameter was roughly nine point six. This effort was directed mainly against Fort Frank and Fort Drum, tiny fortified islets of steel and concrete, but every so often they lobbed a few of their big rounds onto Corregidor.

Captain Ivy, a young West Pointer from the army's coast artillery, had taken his "walkie-talkie" radio and a group of daredevils right into the middle of the Japanese, located that battery, directed the spotting fire, had escaped with his survivors across the eight hundred yards of water to Fort Frank, and received a well-merited Distinguished Service Cross for his leadership. We thought the big 12-inch rifle of Bat-

tery Hearn had forever dissuaded the enemy from the idea
of setting up any more 240s, but after a while the big shells
began coming the way of Fort Frank again, and now and
then a few shells hit Corregidor.

The Japanese lobbed one of those five-hundred-pounders
into the North Mine Dock area of Corregidor along with a
105 salvo. The bursts exploded among a working party. A
soldier's leg was badly injured, a Marine had his arm severed at the shoulder and he later died in the Malinta Hospital, and a first class torpedoman of the navy lay dead, a
bloody, smashed mess of shreds of flesh and bones with
some of the flesh hanging up in the telephone wires, resem-
bling horrid fruit.

The artillery fire was shifted to belabor Middleside barracks with its attentions, but so uncertain was this type of
bombardment that it might fall upon the North Mine Dock
area again at any instant.

Colonel "Donald Duck" was at the regimental command
post hard by in the Queen Tunnel. Hearing of the incident,
he decided to take a look-see, for working parties were still
in the area. He threaded his way past the mouth of the big
Malinta Tunnel, past the bake shop, along the ruined church
in the barrio of San Jose, and finally came to the North
Mine Dock area. The wounded soldier, the dying Marine,
and the dead sailor had already been removed, and a Filipino sailor of the Insular Navy was poking at the shreds of
flesh that festooned the wires, trying to knock them down,
when the colonel came into view.

Up Middleside way the shells burst wildly, for the cannon were not too accurate at such extreme ranges. The
Japanese shifted their fire to Topside, and the working party
breathed a collective sigh of relief, for they knew from past
experience that most of these shells would skim the top of
our island and burst harmlessly in the water.

"Donald Duck" sat down in a convenient shell crater
alongside the road and began to draft a field message that
would again warn men not to huddle up for imagined security. All hands had been told this repeatedly, all hands had

been warned not to run when shellfire came upon them, but to lie down and ride it out before seeking the security of a bombproof. But it was felt that another message to all unit commanders in the Marine regiment, emphasizing the recent tragedy, might help.

As the colonel wrote, there came a salvo in his direction. There was the *meowr-r-r!* and the *boom!* of the 105s, so aptly called by the Filipino Scouts the "wildcats," for the interval between the *meowrr-r-r* and the following *boom* was less than a second. There was a shower of dust and red-hot steel splinters thickened with flying granite rocks, and men flattened themselves to the ground where they were.

The danger had passed, heads were cautiously raised, and the men called to one another to make sure no one was wounded. The colonel's runner called attention to the "Old Man." With an expression of annoyance, he was seen brushing off the dust clinging to the pages of his field message book and resuming his writing. Apparently he had never flattened out on the ground, and so intent had he been on finishing his message that he hardly realized how close Death had been to him.

Near the runner was a very young Marine, Field Music John Corley, from F Company, 2d Battalion, barely twenty years old. He stared goggle-eyed at his colonel, and he may have been thinking of that description of "ice water in his veins for blood." After a moment he recovered his breath and turned around to the men of the working party.

"Old Donald Duck doesn't scare worth a good god damn!" he said in a tone of awestruck reverence.

Note: John Corley received the first Silver Star awarded to a Marine during World War II. He told me this story.

25

LAUGHING WITH DEATH

"Big Mac" McKinney, Headquarters Company, 2d Battalion, 4th Marines, is dead. He lasted less than two months in Japanese jails. Father Frank McManus gave him the last sacraments of his church, with the rain dripping in the dark through the nipa thatch and bamboo floor of the officers' bathhouse, where "Big Mac" lay on the ground. Bacillic dysentery was his killer. Sulfathiazole could not be had, and so he died. We who volunteered to carry him away for burial the next day had no real cause to grumble, for "Big Mac" weighed less than a hundred pounds.

A scant six months before he had tipped the scales at close to three hundred pounds. "Big Mac" admitted that when he went to ship over in San Diego, a kindly navy doctor had recorded his weight at 250, advised him to diet and exercise, and then promptly went on leave. His successor would have to answer any official queries that might arise for passing such a man as "physically fit for reenlistment."

"Big Mac" joined the 4th Marine Regiment in Shanghai right after this. With the knowledge that war was soon to break out, there was furious training with our 1918 weapons, and there was a more furious to-do about physical fitness, with great concern over repeaters in the hospital, with men "dry-docked" with social diseases more than once, with fat men, and with chronic drunkards.

Every boat carried home a large draft, with fewer replacements. The wise men in Washington, D.C., were getting their Marines, as many as they could, away from the Asian death trap before it could be sprung. A token force must be kept up, as the Japanese were not quite ready for their war. As long as those few Marines held the line, the International Settlement in Shanghai was safe. If struck, those sea-soldiers would hit back, the flag would be insulted, and a shooting war would start. So the Japanese held their hand, for their plan for Pearl Harbor was not quite ready.

The Marines' military presence at Cavite was to be increased by forming the 1st Separate Battalion. Shanghai could help furnish men, and so company commanders carefully culled the undesirables. It is something that has been done by military men since the dawn of history, for the "second oldest profession" changes very little.

In the 2d Battalion the billet police sergeant was the lordly, quietly efficient platoon sergeant, "Big Jack" Taylor. He handled his Chinese coolies well, his compound was always spick-and-span, and his duty performance had always earned him a "well done." An ex-heavyweight fighter, it was said that Taylor had knocked down Primo Carnera when the latter was being groomed for the championship before a succession of "tank divers." This woeful lack of tact finished the fistic career of "Big Jack," and he became a Marine. He was now a platoon sergeant, and there was talk of making him a gunnery sergeant, for he was an able man. But a ruthless, adamant doctor found the big Marine overweight, and so he was sent off to Cavite. (I heard that the doctor died years later, on a prison ship that was bombed and sunk.)

When the battalion got "Big Mac," the adjutant, 1st Lt. Hugh A. Nutter, exploded. "Here we just lost a darned good man, even if he was fat. And in his place we get a fatter one, and we don't know if he's any good." The first conditioning march, eleven miles, at a rate of 160 steps to the minute, showed "Big Mac" not very good at this sort of business. His legs gave out quickly, and the first sergeant, Wayne K.

Miller, had him fall out and return to the billet by rickshaw. With "Big Mac," his rifle, and heavy marching pack along with a hundred rounds of ammunition, it's a wonder the springs of the ancient vehicle did not collapse.

The staff put their collective heads together. They decided to relieve the billet police sergeant, a lean, hungry, Cassius-type Marine, and replace him with "Big Mac." They would excuse him from hiking. Being an old-timer of sixteen years in the Marines with a couple of Shanghai tours under his belt, "Big Mac" knew China and the Chinese. In a short time "Big Jack" was only a memory and the compound looked better than ever.

The new police sergeant looked like the traditional Irish policeman, with his six feet four inches of imposing frame marred only by a gigantic "bay window," for "Big Mac" was quite fond of the pleasures of the table, and more than fond of Shanghai's beer. His merry little blue eyes held a perpetual twinkle, his button nose glowed pink upon his face, and he was always perspiring. Like most fat men and red-skinned Irishmen, he had to watch his sunburn, for he blistered terribly when trying to cure his prickly heat. Altogether, "Big Mac" was not exactly happy dealing with the summer heat of Shanghai.

The regiment did not notice his absence from the prescribed conditioning marches, and he was never seen in the parades at Kiaochow Park or the Race Course. Being a non-commissioned officer, no official letter came down from headquarters directing that he reduce his weight, so "Big Mac" took things the easy way. "Ewo" and "U-B" beers were cheap, plentiful, and cold. It is possible that he even gained a few pounds.

In the hurry of the evacuation the 2d Battalion was to make up the first boatload. "Big Mac," checking in his property at the Ferry Road quartermaster, was quite busy. We embarked in our buses in the rain and went aboard our lighters [barges] at the Bund. The *President Madison* sailed without "Big Mac," and Capt. A. C. "Shifty" Shofner, the company commander, was plenty sore. When the big Marine found his battalion gone, he turned in to the regimental headquarters and was sent out on the last boat, the *President Harrison*, two days later. "Big Mac" rejoined his battalion in Olongapo, in the Philippines, his excuse for missing ship was accepted, and the file thought it a fit subject for laughter. But I suspect that the rank did not forget it.

A few days later it came: war and bombing. Olongapo, being a mighty wet place during the rainy season, had a series of concrete ditches, dug long before by prudent captains of the yard. They were two feet wide and about four feet deep. If we filled up some sandbags and made bays every ten feet or so, we had perfect foxholes. The "Old Man," Lieutenant Colonel Anderson, had seen to this before the war broke out.

The first enemy bombing found "Big Mac" near the ammunition pit, where there was ample room for his frame. The sandbagged ditches being a bit too narrow, he resolved to stay as close to the big pit as he could, but his duties took him some distance away. The next bombing caught him a good three hundred yards away. While four little attack bombers, old and obsolete but good enough to destroy our seven lumbering PBYs on the water, were engaged in their work, the Marines of the regiment dove for their ditches and looked to their weapons, for we knew our turn would come.

A ripple of laughter broke out along the lines of the ditches. There was "Big Mac" in a waddling run, heading for his ammunition pit and casting agonized glances at the ditches where we lay. We cheered him on, even forgetting to look at what was happening to the PBYs across the bay. Lumbering down the road, zigzagging from one side to the other, hoping to find a ditch large enough to fit, "Big Mac" was the picture of desperate frustration. The laughter and shouting almost drowned out the sounds of our 20mm cannon and .50-caliber machine guns, for the enemy planes were headed our way. "Big Mac" made a final burst of speed and dived into his shelter. We began firing, for the red balls of the tracers from the planes were all around us.

The danger was over in a matter of seconds. We laughed

at ourselves while water spurted from a dozen places in the high water tank, the damage having been done by the frenzied firing of a young machine gunner, a Private First Class Albert from Company H. Across the bay, sailors were dead or dying, smoke rose in black, billowing clouds, and over at Grande Island the crack of antiaircraft cannon mingled with the dull explosions of bombs, for the Japanese planes were working over the army's Fort Wint. We still laughed while all this action was taking place. Most of all we laughed about "Big Mac," and we were still laughing about him during the five months left to us before we were to be overwhelmed by the enemy.

On Corregidor we got the chance to slip "Big Mac" to another battalion. The hopelessly fat Marine left during the darkness, for it was dangerous to move by day. The rank probably recalled that affair of missing the ship in Shanghai, and they had too vivid a picture of "Mac's" awkward predicament in seeking shelter from being bombed or machine-gunned from the air. Agile and vigorous Marines were needed in the 2d Battalion, not gross hippopotami, and we could let the 1st Battalion worry about him. After the "Shanghai" was made, we seldom saw "Big Mac," for his unit had been assigned to a very dangerous sector. His gunnery sergeant warrant came in by radio from the States, and we heard that the big Marine was doing well, inspiring his men with a show of calm indifference under bomb and shell. In the last fight of all, around Monkey Point, we heard he had been killed repelling the Japanese landing. A few days later, when we were all prisoners, we discovered him, to our joy, safe and unhurt.

Starvation rations slimmed "Big Mac" down quite a bit, but we thought he could live on his fat alone for a long time. Nearly two months after Corregidor fell, bacillic dysentery struck him. Being a clean man, he moved under the empty nipa officers' bath shack to keep from fouling his own nest. His friends brought him his mess kit of rice and vainly urged him to eat. Under our horrified eyes he became a living skeleton in just a few days. The doctors looked him over daily, but he was too far gone to be moved across the road to the isolation hospital, that pitiful collection of nipa shacks.

We got a few cigarettes for him, for they seemed to cheer him up. Father McManus stayed close to him when the end was near. Finally, in darkness and dripping rain, his weary eyes closed forever, and the small crucifix fell from his lifeless hands. We guess he died in a state of grace, in the odor of sanctity, for "Big Mac" was always a decent man and was well liked by his fellow Marines.

We who survived, after our three and a half years and more of nightmare starvation, of seeing countless comrades die and the rest become animated bags of bones, should recall "Big Mac" with reverence and affection. We have plenty of the latter, but we sadly lack the former. All we can readily remember of "Big Mac" is that agonized running waddle of some three hundred yards while looking for shelter in the ditches that were just too small for him. Even when we start to speak of his good qualities, the talk always reverts to that frantic, bewildered, perspiring dash for safety. We laugh with unseemly mirth.

Not all of us who made it back home are entirely sane. Prison life at the hands of the Japanese may have seared and scarred a streak of callous cruelty in us. When we laugh at the memory of a man in a race with death, we wonder.

26

THE LISTER BAG THAT DIDN'T GET THE PURPLE HEART

His name was PFC John Francis Ray, from Headquarters Company, 2d Battalion, 4th Marines. He was as Irish as Paddy's pig, and his devout parents had named him after St. John the Evangelist and the gentle St. Francis of Assisi, as was meet and fitting among the transplanted sons of Erin. The Irish classify themselves as "black Irish," "red-skinned Irish," and "Irish with freckles." Our Johnny was red-skinned, leaning toward the black side.

A typical Scollay Square Irishman, he was a scion of that part of South Boston that should be a shrine of the nation, for John L. Sullivan was born there. Boston is still called the "Athens of America," but many folk today in the city by the Charles are none too well aware of this fact. To them, it is more famous as the birthplace of the immortal "John L."

Our Johnny could not make up his mind in Shanghai whether he wanted to become a corporal in a machine gun company or a field cook in the galley. His indecision gave his first sergeant quite a headache, for 1st Sgt. Richard "Bozo" Duncan had to write his letters to the Marine Corps commandant in Washington, D.C., about the rating of field cook. Johnny finally wound up on Corregidor Island in the spring of 1942 as a private first class on special duty in the galley, striking for the rank of field cook. The mess sergeant, T.Sgt. Leon B. Ellis, was a rugged, severe type of individual where his work was concerned, who spoke well of

Johnny. When the air alarm went off and lesser men scurried for shelter, PFC John Francis Ray stayed with his pots and pans and the galley fires, for he feared that his precious beans might burn.

James Ravine, where he labored in his humble work, was a rather tough place in which to be doing duty during those hectic days. The enemy bombers arose from Nichols Field in the north, went westward over the Bataan Peninsula, and then turned toward the island fortress, heading for Bottomside and the North Mine Dock area. They lined their sights on tiny Mona Islet and James Ravine for their bombing runs. Too often the antiaircraft guns of the 60th Coast Artillery made the Japanese fliers so nervous that they opened the bomb bays, and James Ravine received the load of deadly eggs. There was also scattered artillery fire from the Cavite shores and the hazard of burning ammunition dumps. All in all, the ravine could by no means be recommended as a health resort.

Some twenty-eight Filipino reservists, mess attendants recalled to active duty from the sweets of retirement after sixteen years of service, augmented the galley force. To their labors was added the extra duty of defending the reserve position on the Upper Belt Line Road as part of the defense force given the sergeant major [Jackson]. That individual thought it fit to introduce them to the mysteries of the bayonet drill, for when Bataan fell, a landing might reasonably be expected at James Ravine.

There was fair shelter from bombs in this beach end of the ravine, for the Dirt Tunnel, some one hundred yards from the galley, would accommodate over three hundred men without too much crowding. Capt. Benjamin L. "Big Ben" McMakin, USMC, who commanded the sector, was visiting in the Headquarters Tunnel carved from the living rock and talking with his kind among the staff. The mess attendants were coming in from their arduous bayonet practice, and Johnny as the cook on watch was stewing up a mush of cracked wheat.

There was a warning shouted of "Motors in the west,"

and the railroad iron, suspended from its tripod, was clanged furiously as an air raid was coming. All but Johnny and a Filipino mess attendant called "Punchy," a former prizefighter in his youthful days aboard a battleship, scurried for shelter. Johnny had that meal to get out and was worried about his cooking fires, for the wood was green. "Punchy," one suspects, had not the keen mental perception of a normal Filipino. Perhaps his nickname was well merited.

Captain Ames's "Chicago" Battery, up on Morrison Hill way, opened up with its 3-inch rifles, and the bombers swerved from their course. The observers yelled out, "Bomb bays are opening!" There was a horrid, screaming swish of a stick of five-hundred-pound bombs as they fell, several ear-shattering blasts, and the ravine was a mess again. "Big Ben" tore at top speed down into his sector, for he had heard the cries of "First aid!" The captain found "Punchy" moaning in the remains of his scattered brush lean-to, his legs nearly cut off at the hips. As "Big Ben" tenderly picked up the broken body in his strong arms, a large branch from a tree overhead, torn loose by bomb splinters, fell across his back, almost knocking him from his feet, ripping his shirt, and making a long, bleeding scratch.

The mess sergeant, coming swiftly from the Dirt Tunnel, stumbled over the legs of Johnny, who had, in the last instant of that screaming swish, dived under the only cover he saw, a ten-gallon canvas water container whose contents were purified with chlorine. Named after its inventor, it was called a "Lister bag." The bag was streaming water from several holes, for flying gravel had cut it. Johnny picked himself up, he and the cursing mess sergeant helped steady "Big Ben" from falling, and all three carried the pitiful burden of "Punchy" to the battalion dressing station. The chief cook had yelled to Johnny that the galley was unhurt, to go on up with the wounded man, and that he, the chief cook, would take over. The young Irishman nodded back.

"Punchy," it was seen, could not live very long. Even Doctor Wade's skill could not save him. He was given first aid, a shot of morphine, and rushed by pickup truck over to the Malinta Hospital. We learned he died that night, unconscious to the very end, which was a blessing.

When the blood and bandages were all cleaned up, Dr. Wade applied iodine and a dressing to "Big Ben's" back. "Well, Ben, I guess you get the Purple Heart, for you were bleeding like a stuck pig," said the surgeon. "And you, Johnny, seem to have a big lump and scratch on your forehead. A little iodine and tape for you, my boy, and you will be fixed up all right." The corpsman wrote both Marines down on his casualty list. Whether Doctor Wade saw it or not when he signed it later, I do not know, for there were other air raids that day, and the doctor was quite a busy man.

In due time the army sent down the award, in proper mimeographed orders of the day. The casualty lists were radioed to Washington to be placed in the official records.

As soon as Doctor Wade was through with Johnny, the latter went back to his galley. The mess sergeant and chief cook were tending the cracked wheat mush, and both were cursing over the loss of the Lister bag, for those things were so hard to replace.

A work detail soon had things partially repaired, and Cpl. "Whitey" Morvan, the 2d Battalion's property sergeant and a thief of skill where supplies were involved, soon had a new bag rustled from the unsuspecting army folks on Morrison Hill. They hung the bag in the same place, over the gravel and stones laid down to catch the drippings.

Johnny took over his fires and resumed his watch. There were more air raids in the ravine area that day, wounding a couple of Company F Marines and shattering a concrete machine gun emplacement. The stolid Irishman did not even have to duck; he merely shrugged off the air raids.

The good mess sergeant, when news of the Purple Heart award came down several days later, had much to say. In speaking of the proverbial luck of the Irish, he exclaimed, "Dived under a Lister bag and hit that thick Irish head on the sharp stones beneath! They give this Mick a Purple

Heart, but they ought to give it to the Lister bag" was his
outraged comment.

"Big Ben" never lived to wear his Purple Heart, for he
was killed while on board a Japanese prison ship en route to
the Flowery Kingdom.

The mess sergeant lived to laugh at Johnny when they
saw each other again on Guam, in September 1945, after
both Marines had been released from the prison camps of
Japan. The former thinks it was the funniest thing he ever
saw during the war, even more hilarious than the day enor-
mously fat "Big Mac" McKinney was trying to find shelter
from bombing and strafing enemy planes, and all the foxholes were too small for his elephantine body.

If I could get that mess sergeant to talk about the war
today, he would tell you the most comical incident he recalls
is the "Lister bag that didn't get the Purple Heart," and he'd
laugh uproariously in telling the story.

Johnny does not seem to have the pride in his award that
he should. He laughs, too, when the decoration is mentioned, and agrees with the mess sergeant. But on the back
of his Purple Heart, in raised letters, are the words, "For
Military Merit." The army, on one occasion at least, gave a
Scout captain and some of his men this medal for putting
out the fires in burning ammunition dumps. But, if Johnny's
resoluteness in sticking by his galley under bombing is not
"Military Merit" of the highest order, then just what does
the term really mean?

27

THE EMPEROR'S BIRTHDAY

The birthday of the Son of Heaven, Hirohito, Emperor of Japan, is the twenty-ninth of April. No Corregidor Marine, or anyone who served those long, dismal years as a prisoner of the Japanese Imperial Forces, will ever forget that date.

In 1943 and 1944 there were birthday ceremonies, and in most cases the prisoners had to stand the interminable Japanese army formation, called a *bango*. The *bango* has passed into the limbo of half-forgotten bad dreams, but the extra rice furnished even to the prisoners on those two occasions will always be remembered.

The natal day of his imperial majesty in 1945 was of a more memorable nature, for Lieutenant Asaka, our camp commandant in that Mitsubishi "Three Diamond" copper mine in faraway Akita Prefecture in northwest Honshu Island, graciously announced at his special *bango* ceremony that we would be allowed some of our hoarded Red Cross food, and we were starving. A twelve-pound box was divided among five ravenous men, who snarled over the division like wild dogs.

But the birthday of the emperor in 1942 during the siege of Corregidor will never, ever be forgotten by any of us who survived. We were apprehensive of an enemy landing; yet we had our doubts, for the moon would rise a bit too early for good concealment of the attacking force. We knew the Japanese had some 290 cannons in addition to a large force

of bombers that had been working over our defenses as part
of the softening-up process before they launched their main
assault. We figured on increased activity, for a present of the
stubborn little island and its defenders would have been a
most acceptable offering to the divinity on the throne.

Among those who waited this day with apprehension
was Sgt. Maj. John B. "Bronco" Kelly, USMC, of the 1st
Battalion, 4th Marines. John had some twenty-nine years of
service before he joined us in Shanghai in the summer of
1941. He was a big, tough, imposing looking man who
feared neither man, God, nor the devil. Regimental and battalion commanders delight in his type, for with a few key
men like him as a leaven for the nineteen-year-old Marines
fresh from the recruit depot, those young men, after a little
tempering and some bloodletting, could storm the gates of
hell with a fair chance of success.

One of our 2d Battalion Marines, Sgt. Wendell N. Garden, on duty in that headquarters, kept a war diary. By some
miraculous process he preserved it during his imprisonment
and got it safely back to the States. He gave me a good look
at it recently, and there, under the date of the emperor's
birthday, was a brief note about Sergeant Major Kelly. It
provides some idea of what life was like "living on a bull's-
eye," as some radio commentator cracked during his nightly
spiel, which started with the words, "Corregidor still
stands!"

And so, here follows the pertinent parts, with a minimum
of editing by myself: 29 April 1942, Fort Mills, Corregidor
Island, Harbor Defenses of Manila and Subic Bays.

HOUR EVENT

0655   Three planes (observation) overhead. Air raid alarm.
       All take cover "Photo Joe" has reinforcements this day,
       and is liable to lay his eggs.
0659   Two planes are diving. Bomb bays are open. Here
       they come! Listen to the screams and dull *crump, crump*

crump! No damage in James Ravine. All seem to have landed in the First Battalion area.

0700 Today is the Emperor's Birthday and here is the Overture of death, a salvo of two hundred and forty millimeter shells.

0822 This is the heaviest bombardment we have ever gotten. There seems to be a Two-forty shell in our ravine every few seconds. So far our installations have not been severely damaged, but our camouflage is being knocked down.

0830 The upper seventy-five millimeter gun is knocked out. Seven Filipinos of the 91st Scouts are killed, and five wounded. All of the gun crew, poor fellows.

0844 Master Gunnery Sergeant Olmstead, of Co. F, 2d Bn. (brave old friend) reports the upper seventy-five millimeter gun is hopelessly smashed. Colonel Anderson says, "Let it go."

0850 The lower seventy-five millimeter gun is knocked out. Captain Massey (Rgt. QM), 91 Scouts, wounded. No one killed. Massey is being brought in. Not badly hit. Dr. Wade says, "He'll live." But the gun is gone. All of the seventy-fives we have.

0900 The bombardment seems to be increasing in intensity. God help the poor First Battalion, out in the open, where all the ground is hard rock. Those rock splinters are worse than steel ones.

0931 Here are several entries relating to the intensity of the bombardment, to casualties, destruction of installations, and camouflage, with comments

1105 About the one hundred and fifty and one hundred and five millimeter cannons. Remarks are made about aerial bombing. As none concern First Battalion, for brevity's sake, all are omitted.

1107 Line to First Battalion is out. 1st Lt. Albert ZW. Moffett declines to order any Marine out to repair it. Says, "Suicidal." Corporals Buethe and Breeze of Communications Section volunteered. Damned fools. This is the end of them.

1205   The awful stillness overwhelms us. The bombardment has ceased! Sergeant Garden is getting in the casualty and damage reports.

1230   Corporals Buethe and Breeze are back. We greeted them like men returned from the dead. The 1st Battalion line is in working order. Colonel Anderson talks to Lt. Colonel Beecher. Beecher says his battalion has caught hell, with heavy casualty list. They have no cover.

1238   Colonel Anderson orders Buethe and Breeze written up for the Silver Star.

1301   (These entries are omitted, as not bearing on 1st Battalion. They tell of frenzied efforts to repair our installations, the death of some of the wounded, the patient care Dr.

1720   Wade gave to injured, and the outposts reporting "Battle Stations all manned and ready to repel boarders.)

1735   Reports from Colonel Kohn, Commanding Officer, 91st Scouts, on data received from Group Four, Coast Artillery Headquarters, in which he tells of terrific damage to the Island. He remarks that only two, of our forty-eight, Seventy-five millimeter guns are left. This is bad. All guns ruined, and we were depending on those guns when the landing comes.

Here is an extract from a speech delivered in 1946 by our commanding general, which I recently read. General Wainwright says, in part, "Great emplacements of steel and concrete were literally pulverized. A two hundred and forty-millimeter shell [explodes] on this tiny island every five seconds, or less. Twelve shells a minute, seven hundred and twenty per hour, thirty-six hundred for five hours. Each is a five-hundred-pounder. One million, eight hundred thousand pounds of steel landing on us. It would take a column of trucks eighteen miles long just to haul it."

1737   Colonel Anderson says, "Morale is good."

1740   The Japanese radio in Manila, in English, denounces us as "The Moles of Corregidor."

1905   In writing up Buethe and Breeze for the Silver Star,
       Sergeant Garden was told that when they were out in
       the First Battalion area, near the Command Post, it was
       entirely vacated, so severe was the bombardment, for all
       the men had taken to cover except for one lone Marine,
       old Sergeant Major Kelly. He was sitting, cool as a cu-
       cumber, in a canvas chair, with shells exploding all
       around. Garden, in relating this to the "Old Man" says
       that Colonel Anderson remarked, "To be expected of
       Kelly."
***   (Remainder of day's entries omitted.)

I am glad to add the sequel that Sergeant Major Kelly is
alive, hale, and hearty, and his experiences seem to have
softened him, for he is not nearly as tough as he used to be.
He has a genial twinkle in his eye, and life for him is good,
for he is glad to be alive. The Army Rangers got him out of
that hellhole, Cabanatuan Military Prison, half dead after
nearly three years of slow starvation. His fighting Marine
spirit, his indomitable courage, and his steadfast courage
under fire seem, to a casual glance, as strong as they were
in those early hectic days.

I talked over the emperor's birthday with Kelly, and he
laughed. "Well, I guess I'm living on borrowed time. But the
one thing I really miss is my old canvas chair. You know I
kept it until the Rangers came in. In the hurry of leaving that
accursed place, I forgot all about it. I wish I had it now!"

EPILOGUE

Charles R. Jackson's personal experiences and recorded observations as a prisoner of war from 1942–45 make up a significant military history. The freedom he enjoyed for so many years before it was denied to him was *his* realization of the American dream. His recounting of fellow brave men facing death—Marines, soldiers, and sailors—helps define their horrific treatment at the hands of the Japanese as well as their own personal courage. How we accept it and relate to it helps define us as a nation.

While it has often been lamented that the recorded POW experiences of those men and women imprisoned, starved, brutally tortured, and killed by their Japanese captors should be "required reading" for all citizens of Japan, I would suggest that *I Am Alive!* be added to that "required reading list" for all Americans as well.

Following his release as a prisoner of war in late 1945, Charles R. Jackson returned to duty at the Marine Corps Recruit Depot, San Diego, California. Here he was reunited with the little mongrel dog, Soochow, mascot of the 4th Marine Regiment, where they kept each other's company until December 1949.

Charles R. Jackson, USMC, retired from active service on 1 November 1951. After his retirement, he pursued his hobbies of gardening, painting, and reading as much as his diminished eyesight would permit.

It was on 4 May 1971, in the backyard of his little home in Pacific Beach, California, that Charles R. Jackson, now deeply depressed, blind, and suffering from the advanced stages of Parkinson's disease, took his own life.

BEHIND BAMBOO: AMERICAN POWS IN THE PACIFIC

Estimated number captured, died, and returned
to US control

Captured by Country		
	Philippines	22,000
	Wake	1,555
	Java (Indonesia)	890
	Guam	400
	Japan	300
	Celebes	255
	China	200
		25,600

Killed or Died in Captivity		
	Philippines	5,135
	On prison ships	3,840
	Japan	1,200
	Manchuria (China)	175
	Burma	130
	Wake Island	100
	Korea	70
		10,650

POWs Liberated by Country		
	Japan	11,400
	Philippines	1,500
	Manchuria	1,200
	Burma-Thailand	480
	Celebes	200
	Korea	150
	China	20
		14,950

BIBLIOGRAPHY

Addax Publishing Group. *Faces of Victory, Pacific: The Fall of the Rising Sun*. VFW Magazine, Kansas City, Mo.

Caraccilo, Dominic J., ed. *Surviving Bataan and Beyond: Colonel Irvin Alexander's Odyssey as a Japanese Prisoner of War*. Stackpole Books, 1999.

Considine, Robert, ed., and General Jonathan M. Wainwright. *General Wainwright's Story: The Account of Four Years of Humiliating Defeat, Surrender, and Captivity*. New York, 1946.

Donaldson, Captain W. H., USA. *Biographical Register of the Officers and Graduates of the U.S. Military Academy*. Supplement, Vol. VII, 1920–30.

Evans, William R., and Eugene Jacobs. *Soochow and the 4th Marines*. Rogue River, Ore.: Atwood Publishing Company, 1987.

Fifty Year Book. Published by the Class of 1919, Washington, D.C., August 1969.

Kerr, E. Bartlett. *Surrender and Survival: The Experience of American POWs in the Pacific, 1941–1945*. New York, 1985.

Matloff, Maurice. *American Military History*. Vol. 2: 1902–96. Edited by Matloff. Combined Books, Conshohocken, Pa., 1948.

Morton, Louis. *United States Army in World War II. The War in the Pacific: The Fall of the Philippines*. GPO, 1953.

Thirty-Five Year Book. Published by the Class of 1919, Washington, D.C., August 1954.

INDEX

297

World War II had many heroes . . .

BLACK SHEEP ONE
The Life of Gregory "Pappy" Boyington

by Bruce Gamble

With the onset of World War II, when skilled pilots were in demand, Gregory "Pappy" Boyington became the commander of an ad hoc squadron of flying leathernecks. The legendary Black Sheep set a blistering pace of aerial victories against the enemy. Though many have observed that when the shooting stops, combat heroes typically just fade away, nothing could be further from the truth for Boyington. Blessed with inveterate luck, the stubbornly independent warrior lived a life that went beyond what even the most imaginative might expect. Exhaustively researched and richly detailed, here is the complete story of this American original.

"A DEFINITIVE BIOGRAPHY . . .
The story of this brave and paradoxical Marine
is the stuff of legends."

—W. E. B. Griffin
Author of *The Corps*

Published by Presidio Press
Available wherever books are sold

*Don't miss this valuable contribution
to the history of World War II*

DEATH TRAPS

The Survival of an American Armored
Division in World War II

by Belton Y. Cooper
with a foreword by Stephen E. Ambrose

"The compelling story of one man's assignment
to the famous 3rd Armored Division that spear-
headed the American advance from Normandy into
Germany. [Belton] Cooper served as an ordnance
officer . . . responsible for coordinating the recovery and repair of damaged American tanks. . . .
[He] recalls his service with pride, downplaying
his role in the vast effort that kept the American
forces well equipped and supplied. . . . [Readers]
will be left with an indelible impression of the
importance of the support troops and how dependent combat forces were on them."

—*Library Journal*

Published by Presidio Press
Available wherever books are sold

Look for this remarkable memoir of small-unit leadership and the coming of age of a young soldier in Vietnam

PLATOON LEADER

A Memoir of Command in Combat

by James R. McDonough

"Using a lean style and a sense of pacing drawn from the tautest of novels, McDonough has produced a gripping account of his first command. . . . Rather than present a potpourri of combat yarns . . . McDonough has focused a seasoned storyteller's eye on the details, people, and incidents that best communicate a visceral feel of command under fire. . . . For the author's honesty and literary craftsmanship, *Platoon Leader* seems destined to be read for a long time by second lieutenants trying to prepare for the future, veterans trying to remember the past, and civilians trying to understand what the profession of arms is all about."

—*Army Times*

Published by Presidio Press
Available wherever books are sold